TEN YEARS OF PETER GLEN

One Hundred Essays for the Improvement of Work, Life and Other Matters of Consequence

ST publications inc.

Cincinnati, Ohio

The essays in this book originally appeared in *VM+SD: Visual Merchandising and Store Design*.

Please direct all correspondence to:
ST Publications
Book Division
407 Gilbert Avenue
Cincinnati, Ohio 45202
U.S.A.

ISBN 0-944094-03-1

First Edition

Smythe Sewn Binding

Book design by Carole Winters

Photograph of Peter Glen by Toscani

 Printed on recycled paper in the United States of America

THANKS

Many people at ST Publications helped produce ten years of writing. Some I know, and some just faithfully received and polished and presented all the columns. You are about to experience their work as well as mine. I thank them all.

PK Anderson
Lisa Baird
Therese Bottonari
Leslie Brod
Joan Gallagher Donnelly
Tracy Dougherty
Doris Eiber
Janet Groeber
Laurel Harper
Mark Kissling
Lori Siebert
Stacey Witt Toevs
Carole Winters

TABLE OF CONTENTS

PART SIX: IMPROVEMENT

PART SEVEN: FASHION

PART EIGHT: SERVICE

PART NINE: AIDS

PART TEN: FACING FORWARD

WHAT TO DO WITH THIS BOOK

This book is divided into ten sections:

1. Trends

2. Design

3. Destinations

4. Retail

5. Openings

6. Improvement

7. Fashion

8. Service

9. AIDS

10. Facing Forward

Alice in Wonderland was told,
"Begin at the beginning. Go on reading until you come to the end.
Then stop."

That was bad advice.

Read creatively!

Pick the section that hits you first and start reading there.

If you like controversy, I suggest you start with "Fashion."

If you want tough reviews of famous stores, begin with "Openings."

If you want to improve your boss, try "Improvement" or "Service."

If you are courageous, turn to the last two sections,
where you will find AIDS, the earth and Millennium.

This book is dedicated to people living with AIDS.

To the Reader

WORK AND LIFE

WORK AND LIFE are the same thing, although a lot of people try to separate them. They talk as though their work were one thing, and their life a different thing completely. Work comes first and life comes later—meaning after work or retirement or any time but the present.

Well, they're wrong. Your work and your life cannot be separated; they take place simultaneously. They are, in fact, identical.

I love the marriage of business and spirit. Business is the only work I know that can make money, satisfy the soul, and improve the world at the same time.

Ten Years of Peter Glen is a chronicle of the customer, the person with the money you want, the loud, the uninformed, the irritating, enervating, unpredictable plaintiff, defendant, judge, and jury all-in-one, the real boss of us all, the aim of all our efforts.

Ten years ago I was content talking "work"—trends and pop sociology. I wanted to prod by amusing, pointing fingers, poking holes, and making fun of misdemeanors. But there is only so much anyone can say about the uses of mannequins and slatwall, and there are practitioners more accurate than I who write about it regularly.

My column was a lot about work but not strong enough or deep enough about life. There were far more urgent things to write about than fashion, display, marketing, merchandising and making money. The world itself was getting worse and I wanted to aim my spirit that way.

Eleven years later, I do not find the world a better place. I haven't made enough of a difference yet, so there is plenty of inspiration for the next ten years.

Ten years of writing generated some trash, and I apologize for adding to the planet's wanton extravagance. What is trash to me has been left out. But some of the old chronicles (stores that closed, designers who died, celebrities now unknown, trends totally forgotten) can illuminate the present. We just do it now with different faces and addresses, different dinners and designers.

In ten years I have seen people and companies cheat and lie and steal and disappoint us all. But many times they also dream, aspire, and act, becoming not only successful, but also agents of goodness—and we share that, too.

Everything changes. The human body changes every cell perpetually. Not one cell of yours existed five years ago. What used to be Sears is now Wal-Mart. Santa Fe was hot and now it's not. Many of the icons and ideas of 1984 are gone or, anyway, forgotten. Ten years ago there was not much in the way of catalogs, no interactive marketing, no electronic juggernaut, no global distribution, not much attention paid to AIDS.

The only things that stay are flexibility, morality, memory, enthusiasm and everlasting curiosity.

Ten years of joy! Expressing an opinion and trying to make it matter enough to make a difference—that was my assignment ten years ago. It's as good an assignment as any student ever received.

For ten years I have been writing about action. It is not enough to do nothing. You must act to improve things. I believe with Mother Hale that "Life is our gift from God. What you do with that life is your gift back to God." And my dear teacher, Alethea Mattingly, believes that the purpose of life is to use your abilities; talent is not just a fact; but a responsibility.

The theme of this book, without being planned, turns out to be work and life and how they can both be improved. What begins as a restaurant review or a store critique is also easily an essay on management and customers and vision. It's then an essay on design in the grand sense of the word, and it turns to bigger subjects like motivation, which loads humanity into the mix, with beliefs and prejudices and our environment at large; and so eventually in these realms of emotion, it gradually becomes clear that work and life are indeed the same adventure and that what is being forged in all our efforts can be happiness.

The hardest lesson we ever learn—we learn it over and over and it is painful every time—is the lesson of self-reliance. We look out and up and down and to the side—we look everwhere but IN—to find the blame for every failure, every mediocrity. It is the corporation, the economy. "It's politics that stop me," we say, as if THEY cared. It must be the gods, or my boss, or the color of my skin, or my sex or my age or my mother beat me up—as if THEY cared!

We read books like this one; we scrutinize our tea leaves, analyze our colors, stare at tarot cards and horoscopes; we clutch at birthstones, crucifixes, fortune cookies, stock predictions, group therapies, and lottery tickets; we ask the rabbi and the universe—as if they gave out answers, even if they cared!

You are fortunate if your work and your life coincide in your heart, as well as in fact. You understand that your work and your life are your own responsibility and that harmony must be created anew by each person, for each person.

This book is for the self-reliant reader who rejoices in perpetual improvement, in putting labor and love together, in being paid for being your own best self, and who knows that creative dissatisfaction keeps the spirit alive and can lead the way to our present necessary salvation.

This book can help you answer two important questions about your life and work:

1. What were you doing ten years ago?
2. Are you happier today?

PART ONE
TRENDS

SHARE THE FANTASY

MARCH 1983

FANTASY is the new reality. It's better than the real reality. The worse things get, the more people want to get out of it.

How many of the following "right-now-fantasy-successes" are you aware of? How many have you incorporated into your plans and thinking for 1983? How many influences can you trace in merchandise or merchandise presentation?

• *Cats.* As if Kliban weren't enough already, now we have poor old T.S. Eliot's chamber poetry blown up to the size of the Bible, sold out six months in advance, solely because we lust for "effects." There is one hit song, and no content. No matter. To wit: Bloomingdale's "Cat's Meow Shop"; "Crazy Kats" at Harbor Place, Baltimore; and the backside of every New York City bus.

• *The Dark Crystal.* The movie's out, but in November you also saw the one-hour video special with Jim Henson of Muppets fame.

• Merlin. Another fantasy era—medieval—costing $4 million and open now. The costumes have already focused attention on Theoni Adredge's designs, and designers are watching.

• AT&T Building. The most controversial building built in decades nears completion in Manhattan and hits *Time*, *Newsweek*, *The New York Times* and all the new books on ornamentation—all because it is a new flight from reality squarely launched by America's greatest architect, Phillip Johnson.

• Ornamentation. The best $40 you've spent on a book since High Tech and altogether radically different. Fantasy architecture leads the way to the future, and the scaffolding is up now.

• The Bancshares Building. In Houston, is probably the most outrageous 82-story fantasy since the real Empire State and Chrysler days of skyscraping aspirations, designed by Chicago's renowned Helmut Jahn.

• The Piazza D'Italia. In New Orleans, this classical stage scenery done on the street is a collection of false facades to delight the eye of the public.

• Surrealism. Revived after Magritte, now in the avant-garde advertising of such diverse home furnishings companies as Jack Lenor Larson and Galaxy Carpets.

• New Clothes. People are wearing costumes on the street. All the Tokyo designers; Castelbajac's boy scouts; Hechter's wipsters; Girbaud's road warriors; Lassance's fishermen. (And why are safe stores stocking only blue blazers?)

- The Fantasy World of Neiman Marcus. The big 1982 display person's coffee-table gift book. (Some of you got as many as 18 copies for Christmas!) Best excerpts from all their catalogs.

- Star Magic. A sparkly new store at 743 Broadway, New York City. totally concerned with things celestial, derived from (of course) California. Slogan: "Gifts of Science and Spirit."

- Tokyo. So strong now that even *Time* magazine has published a guide to the current Japanese designers.

- Michael Graves. Designing Sunar's showrooms in New York City, Dallas, Chicago, Houston and Los Angeles, Joffrey Ballet settings, the most astonishing office building in Portland, Ore., and invited to appear at the California Visual Merchandising Market in San Francisco.

- EPCOT. Fantasy as the new reality in Florida, off to a partial start, now functioning as hordes of Americans—including "grown ups"—pour through the doors. EPCOT's opening included for the first time anywhere outdoor daylight fireworks. Let's not hear that the Disney mob is not what it was. It is what it was—the best.

- *Carnevale a Venezia*. Masks and Mardi Gras in the most fabulous book of photos published in years, by Fulvio Roiter. (Go to Rizzoli at 55th and 5th in New York—always go to Rizzoli.) You'll want to skip Rio de Janeiro and go to Venice instead. You'd better get overdressed and go now.

- *Little Shop of Horrors*. Man-eating plants in a musical are certainly fantasy. So is going down to the slums to see it. This little obscure Off-Off-Off-Broadway musical is getting $22.50 a seat—and just try to get a ticket!

- *My Favorite Year*. Becoming another Peter O'Toole cult film. And Peter O'Toole is always fantasy.

- *Alice in Wonderland*. Imperishable from Lewis Carroll through John Tenniel, Walt Disney, Meryl Streep and every child's mind. It's being launched again by Eva Le Galliene 50 years after her own first performance.

- Art Treasures of the Vatican. Transported to the United States for the first time ever, opening early spring at the Met and many dates completely sold out since December 1. This will be the biggest hit since Picasso.

All these appeal to wishes, not to needs. Escape. Retreat. Adventure. Exploration. Danger. The thrilling. The unknown. The occult. The magical. The future. The past. Humor. Wit. Imagination. Envy. Impersonation. The false made real. The unknown revealed. The invisible made manifest.

And we react!

We gasp when a kitty-cat ascends to heaven. We gloat while a plant eats a trio of doo-wops. Big men weep when a wrinkled being wants to "go home."

We recoil from a pit of snakes in Egypt.

We all react—merchants and customers.

Fantasy.

Merchandising.

I THINK I'M TURNING JAPANESE!

JULY 1983

BLOOMINGDALE'S, Macy's, Bendel's and Davison's (and probably lots of other stores) all have the same strange feeling lately—they're turning Japanese.

Of course, for a long time everyone you know has been consulting Japanese watches. Listening to Japanese audio equipment, driving Japanese cars and worrying about these current invasions. But one year ago, nobody was going around blithely saying things like "Issey Miyake," "Rei Kawakubo," "Comme des Garcons," "Yoshi Yamamoto" (as differentiated from "Kansai Yamamoto"), "Mitsuhiro Matsuda," et cetera, except for a very few hysterical trend watchers—and an ever-fewer, very rich people who can afford to buy that stuff and take the chance that anything so radical and gray and unfitted could be thrown away if it met with excessive laughter when worn.

But those are the old days. Now, Japanese fashion has hit so suddenly and so hard that it has even managed to genuinely upset the most upsettable people on the face of the earth—the French. The French are so busy today publishing nasty "hate-statements" about the Japanese designers, that they hardly have any time left at all to design their own collections and, thus, are coming up with not-very-interesting rehashes of the same old stuff that they did last year.

But that's not all! It isn't just the new clothes, although they are certainly news, being put together out of what appears to be bits and swatches and strips, after being twisted, tied and re-tied, knotted, gouged and unlaid, overlain and inlaid (not to mention that there is no trace of the human body once inside a new Japanese garment).

OH, NO!

Now they've hit with the visuals!

The new shops in Japan are something to be seen and marveled at. There's nothing like them here. Just like the clothes, they are gray and gray and gray—with occasional flourishes of black (although Issey Miyake is white and white and white, with occasional arpeggios of gray).

They are concrete, plaster, pipe-racks, understocked and empty looking. (Comme des Garcons has actually achieved one of the great visual non-merchandising feats of all time—there are no clothes whatever in the store. If you should want to actually see something (shudder), you have to bust your way past the black-lipsticked harridan who's guarding the "merch," and state your case in no uncertain terms. You stand in the presence of the Apotheosis of Minimalism, amen!)

But, there's more! There's more to be learned and borrowed about visual presentation in Japan today than in any other single destination. You'll gasp about:

• Skyscraper shop collections geared entirely to teenagers (Alta).

• Department stores' separate divisions, devoting floor-after-floor to exciting boutiques for the home, the body and sports (Parco 1, 2 and 3, division of Seibu; and Di-Di, division of Margui).

• Miles of staggering electric signs, without one single bulb burned out.

• Department store graphics celebrating purchases made and wrapped and going—not trivial merchandise ads.

• Video-selling with a vengeance, from the 50-square-foot television set showing merchandise on the outside front of Alta, to the banks of television previewing the store outside Seibu, to the computers in the banks that offer customers investment counseling.

• Rooftops used for tennis, golf, a shrine or two, a kiddie train, gardens for old folks to rest in, carp pools for kiddies to fish in, bonsai collections and giant fish flags flying over all. It's exhilarating. And the store you work for has a roof you've never seen.

• Themes realized through theater lighting projections. Rainbows (clinched, eh?—think again!) projected onto merchandise signs, balloons, Venetian blinds, walls, shutters, escalators.

The cleanliness, discipline, training and customer service in all Japanese stores are worth 16 visits in themselves, but that may not belong in this column because it isn't "visual?" Wrong! "It's not your department?" Wrong, again!

• Visual exhibitions—every big store has an important art gallery with an important show. Like the restaurants, which are both visual and terrific, these visual activities keep the customer in the store longer.

• Merchandise—after you struggle in and out of "fashion" and pick up a few electricals, you drop right down dead about plates and cups and bowls and boxes and chop-stick rests. None of it is anything we ever set on a table. You'll want to rent a cargo container and throw out every ugly piece of table-ware you own.

Eating is a major visual learning experience. Go to a major (very expensive) private restaurant and prepare to be astounded by what's put down in front of you, what it's put down on, by whom and with what attitude. You'll study the forms, shapes, colors, materials, sequence and feel like you're quite directly eating some imagination.

Visual details, tiny finesses that stay in the mind:
— Never a Styrofoam cup; never!
— White gloves
— Bowing
— Not one burned-out bulb
— Ladies on their hands and knees cleaning up a customer's spilled Coke
— Mickey and Minnie Mouse in kimonos at Disneyland
— One American, one Japanese flag set out on the table at a business meeting.

Et cetera, et cetera, et cetera... With two very special memories for those of you who know how much a detail matters, and how your heart can be included with your talent:

Deep in the safety-deposit reaches of the biggest Tokyo bank, set out on a tray, because they know that people who come to read small print might possibly forget their glasses, is a selection of eye-glasses for customer use.

Order a cappuccino just outside Issey Miyake men's at Parco. The cappuccino arrives—along with a spoon holding a perfectly shaped, fresh, whipped cream rosebud. The server places the spoon with the rose into your cappuccino. The rose immediately blooms. It opens its petals, spreads and vanishes.

Japan is without question one of the most publicized countries in the world today. But we have not begun to tap its visual tradition for merchandising purposes. There's much more to it than a few new fixtures, lights and straggly-expensive designer garments.

The root of all these possibilities is in the ancient screens, kimonos, gardens, sculpture, tea ceremonies, temples, shrines, paper, swords, dyeing, dolls, pottery, calligraphy, bonsai, waterfalls, walkways, carp, stonework, woodwork, glazes, bells, blossoms and the smell of incense.

You won't find any of this in the stores.

But if you bother to explore beyond your usual retail familiarity, grateful for the hospitality and ideas, but still searching—if you go further—you will find these other, different, real things-of-origin. And you will refresh your spirit.

HOW TO RAISE YOUR E.Q.

SEPTEMBER 1983

THERE ARE TWO WAYS to get ideas:
1. Experience of the world.
2. Experience of yourself.
Both kinds of experience lead to ideas. A creative person is the sum of his ideas.

This creativity can be internal if you are a cloistered monk. If not, you need to visit the world. Most visual merchandisers would be lousy monks. A great retailer is one who translates current events into instant merchandising action.

You need to know what's going on—all of it, in every field the customer is interested in. Impossible, but true.

It doesn't matter whether you like what's new or not. But you need to know about it.

You need to read, eat, explore, enquire, taste, try, experience everything. Know every new movie, play, restaurant, product, thought, idea, protest, upset, opinion—all of the above on every subject, architecture to zoology.

This can be called E.Q.—Experience Quotient. How's your E.Q.?

However it is, it's never stable. You need to be "tested" constantly.

These are hot, new ideas. This list changes constantly. The best we can do is to try to keep up.

• Ralph Lauren for the Home. Perry Ellis sheets. The $1 million showroom at J.P. Stevens is the best "display" in America, and soon your stores will imitate it.

• *Megatrends*, *In Search of Excellence*, *The One-Minute Manager*. All three are still at the top of the best-seller list, and some of you have not read them.

• Mexican food (even dressed-up elegant Mexican food). The new hamburger for everyone, along with the elevation of Pizza to couture-designer status (but probably only in Los Angeles).

• Friendship pins. Kids' intermessages, pinned to their sneakers.

• Xanadu House. Prototype living in Orlando.

• Movies, books, et cetera This fall, the 20th anniversary of John F. Kennedy's assassination.

• "Dragon's Lair." Hottest video game.

• *USA Today*. The fastest route to raising your E.Q. is a subscription (along with 1,200,000 other people) to a great newspaper.

• Hello Kitty. The line of Japanese toys that is catching on fast, and vast in its selection.

• *La Cage Aux Folles*. The musical, to be the biggest hit in years. Try to get tickets for 1984.

• The 1984 Olympics. Even now beginning to be advertised, editorialized, merchandised, displayed.

• Buying in bulk. No packaging at all, just help yourself. Already at Safeway, Ralph's, Kroger and Pick 'n' Pay.

• Cameras. In colors.

• Gravity exercise. From boots to slant-boards to books to records. Health goes on and on in brand-new ways.

• Eddie Murphy. Best new comedian in years.

• Saks Fifth Avenue. Video windows, abstract patterns and colors tuned to the clothes.

• *M* magazine. The male *W*, consumer fashion-eat-travel-stunning news.

• Julio Iglesias. Biggest song star on all the earth but here, soon to be here.

• Teleconferencing. May replace your company's annual travels to resorts, bringing you together often on television.

• Sexy men. Incredible hunks, like Richard Gere, Tom Selleck, the new John Travolta, Mel Gibson.

• Compact disc. The greatest change in sound since stereo.

• Aroma disc. The greatest aroma to fill your home with nasal atmosphere.

• Yves St. Laurent. About to be greater than ever, at the Metropolitan Museum, everywhere.

• Convertible cars. Part of the possible salvation of the U.S. auto industry.

• Off-price stores. Including Ross, the Elegant Plum, The Price Club, et cetera. Traditional retailers are reeling.

• MTV. The music video channel, a vast instant influence on television music, graphics.

• And the lowest trend ever, even lower than Bill Blass chocolates: Gucci Scotch Whiskey!

Your E.Q. is the source of "trend awareness." And trend merchandising. And items. And fads. And customer interest. Your E.Q. is your own royal road to ideas and inspiration. Your job is to take your experience and make it visible.

Try gravity boots. Sniff aroma discs. Go to the movies. Go someplace new for lunch. Shop the competition. If you already do this, do it harder. Search. Investigate. Ask. Fight. Criticize. Come back every time with a stolen idea, or change your thinking.

There are people who would hate all this, or endure it to get done with it. Those folks miss the point.

It's fun. It's exciting. It's adventurous. Uncertain. New. Inventive. Thrilling to discover. Urgent to be first. Bearable to know. You'll never know it all. This exploration is one of the best, imaginative parts of the job: a luxury that comes with the territory.

It's so important, that if you are in a visual field, and you don't love knowing that you never know what's coming next—but you ought to, and you want to—you've probably got the wrong job. Knowing what's happening—and using it—is your job.

People with low E.Q. are afraid.

They are afraid of all the movies they haven't seen and all the people they haven't met. They are certainly afraid of all the projects they haven't done yet.

Fear of the unknown.

Fear of failure.

Fear of change.

Fear of new ideas.

Fear of experience.

Wouldn't it be better, much better, if instead we were afraid of *not* knowing what is going on?

Fear of routine.

Fear of being second.

Fear of falling out of date.

Fear of missing something.

The next time you see something new, don't go home, go after it. Whatever it is, try it. You may not like it. It may not produce your next idea. But at least you'll know what you're talking about.

HOW TO RAISE YOUR E.Q. (PART II)

HOW do you improve your ideas? There are two kinds: the experience of the world, and the experience of yourself. It's easier to read about things than to do them. What are the most exciting things you've ever done?

Have you ever climbed Annapurna? Found the best hotel room in Venice? Played mah jongg? Been down in an opal mine? Grown an orchid? Stolen a pomegranate? Read to a blind person? Scanned a line of iambic pentameter? Ridden a kite behind a motorboat? Watched a snail race on the rocks at Valley Trunk Bay? Ridden an air-boat? Run away from home? Listened to Mahler's First through a Walkman in the Grand Canyon?

Why not?

You're a designer. Your ideas come from your experiences. Your experiences need to come from every field. You must be interested in everything. Everything influences design.

We've talked about your experiences of the world (current events, trends, et cetera) Now we're talking about experiences of yourself. The best experiences you've never had are not those you've read about, but those you've experienced yourself.

You can't hate enchiladas unless you've tried them.

Let's check around in various fields to test yourself on actual personal experience.

• Music. Have you ever heard a single song sung by Julio Iglesias? Or Menudo? Or the works of Brian Eno? Or anything by Vangelis other than the theme from *Chariots of Fire*? What is The Police's biggest hit?

• Architecture. Who is Helmut Jahn? What's your opinion of I.M. Pei's new hotel in China? Or the New York Convention Center? Have you persuaded a guard to let you in to see the lobby of the AT&T Building?

• Theater. Will you be among the first 100,00 people to see the musical *La Cage Aux Folles*? Can you hum anything from *The Little Shop of Horrors*? Who is Tommy Tune's co-star in *My One and Only*?

• Books. Name three of the ten "Megatrends?" Will you realize it's the 20th anniversary of JFK's assassination before the books all hit us this November? Who wrote *August*? What did you think of it?

• Sports. Have you seen the store plans, logos, posters, ad campaigns or the program for the 1984 Olympics? What companies are sponsors? How do you get tickets?

• Advertising. How do you suppose the agency ever convinced British Airways to run those commercials? Do you get the Esprit catalog? Who won the "Clio" awards last year?

• Fashion. Do you think Ralph Lauren's home furnishings will sell? Are you going to the Metropolitan Museum Costume Institute's party launching the Yves St. Laurent exhibit? Why does display at Crate & Barrel exactly duplicate its catalog?

Now that you've investigated all that, you need to know about television, poetry, politics, finance, cooking, information services, computers, manufacturing, arts, crafts, education, entertainment, foreign languages and the news.

One great way to improve your personal E.Q. is to resolve to discipline your next trip to New York City. Do you dare...

— stay at a new hotel
— never eat in the same restaurant twice
— eat in new restaurants always
— see three new resources in the market
— visit every new merchant in town
— do anything to see *La Cage Aux Folles*
— do one daring thing that may not be "you" until you try it
— visit one museum you've never been to (There are 54 in New York)
— spend an evening with someone you've never spent an evening with before.

However, if you cannot wait to travel to some great capital, you can do all of this at home. Simple as it is, some people never...

— visit the competition
— jump into some local fountain (all malls have them)
— revolutionize Father's Day
— make an event of Teddy Roosevelt's birthday, October 27 (a teddy bear fest?)
— drive a different way to work
— stop having the same drinks with the same people in the same place at the same time
— go to the movies; read everything
— get out; go other places.

Don't say there aren't great things to do where you live. You just don't find them.

If you don't do all these things, you'll have a rougher time coming up with new ideas. For example, without personal experience...

How could Michael Southgate ever come up with so many variations on the theme of dressing mannequins if he hadn't mastered every style?

How could Sinclair Russell decide to hire 32 lifeguards to dance with 32 unattended maidens at a sales meeting, if he hadn't found 32 lifeguards?

How could Ann Oakes help decide to put red ribbons on the necks of a flock of flying sculpture geese for Christmas if she hadn't studied the geese?

How could Jack Hruska rent a U.S. Coast Guard hangar for a fashion show if he didn't know the building existed?

All these experiences lead to a higher and higher E.Q. And experiences lead to ideas.

T.S. Eliot: "And the end of all our exploration is, that we return to the place we started from, and see it for the first time."

HIGH-TECH AND HIGH-TOUCH

JANUARY 1984

IT'S 1984. The dreaded year is here. You've read the book. Now we get to see the real thing in action. "Big Brother is Watching You!" George Orwell's book *1984* first seized the collective imagination of millions in 1948 (Orwell's juxtaposing the numbers was meant to signify *1984* was already here, to an extent). But to the general public, *1984* seemed unreachable. The complete depersonalization of everything and everyone was safely improbable. Nobody ever thought that Apple, Atari, the IBM Peanut, LaserDisc and Computer Scrabble would come so soon. Or that stores would have computer skin analysis in the cosmetics department.

Or that there would be "electronic catalogs" instead of static, real models modeling brushed nylon gowns. Or that "media walls" and "cubes" would exist where formerly exhausted wig-and-accessory geniuses once fretted and toiled.

The depersonalization of the human race also has become the depersonalization of retailing. The shopping experience has gone to the computer.

Or has it?

Wouldn't it be awful if retailing became, in person, the way it certainly is going to become with cable-video-keypunch-shop-at-home-awful-but-it-works?

John Naisbit (*Megatrends* author) maintains—and so do I—that nothing will ever replace the joy of shopping for surprises.

Nobody needs to go in person to purchase cola drinks, Q-Tips, light bulbs, 2000-Flushes or hair rollers. They all can be ordered better from the keyboard at home.

But just as *1984*-ghost retailing can increase the efficiency of shopping for practical necessities (and lower the selling cost, and therefore the price), all this lack of humanity will make us long (more strongly than ever) for the anticipated adventures of shopping in person.

Nothing, when it's good enough, will ever take the place of the store. Long live the store? If it's good enough.

If the store is full of adventure, surprises, high-touch trying on, great selling coordinators, the picturization of dreams, of foreign places, unreachable stars, the instant reflection of current events, the sound of music, sampling, gift-with-purchase, whole desirable rooms, a brie line in the food department where everyone is planning a party, and as long as this continues and grows stronger, the store will grow as the living alternative to the old idea of *1984.*

If the store is not good enough, it will lose its life to the computer, which does cold things better, cheaper, faster and more accurately.

Many stores are headed in death's direction. They have cut the staff, the budget, the fun and the surprise right out of the store. They have such continuous "sales" that now the customer has been trained never to buy anything at regular price.

Never to expect service.

Never to see a surprise.

The customer is learning to stay at home.

In many instances, the customer is more intelligent than the store.

But if *1984* were the future, then in 1984, we should think again about what the next future will be. (The future is a moving target. The store had better get moving, too.)

The store of the future will balance exactly high technology with "high-touch." This is not my idea. It is the idea and the answer of a public that has divided its shopping into those two co-existent categories.

The public knows and understands already how to crowd into high-tech membership clubs, bulk-buy stores, off-pricers, discounters, telephone and mail-order, and other humanity-starved kinds of stores.

But the public also already knows—and more than ever, loves—the great crescendo of more and more humanity and excitement, in those few stores that value it. When Bloomingdale's opened in Dallas, 20,000 people showed up in the first hour of business. They weren't high-tech. It is almost impossible to get a seat in a restaurant at the South Street Seaport in New York. That, too, is not high-tech. In its first year, EPCOT entered 23 million people (which, amazingly, is one out of every ten people in America). EPCOT, in spite of its high-tech subject matter, is altogether a high-touch, crowded experience.

People like live experience. Cable television has not replaced theater. Catalogs have not replaced the marketplace. Plastic will never replace real plants.

The stores of the future will be one or the other:

A. High-tech

B. High-touch

High-tech stores will get less and less visual attention. The machine will be the message.

High-touch stores will get more and more visual attention. The message will be emotional.

This is very good news for visual presentation people—if they work in stores that believe in high-touch selling.

And even high-tech retailing needs high-touch: Dayton's computer infant registry needed the addition of some storks and the name "The Stork Club" to make it appealing to people.

The Christmas gift list computer printout needed a humorous robot roaming the store at Parisian to make it a warm experience for customers.

Someone said, "Now that I've got a personal computer at home, I feel the need to crochet a cover for it." And it's "the quilt and the computer" at Esprit headquarters in San Francisco. The computer room is in two big horizontal visuals: computers from the floor to halfway up the wall, and then, from there to the ceiling, part of a large collection of rare, old Baltimore quilts.

The lion shall lie down with the lamb. The quilts hang out above the computers.

The best visual merchandisers are attacking 1984 with a sense of this delicate balance. Every time retailing takes another high-tech step, we must be sure to balance it with an equally high-touch touch.

All high-touch, personal, warm, argumentative. More to come.

Big Brother *is* Watching You.

WHERE'S THE STORE IN 1984?

JULY 1984

NEW STORES WILL OPEN across the street from major malls, near malls and anywhere the rent is cheap. And that's because the "entertainment" promised by the malls has hardly changed in 15 years. There still are car shows, boat shows, antique shows and petting zoos, and everyone has seen them all. We have heard environmental music and admired the fountain in the court. Here's a prediction—stores will once again be used for shopping instead of as a substitute for life.

• The store is not a store. It is a revived downtown, and this will work. It works right now in Boston, Baltimore, New York City, Norfolk, Milwaukee, Toronto, Edmonton and San Francisco. These are strong downtowns, with more sense of worthwhile occasions than any mammoth mall in the world. Dirt and danger are being balanced by scope and excitement, architecture and heritage. No two downtowns are alike. Every mall is like every other mall. Instead of leaving hair in rollers and "schlepping" through the mall, people will get dressed and go to town. People want the main store, the headquarters, the best cathedral. Shopping gives their money prestige.

• Retail uproar. As off-price refuses to go away, and this world continues to polarize, discounters will be more like discounters and specialty stores more like themselves. And department stores (presently split between discount and specialization, thereby compromising both) will have to regain their single kind of undeniable advantage of scope, scale, spectacle, ideas, entertainment, adventure and emotion—coordinated ideas on a very big scale.

• Customer service. It will not disappear. It actually has been long gone, although stores keep lying about it by saying they provide it. The difference now may well be simple honesty—there isn't any. Don't expect it. When customers get this message, they will form different expectations and cease to be perpetually disappointed. Some stores will say this is not true. But it is true.

• Direct Marketing. It used to be called mail order. But whatever it's called this week, it works when it's good, and it's often good. Who would trade the Sharper Image, L.L. Bean, White Flower Farm or Harry and David for a lousy store experience! Even retailers with stores also succeed through the mail—Esprit, Eddie Bauer, Neiman-Marcus, Tiffany's. Think what's happened at Spiegel or The Book of the Month Club. Even pizza and

Chinese food can be delivered. Who needs to go to the store!

• Advertising. It will shift from outside advertising to in-store marketing. The problem is not just to get customers into the store, but to sell something to them when they get there. More and more money and attention will be devoted to signage, in-store promotions and gift with purchase—buy one, get one free, so buy 12. In-store marketing is taking the place of sales people.

• Visual presentation. This will be now, more than ever, the only retail factor that actually sells merchandise once the customer is in the store. Recognition of the importance of this profession will grow, and so (maybe) will the power and the pay. One of these days, a merchant will be president once again of some great store.

More to adore in 1984. Here are some things to watch out for this year:

• Radically different architecture. Not only Ornamentalism, but entirely new aspiring tops to buildings; the end of glass as the major outside material and the return of granite, marble, pattern cement, bricks and wood; and entryways with a real sense of occasion—above all real, instead of similar.

• High-tech. Computer panorama and otherwise more and more of the same—but more familiar, less frightening, more common and immediately balanced by innovations in high-touch.

• High-touch. People will crochet a cover for their home computers and display the quilt next to the robot. Every natural material, everything that is or looks handmade, will be prized. And this new balance between high-tech and high-touch is here to stay. There are tremendous retail implications here.

• Home. Going there, staying there and entertaining there. Designers, and then soon everyone else in the world, will discover self-expression, not just in what they wear, but suddenly—and most likely from now on—in where they wear it, and what they do when they get there.

• Entertainment. Whether at retail or the movies or at home. Cooking, game playing, dressing up, Halloween, EPCOT, Egypt, crafts, gardening ... all of these and more are social activities that require participation, competition and not just sitting in the stands and watching. This direction will be the mental and emotional successor to body-building, running and all "self help." We are going out—not just deeper and deeper in, and we'll take people with us.

• The end of the world. Which may not actually be in 1984, but the fight about nuclear everything will get a whole lot bigger right away. This will be more than marches. This will be movies, television ("The Day After"), plays, music and books. If we really are going to get concerned about the excellence of life, then, simultaneously, we will need to think about keeping it.

• The Orient. Not a sales promotion about Japan, but the true infusion of the Orient's "aesthetics system," both in visual things and in the treatment of people. The Orient has our attention by beating us at our own game. Now we must see what else it has to offer to adapt and to exchange.

• Clothing. Imagine a world in which your wardrobe is small and continuous, in which fads are replaced by continuity, in which the reaction of beholder is how you look, not what you're wearing. You don't need to imaging much—it exists now at Comme des Garcons. No wonder designers are going into other fields. We may have actually exhausted this one.

• Sex. In praise of men, hunks, 19-year-old movie stars and Chippendale's; in praise of women, Marilyn Monroe again and again. And sex in advertising ... nudity will hit the magazines and the videowaves, where it is permitted. European advertising has acknowledged the human body for years, while we have coyly covered it. About to be uncovered and discovered—Americans have bodies, too!

• Patriotism. Not just because we have many mini-wars, but because we need a resurrection of the spirit that got us where we were and ought to be. For every recognition of our failures, there must be a balancing, aggressive pride. However bad it is, this is the place we really would like to be most, and we'll start talking about it.

• Quality. Finally, a universal concern, and finally, some action. The car companies see it as their simple, sole salvation, and they have started working on it hard. The quality of goods and services has slipped beyond our tolerance, and we will start to swing back up to where we ought to be—making stuff that makes a profit, surely, but also stuff that's worth the effort. Those who ignore this need will lose their market.

• Excellence. In the way we do the things we do. It is the theme of every 1984 conference (not just a best-selling book), and we mean it. It is the key to the execution of every other activity.

• Heroes. Not just Iacocca, not just Olympic champions and not just those who do things both with quality and excellence. But beyond that, heroes are those who fight to get what they want and believe in. This will lead to leadership and decision-making—two "unpopularizing activities" that we sorely do need.

When *Sports Illustrated* named Mary Decker "Sportswoman of the Year," the headline on the story explained in perfect, poetic terms why heroes thrill us so much—"She runs and we are lifted."

COULD THIS BE REALITY?

WHAT DO THESE WORDS mean to you?

Home

Family

Patriotism

Quality

Religion

Heroes

Humanity

Not very long ago, surprised audiences found themselves in tears when a little extra-terrestrial repeated over and over again, "E.T. phone home." Suddenly, at the height of the fantasy era, an alien being connected with the rest of us, and humanity sparkled. This new humanity now is showing up in marketing. And that includes visual presentation, store design, architecture, advertising, display and every other aspect of the art of the visual image.

You can see the changes everywhere.

American architecture is no longer impersonal high-tech glass. It now has ornaments, towers, statuary—all suggesting that people live and work there. Furniture and furnishings have changed from fierce steel regulation to witty, amusing playthings.

Discos (and their music) are changing from the total-tech metal of The Saint to the watery promise of resident mermaids at Visage. Linda Ronstadt, erstwhile rocker, now sells love songs and this fall will appear as Mimi in *La Boheme*—a vast career leap and a love story if ever there was one.

A few years ago, the hottest stuff on television was brainless comedy sit-coms. Now everything is altered. We sweat out the "soapy" relationships in *Dallas*, *Dynasty* and *Knot's Landing*.

Even Calvin Klein's hefty narcissists seem to have made friends. His perfume ads are no longer love alone. They feature not only one, but two people doing intriguing things.

We're getting high on reality instead of fantasy. Friendship is better than chemicals. And doing unto others is better than doing unto yourself.

Could this be love?

These changes from isolation to companionship, from fantasy to reality, say something good about all of us.

What does all this philosophy and evidence have to do with visual presentation and marketing? Well, here's what—adroit marketing is always a heightened response to what is going on in the customer's mind. The opportunity is so great that when a visual merchant "connects," the creative ideas that result are so powerful their efforts go beyond mere marketing and into the realm of art.

It doesn't happen often. (Who cares, as long as it happens sometimes?)

Immediately the "families" of Ralph Lauren and Esprit (and the Jacksons) come to mind. Here are people who are wonderful, and they also are real, attainable. Identifying with them is possible. Second generation families include Merona. The Gap and Benetton. More human people.

The ultimate appeal of great heroes is not only their superhumanity, but their link with more ordinary mortals. Mary Decker actually lost a race. Lee Iacocca not only saves Chrysler, but heads a committee to restore the Statue of Liberty. And Michael Jackson is shy.

All this applies to modern marketing. If family is what the public wants, we'd better give it to them.

Three years ago, the entire liquor industry advertised beautiful, full-page pictures of bottles—only the product, no people. But in just three years, liquor ads in America have shrunk the bottles and replaced them with two people or a group, people engaged—like Merona, Benetton and Esprit—in mutual adventure and emotion.

It must be a trend.

Celebrity endorsement is stronger than ever. You get to see Larry Hagman and Joan Collins under sheets; Jane Fonda and Victoria Principal selling better bodies; Brooke Shields getting undressed again; and Diana Ross selling pantyhose for Kmart.

People, people, people are more important than product.

We want romance. We want love. We want each other. And on the way, we want Seagram's gin and Calvin Klein perfume.

The paradigm of all this humanity is reached in the most popular single entertainer of all time. Why is Michael Jackson so appealing (after talent, music, stardom, money, fame and publicity)? It's an accumulation of details: llamas in his backyard; his friendship with an 11-year-old; his charity; his glove. And they all add up, after the "success," to certain "terms of endearment." The lesson is important. He is, says Nelson George, a merge—black/white, male/female, exotic/wholesome, adult/child, sexy/religious.

Whatever happened to John Belushi, Lenny Bruce, Donna Summer, Grace Jones, Superman, drugs, crowding, booze, sex with strangers, mediocrity, lousy automobiles, not giving a damn, "It's not my department," and the whole grievous state of the country? Good things are happening. Our protests now seem to be *for* things, not against them.

The best windows I ever saw were done for Tiffany's by Gene Moore. They were a series of miniature-sculpted, New York park bench scenes. One showed three drunks on a bench sharing a flask. One showed two tourists on another bench gaping at, probably, Diana Vreeland. And one showed two bag ladies on a bench, both with shopping bags. One was very rich. One was poor, destitute and hopeless, with a $200,000 diamond necklace in the bag.

The best one (maybe ever) was a young couple together on one end of the bench, both admiring her new engagement ring. At the other end of the same bench was an old, fragile lady looking at her own hand, lonely ... and remembering.

Tiffany's should put those windows back in right now. And so should you.

The times are right. But better than that—they'll bring out the excellence in you.

1986 MARKETING MANIA

APRIL 1986

Sandra Torres of Houston won a car in a drawing at Leonard's department store. When she got it, she told the store to keep it. Why?

It was a 1979 station wagon with 89,000 miles on it, a side door that would not open, a missing headlight knob, a cracked dashboard, no back seat and no hubcaps. The store apologized.

What shopping center has 838 stores, four submarines, a French street, and contributes $5 billion annually to the economy of a city of 700,000?

West Edmonton Mall, Edmonton, Alberta, Canada.

What wonderful store, in a town of 800 people, started advertising "Free Ice Water" in 1931 and now attracts 15,000 people on a busy day in the Badlands of South Dakota?

Wall Drug, Wall, South Dakota.

Name seven social issues being changed by strong public opinion and aggressive legislation.

Drunk driving, missing children, safe sex, drugs, child abuse, seat belts and hunger in America.

What new 65,000-sq.-ft. store had 176,000 customers in its first five days, then closed temporarily when the waiting line was two hours long, and the lines inside at the registers were 90 minutes?

IKEA, Plymouth Meeting, Pennsylvania.

There are enough stores in this country to satisfy a population of 450 million people. What is our population?

258 million.

"A marketing campaign isn't worth doing unless it serves three purposes," said James Robinson, chairman of American Express (spending $500 million on advertising in 1985). What are they?

"It must grow the business, create news, and enhance our image."

One "retailer" expects to sell $320 million of stereos, jewelry and luggage through bill inserts this year. Who is it?

American Express.

What store has a delivery room where you can watch babies being born?

Babyland, Cabbage Patch Doll Headquarters, at 41st and Fifth Avenue, New York City.

What is green, two miles long and 72 stories high?

The dazzling green argon light tubing outlining the InterFirst Plaza Building in Dallas, visible for 15 miles.

What is Australia?

A large, island continent that everyone has ignored for far too long, but won't, if The Limited and Neiman-Marcus have anything to do with it in 1986. (Also look for Down Under, Outback and Olivia Newton John's Koala Blue.)

What are the four worst store names in America?

"Honk 'n' Holler," a truck stop in Tennessee, "Tank 'n' Tummy," same type place in Michigan, "Hide And Chic," a leather boutique in an unnamed department store, and "Aisle of Ewe," which sells handknits in Baltimore. There is also a set of toilets in Indiana marked "Setters" and "Pointers," and a drive-in funeral home in Georgia. H.L. Mencken was right; nobody ever went broke underestimating the taste of the American public.

The U.S.A. is behind. We still haven't had *Starlight Express* or *Chess*. And Andrew Lloyd Webber (*Cats*) has announced his next. Name it.

Phantom of the Opera, *previewed at England's Sydmonton Festival.*

Why do small businesses fail?

Bad management (33 percent). Inadequate capital, lack of experience, and owners not dedicated are the second, third and fourth most frequent reasons.

What would you say are the best consumer items of the past 25 years?

Stanley Marcus lists: disposable lighters, Post-it notes, Polaroid cameras, the Pill, the Water Pik, disposable diapers, felt-tip pens, seat belts, disposable razors, quartz watches, contact lenses, home computers, credit and debit cards, auto-focus cameras, transistorized televisions, instant copiers, supersonic transports, portable hair dryers, video-cassette recorders, electronic typewriters, mobile telephones. We've been busy, haven't we?

Whatever happened to Michael Jackson?

What difference does it make?

Name two national chains and two manufacturers who have banished gender from their vocabulary, using small, medium, and large, instead of his and hers.

Benetton and The Gap; Swatch and Esprit.

Where can you see robots guided by electronic sensors follow shoppers around the store, carrying packages, starting and stopping when they do; calculators attached to shopping carts, spiral escalators, laser-disc screens in dressing rooms to show environment, and more?

Seibu, Tsukuba, Japan.

Speaking of Michael Jackson, what are some of the things we are saying goodbye to right now?

Yuppies, disco, blue margaritas, all-glass buildings and Cajun food.

Name the stores that really blew it in 1985.

Sakowitz, Korvettes, Altman's, and Montgomery Ward.

What did Stanley Blacker allegedly do to collect insurance?

Soaked $30,000 worth of suits in water and filed a claim.

What's the hottest new (old) shopping zone in Paris?

The area called The Marais, behind the Beauborg Museum, near the Forum des Halles, which everyone said was doomed since it opened. Au contraire.

Who made the biggest marketing mistake of 1985?

Coca-Cola.

Who made the biggest garment-manufacturing mistake of 1985?

Coca-Cola Clothes (Murjani). Advertised as "All-American Clothes," it turns out they were made in Macao and Hong Kong. Murjani then said it planned to significantly increase its purchases from domestic producers.

Who canceled about $300 million worth of orders of foreign goods and planned to buy and sell American instead?

Sam Walton of Wal-Mart.

Name the three "stories" in Wendy's Russian fashion show commercial.

Daywear, Eveningwear and Swimwear: "Some people like a choice."

Japan is gadget heaven. Name seven new gadgets they have and we don't.

Electric toilets, self-cleaning mirrors, talking vending machines, electric taxi doors, picture telephones, electric revolving doors, ski jackets with built-in cassette players and speakers and hot coffee in a pop-top can.

What New York store—the most expensive ever built when it opened in 1965—will close this year?

Alexander's.

Merger-mania has hit England, too. Who's involved in their $2.2 billion deal?

Sir Terence Conran's company, Habitat-Mothercare, (which owns over 750 stores, including Conran's USA), is merging with British Home Stores, a department store and food retailer.

What great events in 1986 will certainly make headlines and could influence everything we do?

Reagan's visit to Russia and Gorbachev's visit here.

What shopping center's exterior is painted 528 coordinating colors?

Horton Plaza, San Diego.

What store and showbiz star combined to raise $6 million for muscular dystrophy?

7-Eleven and Jerry Lewis.

Skeptics cry that membership discount clubs won't work. Is this true?

There were 60 in January 1985, and 100 by the end of the year. Predictions now call for five times the present volume, or $20 billion by the early 1990s.

What's the newest trend in food?

Steak and potatoes, home cooking, "country cooking." What you hated in grade school will cost you now. Po Folks of Nashville has annual sales of

$1.5 million. But the company plans 1,000 units by 1995. Watch for Peavines, Zackly's ('zackly like Mother used to make).

A seven-dentist center in Cherry Hill offers a ten-speed bike free with each set of braces, sends roses to patients who refer other patients, and mailed 10,000 $25 gift certificates to prospective customers. What is the center's slogan?

"We cater to cowards."

What's been at L.S. Ayres since January while everyone else is on the back burner?

"Magic Mirror" displays up to ten outfits a minute on your reflected image while you watch. Ayres put the entire Liz Claiborne spring collection on the system, and sales soared 700 percent in one week.

WWD is often wrong, although always belligerent. Give a recent example.

Two pages proclaiming that Japanese fashion is finished, dead, forgotten. The next week Time *magazine ran three pages proclaiming Issey Miyake the best living designer.*

What is the most tasteless product of 1985?

Jim Carlberg, of Important Paper Products in Roseville, Illinois, offers four rolls of "the ultimate personalized toilet tissue" for $20. Any photograph the customer submits is printed on toilet paper. Isn't America wonderful?

Johnson & Johnson and Germaine Monteil are actively marketing to the woman over 40. Who are this customer's heroines?

Catherine Deneuve, 40; Linda Evans, 42; Joan Collins, 51; Sophia Loren, 50. The number of women between 35 and 54 will grow 56 percent by the year 2000. What are you doing about it?

Who said, "The only difference in stores is in the way customers are treated"?

Nordstrom.

Robert Townsend (Avis, American Express and "Up The Organization") was asked, "You travel the country, talking to managers. What's on their minds?"

The number one question is, "How do I get rid of my boss?"

What has seven levels, 12 disc jockeys, 590,000 records, two four-ton video banks of 25 monitors which rise and fall, lots of art, visits by Calvin Klein, Mick Jagger, Andy Warhol, Liza Minelli, and two million other lucky people per year?

The Palladium, a last-gasp disco in New York.

What grows seven times its size when wet?
Grobot: an eraser-sized foam robot.

What did an arsonist do to a retail store in Paris on December 19, 1985?
Set a fire that killed the owner of Fauchon and her daughter and injured 11 others.

What will open in 1990 twenty miles east of Paris, even though the Minister of Culture fought it all the way because it was not French and therefore not perfect?
Euro Disney. Cost: $1 billion.

Houston mayoral candidate Louie Welch, thinking the television cameras were turned off, suggested a curb to the spread of AIDS. What did he say?
"Shoot the queers."

What is seven hours long and has sex, Nazis and 87 costume changes for the star?
Sins *produced by and starring Joan Collins.*

Florida society matron Gregg Dodge attended neither an afternoon polo match nor a party thrown in the evening by Armand Hammer for Prince Charles and Princess Diana. What was the reason?
She told the Miami Herald, *"That's the day I have my legs waxed."*

What privately-owned department store single-handedly saved the down-town of Wilkes-Barre, Pennsylvania, by putting up one million lights throughout the entire city, then did exactly the same thing in Binghampton, New York?
Boscov's.

What new food products are selling?
Wine coolers, tofu desserts and, God save us, hot dogs with chili injected inside. Cabbage Patch Kid cereal is also with us. And more and more frozen foods.

What two great New York City buildings are being either improved or destroyed by flash-in-the-pan architects?
The Guggenheim and Whitney museums.

Whatever happened to Broadway theater?
Nothing.

What is possibly the best show running anywhere in the world right now?
Les Miserables *in London. Opens in New York, Spring, 1987.*

What is worth the two-hour wait to get in?

The Aquarium, Monterey, California.

If you could get a terrific seat for just one event in 1986, what would it be?

A boat in New York Harbor on July 4th.

What sells for $31.50, is wrapped in a blue blanket, has a snap-on, non-toxic, luminescent halo and is available in anglo, black and hispanic versions?

Baby Jesus dolls, with tags that read, "My name is Jesus. Jesus loves you. I am your friend. Please love me."

Who is Julie Brown?

A rocker who recorded, "I Like 'Em Big and Stupid," and said, "Madonna's not the only one who can act like a slut for big dollars."

How does the U.S.A. rank in percentage of women in the work force?

Third. Sweden and Norway rank higher. Almost two-thirds of U.S.A. women aged 15-64 are working.

The Boring Institute of Maplewood, N.J. (wish I'd thought of it) has named the ten most boring people in the nation. Can you?

Number One: Dr. Ruth Westheimer, who has managed the almost unmanageable feat of making sex seem boring; Sylvester Stallone, Mary Lou Retton, George Bush, Prince Charles and Princess Diana, Phil Donahue, Joan Rivers, Jerry Falwell, Madonna, and the entire cast of Dynasty.

"Madison Avenue" has named the ten best Christmas catalogs. Can you?

Neiman-Marcus, Harry and David, I. Magnin, F.R. Tripler, John Wanamaker, National Geographic, Cartier, French Creek Sheep and Wool, Banana Republic. Good Heavens! Whatever happened to The Gap, Pork Avenue, Sharper Image, Sointu, Dean and Deluca, The Nature Company, Crate & Barrel?

Last year, Live Aid, Band Aid, Farm Aid and others gave the music industry a new reason for being. Bob Geldof (now known as St. Bob among London rock 'n' roll circles) is a hero. What will the biggest fund-raising event of 1986 most likely be?

Hands Across America, this May.

If you celebrated New Year's Eve spending as much money as possible, what would you have been doing?

Spending it at the Essex House, New York City, where the party was $2,000 per person, plus whatever it cost to get you there and home again (Concorde?). Julio Iglesias sang.

Who is the first designer ever to open a boutique in the Soviet Union?
Pierre Cardin.

What category of merchandise went from sales of $25 million in 1984 to $200 million in 1985, and will reach $500 million by 1987?
Real juice-based sodas. "Slice" already has 2 percent of the soft drink market, and watch for "Minute Maid," "Perrier," "Max," home dispensers and "Paradise Coolers."

Where can you see entertainment, exhibits from 40 nations, Steam Expo, Tall Ships, a DC-3 Airmada, World in Motion, World in Touch, People Movers, Flying Trains, Jeepneys, gondolas, and Omnimax, for 165 days and nights?
EXPO 86, Vancouver, British Columbia, World Exposition. A great city, even before EXPO.

Who is spending $12 million between now and March to stun the unstunnables on upper Madison Avenue?
Ralph Lauren, who keeps insisting he's not a designer.

Who became the richest man in America in 1985?
Sam Walton, chairman of Wal-Mart.

A hospital ran a full-page ad offering "Custombirth," a complete package for $495, about one-third off. Ninety-six women signed up in three days; then the hospital followed with a special on cataract surgery. Where?
Texas, of course! Fort Worth's All Saints Hospital.

Last year Harrods racked up $10 million in two days advertising its sale-and-airfare package in *The New York Times*. Then what happened?
Air France and Printemps combined to offer a Christmas shopping holiday in Paris. Pan Am teamed up with Harrods, Fauchon, Galleries Lafayette, Porzellanhaus Zoellner and Loden Frey.

What Canadian chain suddenly opened seven stores in the U.S.?
Chateau Stores, Ltd., selling moderately-priced, fashion-forward apparel and shoes for women and men.

What astonishing cultural revelation was made by John Gambling on his WOR radio show?
Midwesterners sleep more than anyone else.

What stirring retail sight takes place in Dallas?
There is a hill from the top of which you can see seven 7-Elevens.

What is the ultimate egotist, Donald Trump, doing now?

He found 66 acres in Manhattan and plans to build the world's tallest building (150 stories), including 2,600 apartments, plus parking, a retail shopping center, television studios, a park and seven other 76-story towers. It will be called Television City.

How many 1985 fad items can you list?

Swatch watches, New Coke, bran in everything, Reebok's, Levi's 501 blues, Liquid Tide, Campbell's soup mix, Rambo, Dovebars, chocolate diet pop, stirrup pants, gummy bears, robots, paisley, caviar, fruit-flavored waters, fake pearls, Miami Vice, organizers, lace, Gone With the Wind on VCR, wine coolers, Madonna, Cabbage Patch Kids redux, Furskins, Teddy Ruxpin, blackened redfish, Mickey Mouse and Coca-Cola clothes, tanning salons, taps, fajitas, earrings for boys, chintz, florals, tapestries, Esprit, jams, hair-body-face-eye-and-dessert mousse, Lee Iacocca shirts, Herbalife, tooth bonding, sun-dried tomatoes, the drug Ecstasy, bagel chips, and the Statue of Liberty.

If you could pick just one big trend that will fascinate consumers, influence their buying habits and make you money, what would that be?

Bicycling. Ten million sold last year. See "Rhode Gear USA" catalog.

What's at The Metropolitan Museum, Bergdorf's and Bloomingdale's in 1986?

India.

What's the best looking store in London?

Jones. Top Man and Sabre are also swell.

Who's afraid of electronic shopping?

Any traditional retailer who suffers enough reality to believe it. You can buy 10,000 terminals for what it costs to renovate one store. By 1989, 50,000 terminals will rack up sales of $5-10 billion. Prediction: five percent of retail sales by 1990 and 20 percent by 2000. If you don't believe this, ask Sears, Penney's, 7-Eleven, Waldenbooks or Record World.

How many stores can you name that started life as a catalog?

Sharper Image, Banana Republic, Eddie Bauer, Brookstone, Royal Silk, Spencer Gifts, Victoria's Secret, Williams-Sonoma, and Sears.

What's a magalog?

A catalog with ads. Bloomingdale's says, "It's the next large medium." Neiman-Marcus has a great new no-ad magazine, and other stores, like

Marshall Field's (according to Time*) are "considering the advantages." There's that "back burner" again.*

Which retailers are doing the worst advertising in America?

Trump Tower copy excerpt: "Now that's a reason to get up in the morning! Beautiful men! Beautiful women! Ah, the Atrium, riding the escalators everyday. Up and down! Too glorious!"

Altman's copy excerpt: "If enemy aliens from outer space caused all the knitting needles on Mother Earth to disappear into some ultra-sonic infundibulum whoosh! like that, 99 percent of the world's would-be best-dressed women would find themselves wearing nothing at all this fall."

Gimbels' headline: "I regret that I have only one life to give for my plaids."

Ladies, would your boss pose nude for an underwear ad?

Send his or her photo and bio to Jockey International. The company's looking for active, interesting women in the workplace. Men, maybe later. If not your boss, send yourself, or someone you feel needs the exposure!

What is the absolutely worst opportunistic ad ever?

Seven days after the Mexican earthquake, this full-page headline blazed through The Los Angeles Times:

"If, God forbid, L.A. is next, our commitment will remain unshaken." The ad was placed by The Rose Hills Mortuary and Forest Lawn Mortuary.

Why did retailers (except Brookstone) ignore Halley's Comet?

Because they didn't realize that this 65-million-ton chunk of dust and ice could sell $1 billion in related merchandise.

Estee Lauder spent $52 million launching "Beautiful" last year, a radical contradiction to "Obsession," "Poison," "Opium," et cetera. Andy Warhol, the great renaissance artist, went to the launch party. What did he say?

"I was thinking it might be fun to start my own perfume line and call it 'Stink.'"

How often are the students of Veteran's High School, Warwick, R.I., allowed to go to the bathroom?

Twice a day. The principal, Edmund Miley, believes there is a link between bathroom visits and falling grades, citing "not biological urges, but an urge to get out of class."

Did Les Wexner buy General Motors?

No.

What did Les Wexner say when asked how he wanted to be remembered?
"As a good sweater buyer."

Looking for quality? See if you agree with this list of the best.
Best image: Esprit
Best designer: Issey Miyake
Best store service: Nordstrom
Best New York restaurant: Jams
Best morale: Mervyn's
Best product extensions: Swatch
Best U.S.A. hotel: The Bel-Air
Best world hotel: Regent, Hong Kong
Best new store: IKEA, Pennsylvania
Best changed retailer: The Gap
Best revised catalog: Neiman-Marcus
Best big New York store: Bloomingdale's
Best new downtown retail center: San Diego
Best theme for meetings: Risk-taking
Best Broadway show: None
Best new magazines: *Elle*, *Details*
Best management idea: Unannounced visits
Best new ways to eat: Nibbling, trolling, grazing.

NO DETAIL IS TOO SMALL

APRIL 1987

How should stores start their meetings?
"Please be brief. We are 25 years late."
    —*Sam LeFrak (NYC construction tycoon)*

What happened on Monday, Nov. 10, 1986?
Bruce Springsteen made $5 million selling his five-record album.

What happened on Tuesday, Nov. 11, 1986?
Only 37.3 percent of 112 million eligible voters went to the polls, the worst showing since 1942. Bruce Springsteen matters more than the U.S. government.

Who is writing a major book, "because I don't get to talk a lot on the show"?
Vanna White

What do you get when you mix America's two biggest passions: television and shopping?
You get home shopping clubs and dozens of other shows. HSC reports sales up 5,000 percent in the last year. Hess's is on TV already. Sears is "experimenting."

Why do people go shopping?
It could be to lift depression. Today, some 14 million Americans suffer from prolonged depression. One in four women and one in ten men can expect to suffer a serious bout at some time in their lives.

Is Ross Perot a villain or a hero?
It depends on whom you ask. Management hates him, fired him and paid him over $7 million to keep his mouth shut. But he did say, "Paying management their big bonuses would be exactly as though the generals at Valley Forge in our revolution decided to buy new uniforms for themselves when the troops were fighting in the snow barefoot." He also said, "People can't be managed ... People must be led." And he said, "It's not robots, it's not technology, it's how we treat our people." And speaking of titles, he said "Titles cost nothing. Titles mean nothing. That's one of the problems in our country. We assign too much emphasis to titles and not enough emphasis to what we're doing."

Not bad for someone who's not talking.

Name six brand new ways of advertising in addition to video shopping.
1. Mobile billboards mounted on trucks in New York City

2. "Buy As You Fly," from flight attendants on TWA flights—mostly close-out merchandise at discounts

3. Pop-up inserts in magazine—vastly expensive, very attention-getting

4. Print ads on restroom walls, the specialty of a San Francisco agency

5. Commercials now showing on 5,000 of the United States' 18,000 first-run movie screens

6. P-o-p radio—48 minutes of music and 12 minutes of commercials each hour now at Eckerd Drugs, People's, Fays, Toys "R" Us.

Will a video fashion magazine ever happen?

It has. Video Fashion Monthly *premiered this past January with all original material, runway footage, interviews, makeovers, service pieces—all in action, as fashion ought to be. $9.95. First run was 30,000 copies, aiming for 100,000 by the end of 1987.*

Pierre Cardin had the first Western store in the Soviet Union. Who said, "We could have two stores in every major city there by 1990"?
A Benetton executive.

How does Atco Properties reward healthy workers?
$500 for a year's worth of walking up 16 flights of office stairs

$500 for smokers who quit for a year

$100 for each pound of flesh lost that stays lost

Out of 27 employees, two-thirds participate. President Dale Hemminger says, "People feel better about themselves, and they do a better job."

If you could read two books to improve and inspire you right now, what would they be?
Made in Japan: Akio Morita and Sony Corporation *(published by E.P. Dutton)*

McDonald's: Behind the Arches *(by John F. Love; published by Bantam).*

How did Arthur Ortenberg, husband and business partner of Liz Claiborne, describe their "rustic retreat lifestyle on Fire Island" in *W*?
"We're just like ordinary people, only richer."

What star has inspired us all to commit ourselves, our souls, and all our resources to fighting AIDS?
Elizabeth Taylor has helped raise over $4 million so far. She said, "I promise you I have committed my life to fight for the cure."

Add one street to the following: Bond Street, Champs Elysees, Fifth Avenue and Rodeo Drive.
Michigan Avenue, Chicago—it's too bad that Marshall Field's and Carsons are on State Street. But Neiman-Marcus, Korshak, Lord & Taylor, another Field's, Crate & Barrel, Watertower Place and a soon-to-be-opened Bloomingdale's are all on Michigan Avenue. All of this is in a town of no population growth, which is giving the suburbs hiccups.

What store decided not to have teddy bears at Christmas?
Target purchased 1.5 million stuffed Shar-pei dogs, called them Kris

Krinkle, and sold them all by December 15.

Why are Americans so fat?

They pig out on dessert, then demand Sweet 'N Low. Consumption of ice cream increased 109 percent in 1986. Cake and cookie eating are up 56 percent. The average child sees 10,000 food commercials a year. Large-size apparel sales will reach $8 billion in 1987. Sixty percent of women wear size 12 or larger. Lane Bryant will open 185 new stores this year. So much for "FITNESS." We are thinking thin and getting fat.

What would increase sales for Father's Day?

A sharper understanding of current fatherhood. Fathers have new roles in many families. Men are more interested in their appearance. More products are appearing. Fathers attend hospital births. Fathers spend more time with their kids. Bill Cosby's book Fatherhood *is a hit.* Fathers Magazine *has been published.*

What is the most original product devised in Murfreesboro, Tennessee?

"Clean" urine samples, at $50 apiece.

Test yourself. Who bought the following?
1. Allied Stores Corp.
2. Associated Dry Goods Corp.
3. Woodward and Lothrop
4. Wanamaker's
5. Macy's
6. Tiffany's
7. Alexander's
8. Zales
9. B. Dalton
10. Brooks Fashion
11. Charles of the Ritz
12. Henri Bendel
13. Genesco
14. Brandeis

Answers:
1. Campeau
2. May Co.
3. Taubman
4. Woodward and Lothrop
5 Management
6. Management
7. Donald Trump
8. Dart Drug
9. Barnes and Noble
10. Dylex
11. Yves St. Laurent
12. The Limited
13. Target
14. Younker's

How did Oscar Wilde define "fashion?"
"Fashion is something so ugly that it must be changed every six months."

Where should you and Benetton open a store in the year 2000?
Not in Chicago—try Nigeria, which might be the world's third most populated country after China and India. With 6.2 billion people on earth, some of them will still want to buy knitwear.

Why do men hate shoes?
Who knows, but they do. The average man purchases two pairs a year; the average woman buys six. Larry Sherman, Detroit shoe merchant says, "A man buys shoes like he buys tires. He buys them because his old ones are worn out, and he needs to replace them."

Now Liz Claiborne is moving into retailing. Will this hurt her business with department stores?
First Boston Corp. analyst Margaret Gilliam said, "Any manufacturer who relies on department stores for distribution has a death wish." Liz Claiborne's second quarter earnings rose 48 percent to $178.9 million.

BABIES ARE OUR BUSINESS

OCTOBER 1987

IT'S been seven years since Wrangler shocked Europe by putting up bill-boards showing an embryo in utero wearing blue jeans. The slogan read: "Get dressed for the adventure."

Now, babies are back. They're forming a marketing force, and you can see it coming. It started with the persistent worldwide appearance of those diamond-shaped yellow car signs warning "Baby on Board." Whoever invented those signs should have patented them—he/she would be very rich.

Yes, retailers have seen the future, and it says "Babies." Look what's happening:

• GapKids—the newest chapter in the resurrection of The Gap.

• Esprit Kids—sprouting all over the world, in "company stores" and franchises.

• 012 ("Baby" Benetton)—instantly identifiable as Benetton stores, but with clouds on the ceiling.

• Gymboree—another hit in Phil Schlein's collection of inspired stores. This one makes you want to get down on the floor and play, and they'll probably let you.

• Waldenkids—a brilliant invention selling books and much, much more. It's really a comprehensive learning center and very exciting, too.

If all this is happening, can Les Wexner and others be far behind? The best way to see all these new stores together is on the upper level of the Westside Pavilion in Los Angeles. The cumulative impact of the group shows the total range of the story. Even the May Company at the end of the hall had a "kids" window. And two important—though not so new—stores are still retailing landmarks: Babyland and FAO Schwarz, in New York City.

The most amazing childcare centers in retail are at IKEA. There, toddlers are deposited in a room with 9,000 colorful balls while parents go shopping. It's called "The Ballroom."

One of the most radical things a retailer has done this year is the ad that's run on several occasions in *The New York Times*, paid for as a public service by Caroll and Milton Petrie. (Milton is chairman of Petrie Stores, Inc.) It's about a baby, too, but in an extremely daring way. The headline reads: "This Baby Has AIDS." And the copy begins: "His name is Michael. He is 15 months old. From birth, Michael tested anti-body positive for AIDS. And now, symptoms of the disease have struck. Sooner or later, probably sooner than later, Michael will die. In the meantime, he has love. He has Mother Hale. For 18 years, Mother Hale has nurtured back to health infants born with in-utero drug addiction. Hale House, established in 1969, has long been recognized as a place of miracles. President Reagan, in his 1985 State of the Union address, described Mother Hale as a 'true American hero.' The most important medicine administered at Hale House is love. Then last year, a baby died. Our worst fears were realized. The epidemic of AIDS has reached the most innocent victims of all—our children."

Babies are creeping into non-baby product advertising. Kodak shows a muscle-bound dad tenderly holding a baby; both are nude. Scandia Down Shop's ad shows a mother and baby in bed together, captioned "Tender is the Night." Stearns and Foster shows and tells viewers how to "sleep like a baby." These portrayals are daring and aim for a very strong emotional response. They get it.

Krementz, the jewelry company, has an ad that people will be tearing out of magazines and putting up on their refrigerators. An almost full-page photo of a man's hand with a big gold ring on the little finger is spread out on a bed sheet. An infant's hand is holding dad's little finger with all its might. The copy reads: "Gold. The mark of a man ... a prized possession to be handed down from generation to generation."

Babies have even invaded IBM advertising. Two-page ads in sober American business journals show two pairs of crocheted baby booties—one pink, one blue. The headline reads "Guess which one will grow up to be the engineer?" IBM says, "We intend to continue supporting programs like these (90 support programs to strengthen women's skills) because we all have a lot to gain with men and women on equal footing." Lo and behold, IBM has announced the strength of women in the workplace begins with babyhood.

Look at the movies. *Raising Arizona* is a surrealistic comedy about a baby. *Three Men and a Baby* is predicted to be the biggest box office hit for Christmas release.

Look at magazines. Europe has had *Vogue Bambini* and others for years. Now, finally, we have a great kids' trend and fashion magazine—*Child* from *The New York Times* magazine operation.

For smart marketing companies, there is definitely a "Baby on Board," and they're doing something about it.

DINO MIGHT

JULY 1993

WHENEVER the world is too much with us, we turn away to other diversions.

Sometimes we escape to art, or even love, sometimes to drugs and disasters. These diversions entertain a lot of people and make a lot of money. The knack is always in knowing what the right diversion is, and that's where vision makes the difference. Steven Spielberg sells more stuff to more people than any other entertainer on earth because he knows perfectly where people wish to escape to, and how, and when, and why—and then he gives it to them in a $60-million package. *E.T.* did it—to almost everyone on earth.

And dinosaurs are supposed to do it now. The world is too much with us. We will escape again. We must go—to Dinotopia. Say "dinosaur," and everybody answers back: "extinct." What's so compelling about the beasts? Pressed for answers, we come up with "awesome," "biggest," "dead," and "extinct." But there's more to the fascination.

"Barney" gives kids a daily television overdose of sweetness in the mornings, and the sitcom "Dinosaurs" circles around prime-time programming. We buy dinosaurs at FAO Schwarz, or else we scoop them up in sets from sidewalk vendors in front of the store at $5 each. The American Museum of Natural History unveils Barausaurus, the largest dinosaur skeleton in the world. The museum then mails educational posters on dinosaurs free to seven million school children, courtesy of McDonald's. What's more, two years ago I was given a pair of battery-operated, dinosaur-foot bedroom slippers, which roared with every footstep. Another friend who sees things coming gave me James Gurney's book *Dinotopia* for Christmas.

And director Steven Spielberg's movie *Jurassic Park* has just opened!

In preparation for this dino-film, in April, Spielberg's company has signed deals with 100 businesses to make and market more than 1,000 *Jurassic Park* products—from action figures and video games to calendars and candy. Spielberg hopes every kid in America will be a dinomaniac.

The trend keeps making the news. April 26, 1993, the cover of *Time* magazine boasted, "The Truth About Dinosaurs. Surprise: Just about everything you believe about them is wrong." On May 3, 1993, the cover of *Fortune* magazine read, "Dinosaurs: Sears, IBM, General Motors: The decline of these three giants is the biggest what-went-wrong story in U.S. business history. There are lessons here for everybody." These three were always among the 20 biggest worldwide companies since 1972. Today IBM is 26th, GM is 40th, and Sears is 81st! They are not alone: Procter & Gamble and Bristol-Myers have also disappeared from the top 20, and Kodak and Exxon are struggling.

Astonishingly, they all seem to have done this to themselves; the enemy was a varied cocktail of arrogance, routine, rigidity and lack of innovation. But there is a far deeper note in our reaction to these images: the real dinosaurs are not the companies which fail, but the people who run them.

Asked to explain what went wrong, GM's Roger Smith said, "I don't know—it's a mysterious thing." As Pogo said, "We have seen the enemy and it is us!"

But there is a lot more to it than the decline of our biggest companies. The United States itself is not (nor is any country) the uncontested power on earth. We are also witnessing—and causing—a planetary and social decline which may get rid of us faster than the dinosaurs.

June 11, 1993: *Jurassic Park* opens. No matter what the film is like, it will be seen—immediately—by many millions of people who want to see dinosaurs.

We love to remind ourselves that dinosaurs are dead. We've come to envy their fortune: they were better off than we are. Dinosaurs dominated the earth for an incomprehensible 165 million years. That's more than 45 times longer than human beings have lived now. We also know, as we go racing toward the millennium, that we have done ourselves grave harm in less than four million years. No wonder we crave dinosaurs.

Today as we sit in darkened cineplexes, wearing dinosaur watches and drinking from dinosaur Coca-Cola cups, watching Velociraptors dance, we are temporarily freed from David Koresh and the Branch Davidians, from Bosnia, Somalia and AIDS, from ozone depletion and from crime out of control outside the cinema door. Dinosaurism is a handy escape from the facts as this brief thousand years comes to an end.

The sweetest imagining can be found in *Dinotopia: A Land Apart from Time*, a romantic fairy tail written and illustrated by James Gurney. Dinotopia is a land where dinosaurs and humans live in peaceful interdependence. The dinosaurs appreciate the skills and liveliness of *homo sapiens*, and the humans benefit from the wisdom and gentleness of the very much older species.

Their land is not ours, and the time is not this, but oh, how we wish it were!

Back in this world, we already compare our biggest companies to long-dead beasts. We know we will not live 165 million years. We do not live in peaceful coexistence with nature or other species or even ourselves. Our infatuation with dinosaurs is evidence of wishing for what we might have been. Sometimes it seems that dinosaurs are more alive than we are. And we can see that as we turn the fairy tale pages. We sit in the cineplex munching popcorn, turned away from our own extinction, watching dinosaurs at play in the land of the living.

PART TWO
DESIGN

FIXTURES THAT ARE NOT FIXTURES

OCTOBER 1983

IN THE RETAIL EPIDEMIC of sameness, nothing is more "the same" than fixtures. There is no store in the world that doesn't lose the customer in a forest of rounders, three-arms, four-arms, waterfalls, shelving, rods and racks.

The "wood era" is followed by the "chrome-and-glass era," and it all looks the same—shiny and reflective.

The world is swept away by slatboard walls and slatboard fixtures, and suddenly the whole world gets grooved to death.

The shoe folks dig up "cubes." Instantly and universally, cubes are used for storage, seating, display ... and all suffer from Acute Cubitis.

These trends come and go. Giant corporations grunt and sweat with sweeping "policies" and "images," and spend vast fortunes changing a look they've finally established in the customer's mind, to some entirely different "new" look, leaving the customer confused all over again.

The basic problem, simply, is that retailers must have some major system of housing for merchandise. It is the most fundamental (and probably the most costly) thing in a store, besides the store itself. And, certainly, the basic fixturing system must be harmonious, flexible, practical and somewhat invisible—to not distract from the merchandise.

But amidst all this sameness, there must be punctuation points—something for the eye to delight in, stop at, rest, refresh itself and get ready to move on into the next forest of fixtures and merchandise.

Consider some exciting uses of fixtures that are *not* fixtures:

A fixture has got to be admitted to be anything that houses and presents merchandise.

Then we can get on with the question: When is a fixture not a fixture? When it is ...

• A cart. Rush to The South Street Seaport in New York City to see the most dazzling and original use of carts, pioneered by The Rouse Co.; in use at Harborplace, Quincy Marketplace and rented even by the week at The Waterside in Norfolk. No "fixture" could take the place of these carts.

• An over-designed cart. At Queen's Quay in Toronto; a masterful Lake Ontario-side restoration of a vast refrigerated warehouse, but the carts have been designed for too many millions of dollars to look like high-tech-ornamental masterpieces, and the modest displays of ware that go best on carts are overwhelmed by Trump Tower-like glitz.

• Armoires and other real antiques. Almost done to death by Britches of Georgetown imitators, but there is still a note of realism that is right for menswear using things with doors and drawers and pigeonholes in roll-top desks. Men feel safe looking at socks in English club-like furniture.

• A billiard table at Outfitters. Northpark, Dallas—really good use of "table space" instead of a counter.

• An all-new slanted paperback book fixture. At Dayton's re-done downtown St. Paul store. Just by using an unexpected angle, an entire book department invites you into the store instead of stopping you with rectangular aisles.

• Moving electric drycleaner's racks. At every Le Sportsac store, keeping the merchandise moving past the customers. How many fixtures move?

• Towel dowels on the cedar walls of a sauna bath. In the dazzling new Ralph Lauren Home Fashion showroom at J.P. Stevens, New York City. When this many towels on dowels are lined up, you can count them as fixtures.

• The ground. In the camel market in Sousse, Tunisia, squared-off ground plots are used by all the shoe sellers, and the geometric neatness that makes any kind of "fixtures" work, works here—on the ground.

• Ordinary tables used for action. The Limited's "buy-one-get-one-free" promotion is simple and (mandatorily) set out on a plain, rectangular table just in the entrance of the store. Hickory Farms simply sets its (mandatory) samples in front of the store. So do cooking demonstrators at Macy's Cellar. A table is a portable stage.

• Giant zinc tubs. Set out on tables, full of fresh fruits, under a vast white tent, at the Esprit International meeting not only provided great fixtures for the fruit, but were handsome objects in themselves and could contain anything.

• Crates, barrels, anything shipped in great containers. See Crate & Barrel, of course, the chain whose very name names its fixtures. All these "authentic" fixture work, and imagination stacks them in many wonderful ways.

• Boats. Yes, boats. The entire famous floating market "klongs" in Bangkok display all the wares of the nation on countless river-streets of boats, and the customers (in their own boats) paddle along from "fixture" to "fixture."

"That's ridiculous," you say. "We don't live on the water. Now he's gone too far."

Go back to The South Street Seaport before your rage expires, and see real boats on dry land used as fixtures.

• A fifties white Cadillac. Jammed with Christmas gifts at Fiorucci.

• Good Humor trucks, hot dog stands. Anything that can be wheeled that moves, with someone to move it.

• A major staircase against a wall with pigeonhole shelf space facing you. Merchandise is danced down the staircase by mannequins, and ordinary shelving is transformed. The whole thing is a modern adaptation of an ancient Japanese set of steps-and-storage; in a children's store at Parco, Tokyo.

• Sprayed white stucco shelving that looks like a cave. At La Gaminerie, Boulevarde Ste. Germaine, Paris. Just like ordinary shelving, but completely different in color, texture and shape.

Now you can go on to fix your asphyxiating fixture fantasies. And demand more of yourself, your sources, your management and your customers than another system of racks.

MUSIC HATH CHARMS

OCTOBER 1984

HOW MANY TIMES can you remember being stirred by sound or music so memorable that it is what you think of first when the memory comes to mind? The Olympic fanfare? Bach's B-Minor Mass at St. Patrick's Cathedral? "The Star-Spangled Banner?" Taps? Bloomingdale's?

It hardly ever happens in stores.

The Saks on Union Square in San Francisco started out life with loud-speakers on the street outside the store. You could hear Saks as you looked at it. The speakers seem to be gone now.

Going into Omo Kamali in New York City, you hear a blast of environmental noises at the entrance, immediately followed by silence in the foyer, followed by the sound of various videos in the background, followed by other changing sounds and music as you go towards the first merchandise. Four sets of sounds, and you're still in the front of the store. It is a rich experience and certainly part of the "presentation" of the store.

But Kamali's kind of sound tailoring and conditioning is confined almost entirely to small, independent boutiques in the three or four biggest cities on earth. The rest are silent—or ought to be because the music experience in most stores is so entirely bland that no one can remember it.

Visual presentation is always concerned with display, props, graphics and merchandise. But there is an area that seems to be ignored and where skills fall far behind the state of the art. That area is music—or sound, to put it more broadly and imaginatively.

⦿ The opening of EPCOT each morning where the crowd that has waited patiently is finally let into the park as the band plays "The William Tell Overture"—unforgettable and funny

• The sound of marches being played at opening in Tokyo department stores as the employees train and train again in bowing to the customer

• The sight and sound of a string quartet live in Paul Stuart in New York City on Madison Avenue

• The minuet at tea-time in Fortnum and Mason in London, as two costumed characters (Mr. Fortnum and Mr. Mason) come down the steps to have tea, dressed in Restoration costume.

All the rest have music "services" or blasting radios or nothing.

Music is a field as vast and various as the field of visual arts, and we tap the visual arts inexhaustibly. But nobody seems to know or care much about music. It only rarely is used in stores. It is always described as "soothing" and "background."

The purpose of retailing is not to lull, soothe and relax, nor is it to irritate. It is supposed to stimulate a variety of responses from the customer. Music hath charms to soothe the savage beasts, but it also can create every other emotional thing. It is, of all the arts, the fastest means of communication.

At Christmas, it is a thrill to walk into the medieval chancel at the metropolitan Museum of Art. The "art" is certainly there each year on the magnificent tree. The instant of shocked emotion every time is not the sight of the tree alone, though. It is the enthralling clarity of the sound of the choir singing Johann Sebastian Bach.

The visual event of a lifetime is to walk—even for the thousandth time—into the Piazza San Marco in Venice. The eyes are occupied every time. But when for an instant you close them, it is the sound of the tinny bands playing sentimental German waltzes that makes you reach for a chair and sit down.

So why have the "visual" geniuses ignored this sense? Is it simply because "nobody else does it either?" Lack of knowledge? Lack of emphasis?

Isn't this very lack of other doing it what gives the first of you the edge and spur to do it?

Do it.

Turn off the garbage. We hear so much noise today that we hear nothing. Think of the thrill it would give you to pull the wires viciously out of the wall. And then begin, as if from the beginning, to rediscover the power of sound and its influence over the person who hears it—in your case, the customer. Add knowledge and variety. Get a music or theater genius to calculate your expectations and bring them back in sounds.

Music should be planned with the care and expertise that you would plan it for a fashion show—a good fashion show. Most fashion shows use just of mess of whatever's newest, with no regard for the clothes or their objective. Last year I actually saw a Chicago show finale where models labored to show clothes to a background of "Liebestod" from "Tristan und Isolde." The music man must have hated models.

In a fashion show, there can be rhythm, pace, syncopation and the entire range of human emotion distilled in sound. In a store, the shopping experience should tap not just the eyes, but every sense. A decision to buy something is an emotional experience, and a store should get there in every way it can.

Sure, music hath charms to soothe the savage beasts. But it also hath charms that can sell.

INVASION OF THE STORE SNATCHERS

NOVEMBER 1984

THE FIGHT IS ON. It is the bloodiest battle in years. Manufacturers are invading stores in a desperate quest for space and brand identification, and they are succeeding.

Many stores are losing what little identities they have. *The New York Times* says, "Stores today are plagued by a lack of distinction and a failure to project their identities to the public." This is partly because all that most stores ever present to the customer is price. But it's also because they don't have very strong identities to fight for in the first place. The sign over the door says Joske's or Burdine's or Marshall Field or Lord & Taylor, but six feet inside the door it all becomes Clinique. You could be anywhere on earth—or nowhere. You could fly 3,500 miles and walk straight into another Clinique counter.

This always has been true, but suddenly it isn't just cosmetics. It's dozens and dozens of manufacturers from every area—all with the same idea.

They enter armed with designers, floor plans, fixtures, advertising, graphics, music, uniforms, total marketing plans and presentations, power and money. Then they have lunch with the president.

The vendors are winning.

Stores have been dying of sameness for years. They have a new "image" every time they have new management. They live by imitation other stores, getting less and less distinct, and they allow themselves to be divided into 40 or 50 little non-stores.

Here is a picture of the apocalypse: Some day soon, some store will be the first store not to be a store at all. It will not have a square inch to call its own. It simply will be a collection of other people's property stretching from door to door and floor to floor—a seamless sea of manufacturer product and presentation. It will be like a miniature wholesale market.

In order to avoid the apocalypse (or closings or mergers or acquisitions), it is worthwhile to set forth what stores can do about this problem. Here's an oversimplified scenario.

Six Steps to Salvation:

• Stop bitching and whining. Right now, the stores have fallen behind the manufacturers because they haven't done anything about it. The problem is happening to them. Unless attitudes change, they'll never be able to go on to the next steps.

• Forge an image and stick to it. Easier said than done. How many stores can you name that any customer could identify? The list is short: Saks, Nordstrom, Bloomingdale's, Lord & Taylor, The Limited, Crate & Barrel, Brookstone, Brooks Bros., Wilkes Bashford, The Sharper Image, Spiegel, L.L. Bean.

How many stores can you list that the customer could be confused by? The list is endless. But the list of clear-image manufacturers is long: Generra, Santa Cruz, 9 West, Liz Claiborne, Esprit, Ralph Lauren, Koret (yes, with 400 shops next year) and many others, including all the cosmetics companies that are opening their own stores because they're so strong.

Forging a strong identity isn't easy, or more stores would have done it. You need unity of ambition, a mission, a statement, courage and a management that can make decisions and stand by them for long-term. Your position needs to be something more than price. Your management needs guts.

• Prepare a statement/presentation of your image and stick to it. How can a store fight for an image when it doesn't have one? Prepare a counter-presentation that clearly states and dramatizes your position. Mervyn's, Parisian and L.S. Ayres can show their "missions" to anyone, missions that are fired up and ready to go.

• Work out rules and pass the work to everyone. Your 140 buyers, merchandise managers, marketing and visual people all need the same word in the same way. The entire army must be armed. Each must know the image, the rules and the presentation. (They do at Saks.) Keep it short and clear, and do not change your mind every time a manufacturer dangles more money in front of your eyes.

• Fight with private label. If your own name has value to the customer, use it. This is the only way you will have both merchandise and presentation that don't exist elsewhere. The genius of The Limited is private label merchandise and marketing. This of Hunter's Run, Forenza and now Kenzo. (Kenzo did $35 million worldwide last year. This year, The Limited plans $55 million for Kenzo.) But many stores haven't explored this.

After Neiman-Marcus, Macy's Cellar, Dayton's and Saks (at Saks, the policy is no merchandise purchased without the Saks label in it, period) how many more stores can you name that sell their image literally?

• Work toward a partnership. This is best of all and inevitable. Cooperate. Manufacturers have great stuff and great designers to show it with. They have the money and marketing skills. And you have your image (maybe) to preserve and market. Develop cooperative design standards. The two of you could come up with something better than each alone. Something new—still yours and still theirs—will be born. But it only works when two strong sides meet and work together. That's why stores need to get stronger before they fight.

A good example of harmonious compromise is the new Esprit shop at Saks, New York City. Both hold their own. Both win. The shop looks like Saks, and it looks like Esprit. It is the result of two entities coordinating the vital concerns of each with image and identity. Instead of whining, they worked together and came out better for it.

The battle is far from over, and there will be more, much more on this subject. Watch for "The Return of the Store Snatchers."

THE UNBEARABLE LIGHTING IN STORES

AUGUST 1985

IN THE BEGINNING God said, "Let there be light." That must have been the first day retailers ignored him. Retailers live in the dark where lighting is concerned. Their efforts with music are bad enough, but lighting is worse. As far as retailers are concerned, God could have rested an extra day.

For years the big excuse for lousy lighting has been money. Back when every store had fluorescent lights and incandescent sources were "new," the incandescent lights were too expensive to buy and too expensive to operate and too hot. But the aggressive stores installed them, and then everyone did. Now every store has incandescent lights.

Then neon came along and was considered too expensive. Meanwhile, the aggressive stores got it. Now everyone has it, and neon is boring. And even neon can be wrong. When Emporium Capwell did its basement as a "cellar," a new neon artwork on a wall showed a whistling pink teapot. Housewares, get it? But the blessed merchants had piled up mattresses under the sign.

Now there are lasers and light boxes and computers and programmed lighting. There is even the odd lighting consultant (a designer, not a store planner). Of course, those people are too expensive, but Chess King has one.

Today we're living through yet another wave of innovation that could be called the New Wave Pierce and Blind School. It's expensive, too. It's also bad. The "method" requires dozens of costly little instruments that swivel and dangle and rise and fall and aim extremely intensive lights at small, isolated patches of merchandise. Jarring pockets of light and darkness are created, with some of the merchandise lit. It gets dangerous when a customer goes to a rack, picks a garment and turns around to be blinded. Uneven, specific focusing is a good idea, but it defeats the purpose when it causes ophthalmologic damage to customers.

One of these days stores will learn that lighting is an art and a science and a specialty—not just a load of equipment. The few retailers who do know about lighting are working wonders. At Seibu in Japan, lasers project rainbows over escalators, and you travel up through them between floors. Macy's uses light paths on main aisle ceilings, providing "streets" as compelling as aisles. For instance, in the Arcade, the lights are white until Christmas, and then the million bulbs go red. The artists at Saks know how to buy the right lights and focus them in their windows, and so do a very few others. But I have an uneasy feeling that most window lighting in the world is just a matter of "on" or "off."

Retail lighting never has been as innovative as lighting in other fields. There are geniuses designing lighting for discos and theater. Lighting can be used to excite and confuse a dance mob. It can be used facing an audience; Joseph Svoboda lit actors from behind, concealing the actual instruments, but projecting a great dramatic glow behind the actors for ominous and thrilling silhouettes. Most store designers are not Joseph Svoboda, though they could learn a lot of magic by taking some lighting courses.

"Let there be light" doesn't necessarily mean fluorescent mixed with incandescent or neon or special effects with lasers, etc. What about daylight? I've never understood why more stores don't use sunlight. Oh, you hear a lot of nonsense about it like, "The sun fades the merchandise." That's a feeble excuse for not thinking about it.

When you do see sunlight in stores, it works wonders. Think of the skylight on "The Main Course" at Bloomingdale's or the radiant effect of the stained-glass dome in The Galleries Lafayette in Paris, or the exuberance of The Galleria in Milan or its descendants in Dallas, Houston and Toronto. As punctuation, it has no comparison. Of course there are disadvantages to either sunlight alone or only artificial light. Obviously stores lit by sunlight are in trouble when the sun goes down.

I've only seen the right combination once, and it is the most exhilarating experience. The dazzling new Esprit store in Los Angeles went through a couple of prior existences as a bowling alley and a disco, including the addition of a dozen major skylights.

When Joe D'Urso turned that space into Esprit, he used the skylights as departure points for an entirely new idea, instead of covering them up. He devised a near-miraculous computerized lighting system that "reads" daylight all day as it changes with the weather. The computer directs all the artificial lighting in the store into a constantly changing, always harmonious balance. It's a treat to spend time in the store and actually watch (and feel) the lighting spend the day with you. It's a great example of using high technology for high-touch objectives. It creates fun, excitement and warmth. The system has not lost sight of its objectivity, though; this highly sophisticated equipment makes the merchandise look its best, and that makes customers try it on and buy it.

To sum it up, the technology exists, and so do the products. But the risks aren't being taken and tried at retail. Store designers and visual merchandisers just go on "lighting" the place with too little concern for the powerful persuasion lighting can provide.

As usual, there are those who lead and those who follow. The field's wide open, folks! The world's still waiting to be created.

EATING FOR INSPIRATION

DECEMBER 1985

DO YOU "GRAZE?" Can you "nibble" and "troll?" Are you thirsting for a "flight of wines?" Or are you still "Dining?" If you still go back to that favorite earthy downstairs slum in Little Italy every time you visit New York City, then you just don't know what's going on.

You are where you eat. According to *California* magazine, "Restaurants have become multi-sensory events." People want food and a visual feast as well. They are getting it. And the best place to find out about it is New York City.

The food came first. We lived through Mexican, Mesquite, Japanese, Cajun, Creole, Southern and all the old anorexic dishes of California. Now, meat and potatoes are suddenly hanging around. "American food" hit the cover of *Time* magazine. Now, you need a new vocabulary. You're getting ready for "sport eating." You'll drink your way through a "flight of wines," order a "couturier" pizza, nibble some little perfections. These are the apotheosis of the appetizer, son of sushi and nachos and tapas and Middle Eastern dips. You can have 20 little bits in one restaurant, or you can have one little bit in each of 20 restaurants. This is called "medley eating." It's great.

Whoever said you have to spend your whole life eating an appetizer, soup, salad and then some gigantic main course heavy thing on a plate—all before dessert? You don't have to do that. It's just habit. It's something your mother told you.

As the food changed, so did the restaurants. Suddenly all the new ideas aren't in the stores. The restaurants have hired every hot designer, decorator and architect as well as light, music and display person around. So when that smog goes down, head for the "grande cafes"—the new kinds of places to do the new way of eating (nibbling, grazing, trolling).

Grand cafes are already in Chicago, Los Angeles and San Francisco, but most of them are in New York, the city that never stops eating. Grand cafes are food plus everything else—the plates, the silver, the salt and pepper shakers, the napkins, the restrooms, the "waitfolks" and what they wear, how they talk, and the lights, the music and on and on.

There is a big difference between trend and design. Right now, we have abandoned good design for experimentation, including a big bag of tricks, cheap laughs, visual witticisms and jokes on dinner. We have taken Michael

Graves, Memphis, Sam Lopata and Milton Glaser far too seriously—although they work. (Two Memphis apartment buildings were sold out as soon as they appeared. Imagine living in a Memphis room when you have the flu.)

Like any great stores or companies, grand cafes have total images that are the collective impact of every detail in these places. Grand cafes are mint or peach and pink and pearlized pastel, unless they're zolotoned, and then they're still pastel, but also mottled and matted and marbled. Everything is fake, except the flowers. There are stylized murals, adorable details, surrealism, trompe l'oeil, amputated columns, false arches, painted windows with artificial views. High-tech is still around, recolored and revised. However, you still get to see a ruthless, realistic array of plumbing and heating ductwork and warehouse flooring. The lighting is better than in most stores, with the key being variety and even programming. One grand cafe has a program that changes the colors of the lights every 20 minutes.

Grand cafes are very large and very loud. They are subdivided spaces, generally starting as lofts, but then terraced and balconied. Everyone has great seats from which they can see everyone else from everywhere, and they watch the waiters fall all over the place because of the steps. There is absolutely no sound dampening anywhere. (Brookstone sells rifle firing range sound deadeners, great fashion accessories that may save your auditory canal.) Lip reading would work, except that you can't see through the haze created by the big, open mesquite pit on which all these bits are grilling. Just wave an armload of jewelry and somebody will bring you something. What is brought doesn't matter much; the food is either indifferent or terrible. That's never the point.

Reservations are hardly possible. If you want one tomorrow, they'll laugh at you over the phone. If you do get one, they'll threaten that if you don't call to reconfirm, you'll be out of luck.

Credit cards are vanishing. These entrepreneurs are sick of paying AmEx seven percent. Bring money.

Dress codes are dead, as long as you look terrific—whatever that means. Only old uptown Protestant eateries hassle you about jackets. Just act like you're going to Palladium.

The bar is the eye of the hurricane. It has nothing to do with eating, and not much to do with drinking. The verbs that come to mind instead are hassling, hunting, hoping, fashion parading—all spiced with repeated trips to the telephones and gang safaris to the bathrooms to replace lipstick left on Heinekens.

The music matters, but no matter what it once was. It gets drowned out, and what you're left with is the basic thump of the lowest bass notes.

The waitfolks (you just can't get the word "waitpersons" out, can you?) are all really architects and actors disguised as servants. They are part of the image, so they are inevitably much cuter than anyone at your table. And they must be rich, too, because they certainly spend a lot of time at gyms and tanning parlors. They enjoy what they do and make you like it, too. The service is usually pretty good (better than in department stores) because they don't hate their jobs and the customers. Imagine real service, even after the customer is seated and going to spend money, no longer "just looking." This may be why customers are spending money on eating out and not on clothes.

You need to see all of the following 19 places. Here's a battle plan. Get a car and driver and stop at the bar in every grand cafe. Have a blue margarita or some other spiffy contempo drink. If you have the stamina, you can snack your way through the whole itinerary—eating for inspiration.

Chelsea:
    Positano (250 Park Ave.)
    Joanna (18 E. 18th St.)
    Cafe Seiyoken (18 W. 18th St.)
    America (9 E. 18th St.)
    Gotham (12 E. 12th St.)
    5th Avenue Grill (102-Fifth Ave.)
SoHo:
    Bar Lui (625 Broadway)
    SoHo Kitchen and Bar (103 Greene St.)
    El Internacional (219 W. Broadway)
    Odeon (145 W. Broadway)

The following also may have opened by the time you get here:
    Cafe Roma (3 W. 18th St.)
    Batons (62 W. 11th St.)
    Metropolis Cafe (31 Union Square West)
    El Rio Grande/Mexico City (260 W. Broadway)

Eventually, you'll have to eat some food. Of all the grand cafes, the best food—both imaginative and excellent—is at Odeon. And *The New York*

Times recently gave three stars to Gotham. "It is the most improved food in any New York restaurant, trendy or otherwise."

First we all said, "Retail is theater." Then we said that disco was theater. Now, restaurants are theater. After a night at the grand cafes, you—and your work—may never be the same.

DISPLAYGATE

JUNE 1988

SOMEONE HAS BEEN CAUGHT. It's happened in banking, trading, politics and religion. Why shouldn't it happen here?

Any day now we'll be treated to the sight of prominent visual merchandisers standing in front of cast national audiences weeping, writhing and saying to the world, "I have sinned. I am a sinner. I take all the blame. I am taking kickbacks from Woo Woo Display Company. I beg your forgiveness. Forgive me, Lord."

It can be tempting. The system gives display people a per diem for expenses that a gnat couldn't survive on in New York, asking them to search out cheap, dirty hotels and means in greasy coffee shops. They're supposed to travel by subway to see what's new and try to ignore the markdowns on the Issey Miyake racks at Bergdorf's. So, when a big decoratives company offers them a second cup of coffee, they take it.

And everybody knows that stealing from a store is easy. Everybody knows a lot of stories like the one about an assistant display manager who was stopped by security on his way out the employees' entrance and found to have 28 teddy bears under his clothes. He was wearing Japanese clothes or else he couldn't have done it. When they went to his apartment with a search warrant, they discovered an environment as convincing as—and identical to—one of their store's own perfect room settings.

Admittedly, there's a thin line between manufacturers offering you a cup of coffee in their showroom and getting you theater tickets; and between theater tickets and a check for $50,000. Just exactly where it becomes illegal or immoral is not a matter of fact.

So, say the manufacturers, "You write me a $1 million order for fiberglass urns, and I will pay you a salesperson's 15-percent commission and send the check to the house. Have a nice day." Or they invite you to spend the weekend in their Key West condo where there are endless (and sometimes very animated) amenities, or to attend the company's golf outing in Mazatlan.

And if you don't get it, ask. The biggest store in America asked a California manufacturer for ten free tickets to a charity function ("Ninety Minutes For Life") in which giving was the entire objective. The manufacturer refused.

Display industry parties are populated almost entirely by the "buyers" who have been bought tickets by manufacturers. Limousines pile up outside the disco "Du Jour" to take exhausted party-goers somewhere—anywhere—else, after the party in hopes that the coddled masses will show up at their showrooms the next day.

Then there are "corporate breakfasts" with Bloody Mary's for which manufacturers invite entire chains. And they sit there tapping their toes while they eat, hoping they'll be asked to bring out their order books. How much you get depends almost entirely on how big your pencil is. Big order—big lunch. Little order—Mr. Coffee, sweet roll, plastic cup.

Here's a handy guide to the game for newcomers—The Displaygate Frequent Buyers' Program:

Big order = dinner at The Sign of the Dove

Small order = deli sandwich in the showroom

Big order = tickets to *The Phantom of the Opera*

Small order = tickets to *I'm Not Rappaport*

Big order = tickets to the Met including dinner

Small order = tickets to the Met without dinner

Big order = free weekend in a sprawling Palm Springs hacienda

Small order = free admission to the Empire State Building observatory

Big order = six nights, seven days on Fire Island

Small order = free blue drink with gardenia at Trader Vic's

Big order = vendor calling two days before Thanksgiving to ask for home address

Small order = store calling vendor on WATS line to wish a "Merry Christmas."

Some companies send notices to their resources just before Christmas explaining that their employees do not receive gifts, and that if gifts are sent, they will be refused. But nobody knows if this works or not. One buyer was told by a shirt manufacturer who was already his biggest resource that he could expect 25 cents on every shirt he bought over a certain amount.

Imagine the manufacturer's surprise when the buyer dropped the account. This is rare.

What is not rare is breakfast, lunch, dinner, gifts, tickets, weekends and cocaine. Every now and then such shenanigans are "exposed." *Women's Wear Daily* did a Seventh Avenue coke story a few years ago. But this publicity seems to flourish and then die down, as if occasionally admitting it out loud cleans up your sins. Everyone gets reborn after confession.

Someone has just been fired. And many said, "There but for the grace of God go I." Now we have our first Jimmy Swaggart, groaning regrets and penitence into the national microphones. Are we really going to have a display scandal? Displaygate?

Surely there will be more. And they will be regarded by both buyers and manufacturers as unlucky and unfortunate. It may stop for awhile, but human nature and vendor/buyer nature being what they are, and this being the land of free enterprise and competition (as well as the country that begrudgingly ostracizes Ivan Boesky, Oliver North and Jim Bakker), it will begin again.

The offers will return—from that perfectly legitimate free cup of coffee with free sugar and free cream to a couple of third row center seats for the Liza Minnelli extravaganza. And, as T.S. Eliot said, "This is the way the world ends, not with a bang, but a whimper."

So it seems the visual merchandising field is right up to the end of the greedy eighties. But wouldn't it be wonderful if, as we head into the caring nineties, we seized the opportunity to be among the leaders who are first to be honest?

FRIEND OR FAUX

DECEMBER 1988

I'VE HAD IT with faux. I want some real. I put my drink down on a table in a restaurant recently, and suddenly appreciated the fact that the tabletop was marble—real marble, not faux.

May we've had enough. Faux is a fad. And I'm tired of it. Fiber is a big fad, too. If you eat it, you'll live forever. This is a faux pas. Coca-Cola tried to do a faux Coke once. Imagine sucking up a faux Cole after years of hearing "Coke, it's the real thing." Fooey. And fashion is the biggest fad of all. It's faux. Starving merchants think up fashion in a passion and then pass it on the public. The same day I felt real marble under my cocktail, I saw a Gianni Versace shirt at Charivari for $790. "It's the fabric," said a salesperson. "It's imported." I had to ask myself, "What faux?"

Real marble isn't fake. That's what's good about it. Real feelings come close behind. That's what's good about them. I'm not the only one feeling this way. The folks over at the beef board are advertising, "I want real food. Beef." Yeah. And we want real gold medals, but the real gold medals are worn by faux Olympic athletes with strength by way of steroids.

Faux is an f-word. The word "faux" is generally used to describe fake finishes, perspectives and design features. It's been used a lot lately. Mantegna painted faux in the 15th century, and Palladio added faux perspectives to some of his villas in the Veneto. His masterpiece is the Teatro Olmpico in Vicenza, one of architecture's turning points. The stage is an entire Renaissance city convincingly rendered as the basic scenery presented to admiring audiences for 400 years. Nobody has ever done it better. But Lord how they try!

Right now, *HG* (formerly *House and Garden*) is braying about faux tortise glass plates and glassware. There's also faux granite laminate and fixturing finishes. The postmodernists have messed around with faux. And by the way, what ever happened to postmodern? Okay, Michael Graves did design a Napa Valley winery five years ago.

Jessica McClintock has just about "fauxed" herself into eternity with her new store at The Crystal Court at South Coast Plaza. But she's been "fauxing" things ever since she put clouds on the ceiling of her San Francisco store on Sutter Street. And Bergdorf Goodman has fauxed the Gaultier department.

New York City restaurants started fauxing murals a few years ago. Now they only things that aren't faux in the restaurant of the week are the ridiculous prices. Faux perspectives go up the stairs and walls of nouvelle eateries all over the country, with more happening every day.

The Banana Republic stocked the same faux safari jacket once too often. People are having pricey "fauxers" paint faux marble floors and walls and tiny entryway foyers in their tiny New York apartments. Tammy Faye Bakker painted the ceiling of her ill-fated shopping center with a faux-view of Paradise. The Sistine Chapel it ain't. But it's consistent. Of course everything about Tammy turned out to be faux.

So what's real?

• Real materials like marble, earth, wood, plants, sunlight

• Real perspective views that are beautiful because they're true, instead of trompe l'oeil, which nobody can pronounce anyway

• Real clothing, goods things to wear, seasonally presented, fad-free, instead of the tricks of the designers who stay too long in limos

• Stores that look like stores, instead of converted, deserted theme parks

• Service performed by people who like to serve instead of waiters who are all really actors and therefore hate their jobs and you

• Design that is genuine and a love that is true.

THE CORN FLAKES SHELVING TASK FORCE

SEPTEMBER 1989

EVENTUALLY, supermarket chains will do what department stores have finally started doing. They'll fight back saying, "You can't put so much of your image in here that we lose our identity." Today, department stores fight with vendors about whose image will be the winner. But supermarkets are a long way off from having that kind of dialogue.

Companies like Coca-Cola and PepsiCo, however, *are* concerned with shelf space and what goes on it. They're just beginning to wonder whether they could make that shelf space produce more if it looked better and if they did something in addition to cramming those shelves with as much product as possible. But while Coke and Pepsi fight for shelf space, and occasionally fight for what goes onto precious shelves visually, hundreds of other suppliers just accept the space they've been given. They stack their products in as fast as possible before someone else beats them to it.

Display manufacturers could really do business with these potential customers if they ever bothered to find out about them. Let's suppose that one day some display manufacturers get out of their catered showrooms and into the field. They would be astonished at what they would find. They would find an interested, inexperienced, unknowing rich universe of possibilities. They would find monster companies who have never heard of the display industry, much less devoted any thought to "visual presentation." This country's largest store groups and manufacturers don't go to display shows. In fact, they don't even know of such a thing.

Since they never heard of the display industry, they're scratching around in their own resources with the best will in the world trying to take advantage of the opportunities. They ask their advertising agencies. Most big agencies have a few second-rate people who try to sketch out "visuals" for clients. But those agencies would rather make giant media buys than waste their time dealing with supermarket shelves, so they give the work to their worst people who produce dead, dull results.

Then the manufacturers ask their in-house product designers to come up with stuff, and that's exactly what they come up with. Those same people who decorate the executive dining room for Christmas try real hard to develop supermarket presentations, but they, too, would rather be doing something else—and it looks it. Next, the assignment is given to packaging geniuses who know a lot about packaging and nothing at all about store design.

Sometimes the product executives go to supermarkets in person and try to figure out how to make their products look better on the shelves. And occasionally they go into some mall to admire Units and Limited and Estee Lauder. They wish they could make some connections between what they're looking at and what they see when they look at their own products. Finally, they appoint a committee back home in the office consisting of anyone who wants to work on "display" until the management stops demanding. This results in something called (I swear this is true) "the Corn Flakes shelving task force"—a group who usually gets paid for doing something else, but sits down every third Friday for an hour or so to discuss shelving. This goes on until the ad agencies, the product designers, the packaging people and the executives themselves are satisfied they haven't come up with anything new. Then the task force is dissolved unit someone brings up "display" again.

And so these giant industries keep waiting to be enlightened about the power of visual merchandising. Is it possible that the display industry is so self-centered that it expects to be solicited by new industries. Oh, I know, the big boys never buy anything, and they make their own stuff, and they want discounts and graft and bribes and 10,000 other excuses.

If the display industry spent one-tenth of the time exploring new business that it now spends explaining why it can't sell to new businesses, it would probably triple sales within a month. Why is selling such a dirty word? Why is the display industry so incestuous? Why does it keep feeding upon itself? Why doesn't it ever enter the real world? How bad will the established retail industry have to get? How many display people will have to go out of business to sound a genuine alarm?

Every day display companies shut down in direct response to the stores that merge, acquire and vanish. Meanwhile, food companies, discounters, direct mail, television and all the other living kinds of marketing flourish, thrive and actually manage to get through the week without visiting a display show?

Ain't it a shame? The display industry ought to celebrate selling instead of licking its wounds, giving bad parties and praising its oldest inhabitants. It ought to wake up and live.

SEARCHING FOR THE SANTA FE STYLE

OCTOBER 1989

"SANTA FE" STYLE is almost out of control. It's more than the sum of its parts. It is both beautiful and strong.

The chef from the SantaCafe is on "The Today Show." The book *Santa Fe Style* sits on every self-respecting coffee table in Connecticut. There is no Mexican food. It has been splintered into Tex-Mex, New Mex-Mex and Nouvelle Mex. And any tortilla that is a corn tortilla instead of a blue corn tortilla isn't a tortilla worth eating in Santa Fe.

Santa Fe's Ombrello of Canyon Road has opened a store in New York City's SoHo, while Zona of SoHo has just opened a store in Tokyo. Carved coyotes sell in Florida mall; chili pepper Christmas tree lights are in every store in Michigan; and every department store in St. Louis has at least one room setting featuring irregular adobe walls, timbered ceilings and terra cotta tile floors—all accessorized with Indian pots and bright, good-humored folk art.

Georgia O'Keeffe hangs on dorm room walls around the world. Bruce Weber photographs Calvin Klein models flexing "pecs" in the pueblos. People at London dinner parties wear Indian blankets fashioned into jackets by Ralph Lauren. And back in Santa Fe, the gossip fills the galleries: "Jackie O may be looking at houses here!"

Has fashion ruined Santa Fe? No. Today Santa Fe is ahead of itself. There is a poster for sale in every store called, "Victim of the Santa Fe style." In bright cartoon style, it shows a woman dead on the floor of her smart adobe home who's been killed by the weight of too much Indian jewelry. She's wearing a SantaCafe T-shirt in space crammed with howling carved coyotes, hanging strings of dried chilis, R.C. Gorham art and sagging walls and ceilings.

The Santa Fe metaphor can be extended to create new style. Zona has done it. The store sells all the Santa Fe trademarks, but has added the top ten New Age tapes, goat-skin gardening gloves from England and white cotton pajamas, as well as the world's best gift boxes from Italy.

Santa Fe style, though, is not just material. It's drinks and dinner at the Pink Adobe. This is truly an eccentric hangout. Coyote cafes and SantaCafes come and go, but the Pink Adobe endures. It's the Santa Fe Opera that sells out. People sit through operas that are either 400 years old or finished just last week, though they secretly wish they were seeing *La Boheme*. But they still go. Galleries stock everything from Disney cartoon cels to Degas. In the museums, locals peer at cases filled with architectural rarities like mummified missionaries' fingers while they wonder if that is Barbra Streisand in the next room.

In the Plaza, ladies clutching cardigans and handbags come out into the heat after listening to Schubert. They pass by the Lycra-spandexed skateboarders who terrify the Plaza. Haagen-Daas is jammed. There are book shops staffed by people who know books. Heavy drinkers pass out during dinner at Victor's. Mariachis pluck away at private cocktail parties up on Canyon Road. Most people dress white ethnic (there is a lot of commotion about concha belts and men wear boots). You can get blue corn tamales for 50 cents in a dump or $15 in a restaurant that once was mentioned in *Town & Country*. Both tamales will be delicious.

Other substyles mix in. The bath house out in the desert is Japanese. You must leave your car in the parking lot and climb one hundred steps to Ten Thousand ·Waves where you lie in hot tubs up and down the mountain landscape, ecstatic under the nighttime desert sky. The Santa Fe and Japanese styles are related. They both leave out everything that is not essential. Japan and Santa Fe don't look anything alike, but they feel it.

You can experience the Santa Fe style in three dimensions by getting a real estate agent to give you a house tour. Santa Fe living rooms show you drama, dazzle and lots of "design." The architects are very busy. There's even a house in the hills with an electronic surveillance system that can be controlled by the owner of the house from car on a freeway in Houston.

While there are a lot of amazing houses and other buildings, there's nothing as powerful as the real, original Santa Fe architecture. And you can find it if you just keep going out of town, backward in time. The best buildings are those constructed ages ago, before designers lived or architects improved things. Buildings took shape out of necessity and purpose. They sat where they had to be, made of what they had to be made of and made as they had to be made. Because they were inevitable, they were great.

The greatest one is the Mission Church in Pecos Pueblo. It was built in 1100, a good long time before the puny derivative English style arrived in New England. But not many tourists bother to travel 25 stunning miles from the Plaza to see it. And yet everyone who does come is hushed by the sight of it, though not because they know history or long for the vanished Indians. Suddenly they see they layerings of Santa Fe style stripped away to reveal its elements of greatness.

Standing in the church under the giant sky, it is clear that any great building must be connected to the site in such a way that it makes the most of both. And every design idea must seem necessary. This hardly ever happens; it happens there.

The church sits on a hill in a mighty valley, astride the rubble of a pueblo city which housed 6,000 people. The city now has just three walls, and it has been 500 years since anyone lived within them. All anyone needs to know about the possibilities of building exists in that city where Santa Fe style meets substance. Every element is there that makes up what has come to be known as the Santa Fe style—the materials, colors, textures, position, scale and, most of all, the absolute connection to the landscape.

Wouldn't the poverty-stricken Indians and Mexicans who made those buildings have been amazed at the sight of all the visitors dressed in diamond-studded denim who climb the ancient walls and are struck into silence by the majesty of the place? It is possible to find the real thing and be exalted by it. The elements of design experienced there are all shared back in town by both the grandest hotel and the humblest house. It is so strong that not even all of the architects from Los Angeles can dim the simple power of the pueblo buildings.

The activists in Santa Fe have legislated certain colors, materials and proportions. Even the most ordinary house and the most pretentious palazzo share the same ideas. Adobe is adobe, and it works whether the building is going to be a Hilton or a hardware store. Aside from two minor disasters (a nondescript cathedral and a non-plaza plaza) there is not a genuinely ugly building in town.

Santa Fe is still an unspoiled place, a design for living today. Or tomorrow. Santa Fe is what the future ought to be.

REVERENCE AND RESTORATION

JULY 1991

"We feel better when we find our selves in the presence of the past."
—Brendan Gill, *The New Yorker*

THE CURRENT MARRIAGE of commerce and existing architecture began with James Rouse (The Rouse Company, Columbia, Md.), who conceived and implemented the festival marketplace with the development of Fanueil Hall in Boston in the mid-seventies. Others soon followed: Harborplace, Baltimore; South Street Seaport, New York; the Union Stations in St. Louis and Washington, D.C.; Waterside, Norfolk; Portside, Toledo; Plankington Arcade, Milwaukee; Jackson Brewery, New Orleans. Compare those restorations to any wholly contemporary shopping center where you lose your location and yourself.

The restorations, though, are entirely individual, each with a genuine sense of place and time. But developers must be prepared to send an extra million if they insist on authenticity, as Rouse did when it had to fireproof the wooden decks that were best for keeping the flavor of New York City's South Street Seaport. Concrete would have been cheaper.

Union Station in Washington, D.C., is a real shock to anyone who thinks that arriving by train is always a humiliation. The station and its shops and restaurants take your breath away. The building has a soaring nobility and a strong inscription over the portico: "If you are to bring back the riches of India, you must take them with you." These trains don't go to India, but they do go to Indiana, and the glorious restored station begins or ends a journey with a sense of ceremony. The restaurants and stores beneath the high white roofs meet and match the architecture in almost every case.

The Rhinelander Mansion stood decaying on the genteel corner of Madison Avenue and 72nd Street until Ralph Lauren bought it and put $16 million into its respectful renovation which opened in 1986. The building had been ignored for a generation, but now yields shopping pleasure and excitement to mobs of identity seekers—and about $1 million a week to Ralph.

It is a joy to spend the day—and money, too—at the restored Covent Garden in London. The famous building is far better used and appreciated than it was for its first 200 years. Like Eliza Doolittle in *My Fair Lady*, the old Covent Garden market has been changed. What was a run-down, under-used produce market is now a shopping center where Londoners and visitors come to divert themselves and experience the city.

You can hike right through the world's most dramatic cruciform piazza. It is the Galleria Vittorio Emmanuele in Milano (even if you don't speak Italian, just *try* to say all that; it makes you want to go there). This astonishing urban street was the world's first shopping center, and it is as exhilarating today as it was the day it opened in 1875. Not much has changed. Even over a century later, people still promenade there—in a shopping center— spending money, talking art, celebrating lunch and one another and having an Italian day.

You could enjoy an essential Italian day without ever leaving the Galleria Vittorio Emmanuele. You could experience the cathedral, stroll the shops, dine diversely, read and relax, admire the parade or join it—all under glass in the original Galleria. Or you could sit in La Scala, the grand opera house anchoring the Galleria, watching *Tosca* spellbound for hours until Tosca finally jumps off the walls of the castle Sant'Angelo into the River Tiber. And then after that, you could sip capuccino in the Galleria.

Meanwhile, back in the states we are "un-making" malls and re-making genuine towns. At Mashpee Commons in Mashpee, Mass., two developers have transformed an old mall into a three-block town center, complete with streets, sidewalks, benches, storefronts, plaza and throngs of strolling pedestrians. A suburban mall is now "downtown." At the same moment, all across America—as reported in *Amtrak Express*—declining downtowns are being restored, as are some old-fashioned civic values and a sense of belonging.

This is more than architectural activity. Respect for genuine architecture can improve the quality of life. Witness a new "mall" phenomenon in mid-America: Jackson, Mich., and Champaign, Ill., have turned their downtown malls back into streets again. The "mall" destroyed the real downtown and people hated it. Even big downtowns are going back to their original architecture. Visit Minneapolis, Chicago or Decatur, Ill. Their downtown malls are being redesigned.

Years of neglect are being erased by lavish amounts of love and redevelopment in the "main streets" of Rome, Ga.; Lowell, Mass.; Lawrence, Kansas; Sonora, Calif.; Madison, Ind. and many others. There are few new brilliant little towns being designed and built from scratch, but based on very traditional architecture. A visit to Seaside, Fla., makes you want to move there, and the folks who have created that town are now building Blount Springs Ala., and Friday Mountain, Texas. They are a little like Main Street or Disneyland, but you can live there.

New/old revised small towns like Mashpee are saving the decayed or failing properties (including stores and other businesses) in Metuchen, N.J., and Clarksburg, W. Va.—all troubled areas economically. Revitalizing the original architecture is also restoring the towns to good health and energetic enterprise.

We are moving forward into the past.

DESIGNING THE FUTURE

DECEMBER 1991

TWO DAYS BEFORE the annual conference of the Industrial Designers Society of America, the world was shocked to learn that one of the 20th century's most familiar design icons, the Barbie Doll, has been dealt a decisive blow. A new doll has been designed and positioned as the logical successor to Barbie—an unthinkable thought in a century that longs for permanence, but rarely experiences it.

The new Barbie—called "I Got to be Me!"—is radically different from the original in all its vital statistics, less bust, less hips, more waist. Reality has smacked Barbie as surely as it smacks us all each day. And all the designers are coming to a fundamental realization that will change their livelihood: Suddenly, the world is demanding simplification, and award-winning stuff like the over-designed Alessi orange juice squeezer seems slightly ridiculous.

We are witnessing the end of the old incestuous thinking of "design for design's sake" because we know in our hearts that good design can simplify life and make it beautiful and we like it. This hasn't happened much yet, but it's going to. Industrial designers—all designers, in fact—will have to get over the old familiar "complexification" quickly and start designing the future.

A lot of design types at the conference in Ballroom E have never dealt with simplification. I listened to a panel argument about the current merits of Rolex versus Timex. Rolex lost. I listened to designers talk about the connection between designers and business school, designers and production, and designers and business community. I didn't hear much at all about designers and consumers, but I guess it's merely assumed that someday after the designers and the business schools and engineers and stylists and producers and the business community all get clear about what they do, that consumers will finally be able to buy something simple.

There was a revolution at the International Italian Furniture Fair this year. *The New York Times* headline proclaimed: "Reality Hits Milan Like a Flashback." The school desk, the old-fashioned office cabinet and the plain kitchen table are redefining and reviving the ultra-sophisticated Italian design scene. Designer Aldo Cobic of Standard described his new table, chairs and porcelain as "nice, normal things." Simple.

A recent cover of *Business Week* said it all. Pictured was one of those totally incomprehensible, frustrating, ubiquitous design items that seems to sum it all up—an endlessly capable, hideously complex VCR remote control programmer coupled with a quote from the customer, the only critic whose opinion really matters: "I CAN'T WORK THIS _____ THING!"

Gemstar Corp. responded with the $70 "VCR Plus+," a remote control device that simplifies the recording of programs on VCRs. With the cooperation of *TV Guide* and, by now, most national television listings, you simply punch the six digits listed in the guide (six, not half-an-hour's worth that results in no-show programs at the wrong time on the wrong channel at the wrong speed with the wrong tape and all because you couldn't follow the designer complexification). Then the machine does the work of finding, programming and recording accurately. You, meanwhile, spend the time you gained opening one more Rolling Rock and enjoying your evening in the serene confidence that even without a degree from M.I.T., you will get to see what you want to see when you want to see it.

Suddenly a sandal called "TEVA" appears on the glutted footwear scene, an extraordinary new design blowing off the shelves in 30 different styles retailing from $35 to $85. And Birkenstocks reappear in *People* magazine, with skyrocketing sales.

Advertising is becoming simplified at lightning speed. Campbell's Soup is re-running 30-year-old commercials instead of producing new ones. Liz Claiborne's ads are the essence of simplification—a family gathered around the bathtub in black and white. There's just one sentence: "Reality is the best fantasy of all." What's important is what's left out. The ads have no "models," no copy, no background, no location, no "styling." They announce their presence with the utmost simplicity.

The Gap doesn't even use an agency. And the retailer is also the most successful example of simplification in its store design as well. There are no mannequins, no props at all—just informative and clear unadulterated signage and no visual distractions. The merchandise is the message.

The lingerie from Triumph International of Japan has come up with a remarkable product celebrating the 200th anniversary of the death of Mozart. A unique limited-edition souvenir: a bra that plays the maestro's music (from under the armpit) when fastened. Just to make the garment more tasteful, it's covered with blinking lights. All this costs $71. Over-design is not entirely bad.

There was a second theme at ISDA: environment-conscious design. Environmental design finally seems to be underway, and what an inspiration (and what a challenge) it is. The public demands it, and designers must respond. Industrial designers are certainly aware that the products they designed in the last 40 years are the same products now choking the planet. They invented mediocre quality and deliberate obsolescence in order to get a rich and willing public to buy more and more and more and more. But now we know that all those innovations turned to trash and refused to go away.

Several new products are making disposal easier by design. BMW introduced the limited production model Z1, a two-seat roadster whose plastic body is designed to come off easily with the removal of a few fasteners. And 3M plans to bring out a plastic desk organizer that is designed for recycling. It snaps together and can easily be disassembled.

Sam Walton has bullied companies such as Procter & Gamble, and now products like "Sure" deodorant are appearing on supermarket shelves with boxes—a stupendous revolution. The designers proved again that less is more, much more in the case of the earth. The famous plastic "L'eggs" pantyhose container is gone. A new, simple, recyclable box is here. A big design competition is underway to solve the problem of compact disc packaging. Many solutions were seen at the conference.

The same week as the conference, Nissan showed an electric car that can be recharged in 15 minutes. Japan again. But most amazingly General Motors also made an announcement the same week: It will build an electric car in the mid-nineties called the Impact that will travel for 120 miles at 55 miles per hour before needing to be recharged.

Designing the future will mean using new tools, making more of less and speaking directly and sincerely to consumers. The simplification designers must now undergo will match the stripped-down simplification of the customer's language. Merchants and customers must meet on common ground of the new simplicity. This will be a productive—and profitable—connection.

PART THREE
DESTINATIONS

BOREDOM IN PARIS

MARCH 1984

GOING TO PARIS is always an exercise in expectation. The words "What's new?" have always been answered in Paris, the source of ideas and the capital of fashion. However, the boutiques look the same—plain, tasteful, with perhaps a new wooden form or an old, rediscovered mannequin. The department stores, like most European department stores, are awful. On this occasion, Galeries Lafayette—once you find the windows behind the trashy kiosk vendors—was featuring a store-wide promotion called "Grande, Grande Bretagne," which actually had a lot of shabby-looking British merchandise standing among plants on a green shag run. Awful.

When you look carefully, there is actually no display. There is placement. There is arrangement. There is accessorization. There are no ideas.

But among the small stores, Halles Capone is good, along with 12 rue de Turbigo which has tons of Marithe and Francois Girbaud designs. Nearby is the Forum des Halles. People have finally tired of hating it, and, now, they like when they see the five subterranean floors of excellent merchandise. It has motion and activity. It sells.

Around the same neighborhood are lots and lots of other shops. Just eating Tarte Tatin at Au Diable des Lombard (64 rue des Lombards) is worth a trip. Also, don't miss Upla at 17 rue des Halles, and Scooter at 10 rue de Turbigo. Nice shops.

Skip the embalmed rue de Fauborg St. Honore. You can buy all that Louis Vuitton in the Trump Tower, various gallerias and on Rodeo Drive. The Rive Gauche is simple and exciting. Go sit at the Cafe Deux Magots on Boulevard St. Germaine and watch from there. Walk up and down every street in every direction. In half a day, you'll see that accessories and the accessory shops are more interesting than clothing.

There are two other reasons to go to Paris now; they are on the rue Etienne Marcel. One, at number 42, is Comme des Garcons. The other is Yohji Yamamoto, two blocks away.

Everything in Paris, except these two stores is going along a smooth, slightly different, evolutionary way that things go in the fashion world. These two have changed everything! Those two designers have started with cloth and have made clothing. But then, they have added the most detailed, thorough extension to every aspect of selling clothing. Nothing is left to chance. Nothing is familiar. No detail is beyond consideration....

- Visual. Industrialized; all black and white with concrete and rubber, and pipe racks, but planned—envisioned, organized, pleasing, subtle, not a joke. (First impressions are startling.)

- Music. Soothing, pastoral, unknown. (It's sent from Japan.) You want to buy the tapes, but you can't.

- Photography. The most amazing catalogs—costly, 10-part, black-and-white oversized foldout with modes—faces turned away—sailing through the air, robed in flying fabrics.

- Catalogs. Take the foldout you've admired (expensive) and put it into the severe tan envelope sealed with transparent Scotch brand tape that says "Comme des Garcons." Even that is special.

- Salesmanship. The employees look like nobody you know, in clothes you have never seen, with makeup you couldn't have imagined five minutes before. It's hard to tell a dress from a skirt, or a sweater from a jacket. The shoes are ragged (but cost $200), and everything has many sleeves. Now comes the shock—these employees look more beautiful rather than peculiar. They move radiantly. They are amazing, but polite. They are beautiful. *You* figure it out.

- Price. Don't even think about it. Some of the fabrics have been soaked in indigo dye for six months before being cut, sewn, torn and resewn! The more you watch, the more (and more) you see.

- Customers. Most of them might be buyers from Bloomingdale's. They are not only buying the clothes, but wearing them—right now. They usually look terrible. They've got the money and the savvy, but they don't look right. They are still wearing the clothes, but they are not convinced of the revolutionary ideas. Like most revolutionary ideas, they look extreme, too far in advance. But they look right, if not to anyone else, then certainly to themselves.

At Yohji, all the hangers are completely original. Study them. Even the electric extension cords have been designed. Try a few things on (you'll need help). You'll understand the trouble those people are in, those who just bought the clothes and are still trying to figure out how to tie them onto their bodies. But you will learn new things about your business and yourself. This is serious. Isn't it worth traveling for that?

For supplementary adventures of the same kind, continue on to Kenzo in the Place des Victoires. Here you can see comparatively frantic activity as people who don't dare Comme des Garcons and Yohji Yamamoto grab for the more acceptable version. This place does a lot of business.

Definitely make a trip in a taxi from Kenzo to Issey Miyake at 201 Blvd. St. Germaine. This man combines mastery with revolution, making beautiful clothes and putting them in handsome surroundings.

When you leave Paris, you might wonder: How could an authentic revolution look so calm, serene, confident? Nobody announces, shouts or describes. Nobody sells. But you are there, and must be. You want to be. You have seen and experienced the things we all continuously search for and often lament the lack of—genuine creativity.

IN SEARCH OF

APRIL 1984

SOON, WE'LL ALL GO to California searching relentlessly for new Cabbage Patch Kids, Memphis furniture, the latest thrashings of the Japanese designers, plus a few garlands for Christmas decorating. Here, then, are just some of the things to look for while perusing the California Visual Merchandising Market and those West Coast-cool stores:

• Androgyny. This is a big word that doesn't mean unisex—it means Michael Jackson and Boy George and the fact that these two universal types are really popular. Boy George appears on the cover of *Newsweek* in January. Michael Jackson has sold more records than anyone ever—even before burning his hair off. It is a sign of 1984 that the average teenage girl's bedroom walls can have side-by-side posters of both Michael Jackson and macho Tom Selleck, two seemingly incompatible heroes.

• Youth. And it's all so very young! It is startling that the little-girl model in Calvin Klein's new men's underwear ads is not only a girl who looks and dresses like a boy, but appears to be only about 14 years old. Menudo singers have to "retire" at 16. And how old *is* Michael Jackson?

Remember the old button saying "Never trust anyone over 30?" We might have to change that to "Never trust anyone over 11."

• Off-Price. You can visit Mervyn's, Ross Dress-for-Less, Plum's and the Price Club, all in California. They are each amazing—even those that are less successful than others. So don't underrate them! They, too, are selling the goods that used to be the private property of department and specialty stores.

• Private Label. Nordstrom is doing the best job here. The company has genuine customer confidence to begin with, and is capitalizing on it with an aggressive private label program.

• Merging. Macy's California has bought Liberty House. Obviously one way to get rid of the competition is to buy it!

Whatever Happened To: the regulars? I. Magnin, Saks Fifth Avenue, Wilkes Bashford, Neiman-Marcus, Emporium Capwell? Well, have a look while you're there. These traditional stores are re-evaluating their strengths, but they have never had such unexpected competition. By the time you get to California, they should either be more panicked or more aggressive. In either case, we'll be seeing some new development.

• Change Your Habits. You can't find out what's happening now or next if you plan to go back to the same old places. California is a *Megatrends* state, and whatever is happening is happening there first!

• Olympics. Don't underrate the Olympics. The Olympics is the largest peace-time (wars don't count) event in the world. How are retailers and visual merchandisers acting and reacting to this major even? Some have decided to just let it pass by—they're not "big" enough. Some have let the Japanese take over. (Fuji Film, not Kodak, is the official sponsor.) But the customer—every customer—is fascinated, and smart stores are recognizing this.

• Biggies. The most news-making stores in America are not the usual elite. They are the battered and resurrecting Big Mass Merchandisers. Sears and J.C. Penney both have monumental rejuvenation plans, and a trip to any of their new stores is a thrilling experience. Montgomery Ward has declared a profit for the first time in five years. And if you are not on the mailing lists that bring you all the Spiegel catalogs, then you are just not with it. If you want to see Kansai, Norma Kamali, Laura Ashley and others, and if you care who's selling their merchandise, you must get the Spiegel catalogs.

More evidence of biggies: Perry Ellis has signed with Levi's (Levi's first-ever designer), and Kenzo is designing for The Limited.

• New Ways of Saying It. It's worth a trip to Los Angeles just to see all those Nike billboards, where athletes leap right off the walls toward speeding motorists. In a city glutted with "Olympic-mania," Nike has found a way to stand out of all the clutter the way a great athlete runs—apart. So much advertising and display work is so busy being just like everyone else's work that it takes real guts to start all over again and change even the media. When you see the billboards, ask yourself what Nike would have gotten if it had invested the same talent, time and money in "normal" visual presentation.

More trends that may exist in California: Primitive, Africa, Australia, Dolls of All Kinds, Riptide Helicopters, Anything Hispanic, *Footloose*, Beatlemania, New Orleans World's Fair, Michael Jackson as "Peter Pan," Men and Women Wearing Hats, Rubber-Fabric, Floors, Accessories.

• Refreshment for your Soul. And, finally, if you're tired of trends and have "shopped 'til you dropped," get a hide-away room at Ventana Big Sur resort, 1,200 ft. above the Pacific (a few hours south of San Francisco), where you can smorgasbord-plus-nature-out in the best looking resort in America. Although it will refresh your eyes and spirit, it will deplete your wallet—but worth every cent!

Same neighborhood, but less money and rustic, is Big Sur Inn, with cabins in the Deetjen's woods and "The Magic Flute" with your oatmeal for breakfast.

In any case, go to Nepenthe for steak, early enough to sit on the cliffs with everyone else and applaud the sunset.

If you can't justify this expense to your company as "visual presentation," you might want to do it anyway on your own. It will present a few "visuals" for you to cherish for a long time.

AN ENGLISH LESSON

MARCH 1985

DRINKING CHAMPAGNE fuels the anticipation when flying to London .... Are men wearing skirts? Is there life after punk? Is everything plaid? Who is "Body Map?" What's happening in music? Graphics? Theatre?

For years there wasn't much fashion news to look forward to. London was only a duty stop on the European "idea route." But it's changed.

Buy three magazines as soon as you get off the plane—*The Face*, *I.D.* and *Blitz*. All three are strongly graphic, and each has a different look. They'll sum up the London fashion subculture for you in twenty minutes.

And then there's the city itself. Samuel Johnson said, "He who is bored with London is bored with life." Even the punks are polite most of the time, and it's rare to encounter "attitude." Then, too, where else but in London can you see Glenda Jackson, Maggie Smith and Joan Plowright in great plays and simultaneously see Princess Margaret in the lobby?

Target Walks

• For high impact, start at Harrods (in Knightsbridge at Brompton Road). Did you know this retailer did $10 million in the first two days of its January sale? Harrods looks terrific, especially at night. The windows always are terrible, but they look like Harrods. Check the Hall of Foods and the old ladies nodding off in chairs while patient salespeople explain things.

• At the next corner is Sloane Street. From there, in just three blocks you will encounter a design adventure. All the new store designs are there, including those designed by Eva Jiricna. Each one is a total statement—from the pavement to the shopping bags, fixtures and merchandise. Each is individual, yet all seem to be related by a certain design viewpoint. You'll find Apostrophe, Kenzo and Issey Miyake as well as the empire of Joseph (Joseph Tricot, Joseph Sport and Joseph Pour la Maison). Joseph Pour la Maison is a store of high-design household items. You will want to own everything. The sleek restaurant in the basement is a design masterpiece, and so are the people who eat in it. Go.

Also on Sloan Street is the new prototype branch of Woodhouse, a menswear retailer. I found more good ideas for merchandising in this little shop than I've seen for quite a long time. The architect's name is Graeme Noble of Ashton Hill Noble partnership, and everyone working in the store knew him.

Not to be missed

• South Molton Street: Browns, Chinese Laundry, Kenneth J. Lane, Gaultier, Ebony, Gee 2, Bazaar, Yamamoto, Rocks and others.

• When you get to the end of South Molton, beyond Gianni Versace and Gianfranco Ferre with their same old costly leathers, look for an alley that's known as Avery Row. There, look at Paul Smith, an exotic menswear shop. And don't miss Kenneth Turner (No. 8), a shop with a vision (the merchandise is entirely dried flowers) carried through superb and extreme fantasy.

• New Bond Street is very nearby where you'll find Ralph Lauren (No. 142). He owns this one. It's so totally merchandised that you don't even need to think. Just reach and pay. It's great.

• St. Christopher's Place is emerging as a brand new shopping street. Visit: Ice (No. 14) with big deal London fashion; Collection Premier (20-21); Cutler and Gross (No. 18) with eyewear; Gees Court; Taverniti; Ixi:z (that's the way it's really spelled); Doddles; and Metropolis.

• Around Covent Garden, you'll find a marketplace and all sorts of little side streets. Specialties to see are: Freelance Shoes (39 Floral Street); Spring (29 Longacre); Sabre (120 Longacre); and Hobbs at The Piazza.

• The King's Road route seems tired to me, but you could rush down it. There are a million shops.

• On Fulham Road, there are three great stores together. Go see the original Conran's (not Habitat). Then walk down to Ogetti (133 Fulham) and London Lighting (135). Eat at the Brasserie, right across from Conran's. Mmm....

• On Kensington High Street, see Head Over Heels (159) and Amazon (3 Kensington Church Street), which is around the corner.

• When you see a Team Detroit, Detroit Clothing Co., go in even though it looks tired. The merchandise is not. (Team Detroits are scattered all over London. You'll find one on Oxford Street at the head of Molton.)

• There is a new "urban mall" called the Trocadero. If you are having "mall withdrawl," go there. It will only take a minute. The HMV, a record store there, is the best. (Trocadero is on Shaftesbury Avenue near Piccadilly Circus.)

• And don't miss visiting Fortnum and Mason (at Piccadilly) to see ordinary foodstuffs transfigured into personal customer service. People walk with you out of the shops and halfway down the block to point your way to something you've asked about or they've recommended.

Then go to the theater

• *Starlight Express* has been sold out forever, but try to track down a scalper. This is a thrilling, spine-tingling, jingling big show without much content. But it's big on energy and has absolutely the most terrifying amount of sets, props, videos, junk, lights, tricks and costumes. And it has, of all things, rather sweet emotion. Everybody in it is a railroad train. Go.

Then eat

• Everyone should have a most favorite restaurant which probably won't be the fastest, choicest, newest, etc. Here's mine in London: La Poule au Pot (231 Ebury Street in the Pimlico area). Who says you can't get good food in London? That's ridiculous. The old myth about soggy boiled vegetables is not true.

Nothing in London is going to change your visual life or deliver mystical experiences. But it is a good stop for the soul. It's civilized. It has crank trends that somehow materialize later. The young life in the streets is definitely "trendy."

If nothing else, you might come back wearing one orange, and one lime green glove. You can trade hands occasionally and wear out both pairs evenly. (You have to buy two pairs.) You can't imagine the uproar such small eccentricities will cause when people look at you in your store. But that's the English lesson—life needs wit, and the blessing is that you are saved from taking yourself too seriously.

GROWING UP IN PARIS

MAY 1985

AFTER YOU'VE BEEN SHOCKED, jolted, entertained, informed, amazed and coddled in London, you can hit the shops in Paris—entirely for the pleasure of it. You'll find punks and principessas, red-eyed American buyers, Japanese businessmen, and universal lovers. Although everything in the world goes into Paris, what comes out is Paris itself—its standards, styles and quality.

The shops of Paris are not like Paris; they're like the world, condensed. London is trendier, Tokyo more advanced, Milan more singularly tasteful, Beverly Hills more humorous, and New York more aggressive. The best of it all is in Paris—refined, edited down and synthesized through the French mentality.

Visit the Forum des Halles and the streets around it. When it first opened, everyone hated it and mourned the loss of the trashy vegetable markets it replaced. The all-night dives and the late-morning prostitutes are still standing, but there are 40 or 50 shopping stops that are the best way to see Paris shops in a hurry.

Not to be missed in the Forum

• Four floors of shops, including: all the couture; the department store branches and the boutiques like Le Jour Apres (the day after), designed like the day after a nuclear disaster.

• Outside, nearby: Scooter and Halles Capone, both on the Rue de Turbigo; Comme des Garcons, Yohji Yamamoto, Kenzo and others on Rue Etiene-Marcel; a new Girbaud mini-skyscraper; and lunch at Au Diable des Lombards at 64 Rue des Lombards.

The Left Bank

• Fabrice, Maud Frizon, Sonia Rykiel, all near Rue Bonaparte.

• Taverniti and others on Rue de Four; antiques on Rue Jacob; and lots more right near your table outdoors at Deux Magot, the cafe at Boulevard St. Germaine. Order d'agneau at Brasserie Lipp, right across the street. Yum.

The Right Bank

• The Champs Elysee shops and the Rue de Faubourg St. Honore—elegant, rich and boring. So are the two big department stores, Galeries Lafayette and Au Printemps.

• The food store Fauchon at Place Madeleine is the ancestor of Dean and DeLuca, Balducci's and Zabar's—except better.

The best thing you'll get out of Paris is not display or architectural ideas, but style, class, refinement, elegance, service and quality. It will condition your thinking.

For example, if you want the best meal you've ever had in your life, do anything to get a dinner reservation at Taillevent, 15 Rue Lamennais. Reservations usually are not accepted, and you can't get in at all without two months' notice. But write to an important hotel concierge to do it for you, *long* before you go. Now, all that nonsense aside, when you're safe at your table, you will learn more about excellence (and enjoyment) in one night than you ever will "schlepping" through stores.

On that day, don't each lunch. Take a long bath. Get dressed up (this is for adults). Find someone you love to go with you. Get that someone to skip lunch, take a long bath and dress up.

Study the decor, plates, service, bathrooms, tapestries, menu, flowers, wine and food. After the house apertif, the first course, and the first bottle of wine, you'll drop your alertness and wallow in perfection.

You'll grin. You'll want more. When you get up to leave, the coat-check woman already will be standing in the hall with your coat open and ready for you. You won't know how she did it, or, for that matter, how any of them did the other things that delighted you so. But you will know what Mies van der Rohe meant when he said, "God is in the details."

When you get outside, you'll probably laugh hysterically for half an hour.

What does this have to do with your profession?

What does absolute excellence have to do with anything? It recharges your ambition and fires your soul. This all costs about $75, and it is a grand investment. You will go home meaner and more inspired than ever.

When you get tired of "shop till you drop," and "born to shop," and "when the going gets tough, the tough go shopping," get a car and drive 60 miles south to Chartres, and visit the cathedral. This is important. It must have been the greatest management feat of all time to get this building built, and nothing built since 1250 A.D. is better than this.

What does it have to do with "visuals"?

The question is beneath consideration. The answer is in the "sight" that briefly will stop your heart as you walk through the front door. The effect will push your brain to higher aspirations in a single moment, and you will experience the "visuals" as direct evidence of God. You will never find the word "window" the same again.

You'll get ideas in Paris: the odd, illuminated mannequin; the eyeglass store with windows like gigantic lenses; the Christmas majesty of the lights in the trees up the Champs Elysees; the obelisks made of grapes behind the waterfalls in the windows at Fauchon; the old car cutouts suspended over the street in the Rue de Rivoli. Most of all, though, you'll acquire an overall sense of how to do things with greater conviction. You'll know your effect before you do it, and you'll do it proudly. Like Paris, you can take your time, deliver, and then sit back. Watch the action take place with absolute certainty.

P.S. Before you point it out to me, let me point out to you that in an article I wrote last year, "Boredom in Paris," I explained how you should not bother to go there. Well, the funny thing is, that it might take you 12 trips to Paris to get its strong, but elusive message. It's worth it, and it works. Nobody has ever gone to Paris again and again and come back loving it less.

It grows on you. And you grow, too.

EUROPEAN GASP ATTACKS

JULY 1987

WE'VE ALWAYS BEEN INTIMIDATED by lovable old Europe. We're always running right back there in case we miss something. We rush to pret-a-porter and Pitti Uomo. We keep going to Harrods as if we expect to learn something, and we wander up and down the Via Montenapoleone trying to pronounce it and wondering why it isn't more exciting.

We suffer jet lag, lack of language and evaluation. We go to places like Dusseldorf, a place nobody would ever go otherwise, to look long and hard at innovations in refrigerator units.

And then we shop. We look at 3,500 all-gray stores, finished to perfection. But they're just the same, whether they're on the Rue Etienne Marcel or Sloan Street. The common market has produced common merchandise, common fixtures and common presentation. Milan, Paris and London are the same cities in different locations. And still we long to be surprised.

We trek through Europe in orderly herds. We see what everybody sees. We try to find trends and tendencies, but often the European gasp eludes us once again. And we come home.

A gasp is that rare, involuntary thrill we long to have at moments of great surprise. We always hope to be astounded. Usually we are merely informed or entertained. But I did find two gasps in two weeks when there recently. Because of the lousy dollar, though, they were very expensive gasps.

Just when every store in Europe is gray and crude and cold, the store Ettore Sottsass, designed for Esprit in Cologne, is suddenly before us—in absolute contradiction combining 50 colors and 50 materials and suddenly making sense of Memphis. It is the totality that matters. A single twisted Memphis table still looks silly by itself, but you learn not to make up your mind too fast standing in the middle of "thorough design." Every doorknob, every light, every single chair is there in perfect coinciding combination.

The best thing about Ettore Sottsass (after the excellence of execution) is the way it flies in the face of every gray store in Europe. There is nothing but color and variety of materials (instead of "less is more"). Most important, there is exuberance, fun and animation instead of cowering Japanese austerity.

It's worth a trip to Europe. It gives you a gasp attack. How many people who schlepped through EuroShop took the extra 30 minutes to drive to Cologne and see this store?

And just as you're about to say that there's nothing much new in Europe, you get your second gasp. There is an absolutely staggering radical skyscraper in, of all places, London. Generally, London has the grimmest modern architecture this side of Lebanon. But this is an exception so important that it almost changes the face of the city.

The building is the world headquarters of Lloyd's of London, the 300-year-old insurance company that ought to occupy dignified-but-decrepit surroundings absolutely not later than the Victorian era. Very wrong. The architect is Richard Rogers, best known (and here's your first clue) for the scandalous Beauborg Museum, the Centre Pompidou in France. When that opened, the French got something new to hate. They have never been happier. Maybe not even I.M. Pei's pyramid in front of the Louvre will give them so much to dislike. But the Pompidou Centre stayed, and any afternoon you can see hordes of school children escalating up the outside walls and playing in the Hommage a Stravinksy fountain. The French have learned to love it.

It is safe to say that there isn't one mid-city skyscraper anywhere in Europe that differs from any square glass box in Denver—until now. Now, down in the deepest part of London (the staunchest conservative part called "The City," where thousands of identical bankers in black shoes, blue suits and hair identically trimmed to regulation length, and with only the occasional flagrant lawyer darting through the crowds in a long black coat and a wig, and only a few hundred yards from the Tower of London, the Crown Jewels, and St. Paul's Cathedral) rises the astonishing Lloyd's of London Tower, home at last after 300 years of various residences.

It's better to describe the experience than the building itself. It has no buildup, no concourse, no piazza, not a word of warning. You burrow down through narrow sunless streets, walled in by undistinguished towers, and suddenly you are standing face to face, at a distance of inches, with a monstrous metal tower showing you every bit of its inside works. You are politely turned away from the front door and directed to a visitor's gallery. Another narrow street, another jumble of steelwork, nothing welcoming anywhere. Looking up, you see a fortress of steel and bolts and rivets with real turrets like the Tower of London, except that these are metal and tubes and troughs, and you can't assign a specific function to anything you see.

You rise to the sixth floor in an elevator made of much assorted hardware, and then emerge into a disconcerting "Disneyland" museum exhibit showing you the history of Lloyd's (not especially interesting). When you have survived this, finally you emerge into a corridor halfway up the inside interior atrium and there—you gasp.

You are stationed on a balcony inside a gigantic interior clockwork, 40 stories of wheels and spokes and gadgets. You can see the works inside the walls, the floor, the escalators. Everything moves. Business is "busy-ness," and you can see it all. But it is the inhabitants who make the masterpiece. The people who work here move around a lot—from desk to desk, from side to side, upstairs and downstairs, backwards, in and out. And the people and the works all work together to form an animated landscape of perfectly synchronized action. It is a labyrinth of busy bees, all centered by a plan as logical as Nature's. The visitor gets the same sort of shock that greets a person looking through glass at the cross section of an anthill. This anthill is a heap of metal, and the moving hordes of ants are all employees.

All this movement is elegant. It takes place almost silently. You shut out specifics and squint to look at patterns. This is, after all, England.

What details—from the finish of each writing desk to the magnets on the black mesh bulletin boards. The wastebaskets do not have plastic liners. Nobody has un-shined shoes. The whole ensemble inspires confidence. It is, in modern terms, what the very first builders of skyscrapers all were trying to build—a monumental Temple of Commerce.

This building isn't funny, trendy or decorated in any ordinary way. Its means of effect are entirely integrated into its function, and the form follows truly, as it should, giving the entire enterprise a solid unity.

How many people took the 10-minute cab ride into "The City" to see the Lloyds of London Tower? In a world where everything seems to have been done and nothing seems to be new, this is new. Lots of people hate it. Lots of people get a sense of their own identity by hating anything that's new.

Ideas are not where you expect to find them. Go to where everyone is, and you'll find everyone and everything the same—a pile of tourists comparing notes to be sure they all come up with the same acceptable observations.

Hail to you adventurers who go the extra step on a chance that you will become an explorer instead of a tourist. The thrill of discovery is often just ten steps farther than the familiar.

So next time you're preparing to go see all the things you're told to see by people who have already seen them, take time out to travel one more mile down the road. Bribe your way into *Phantom of the Opera*, go see Ettore Sottsass in Cologne, forge on to see new anthills scraping at the London sky. You may only gasp twice in two weeks in Europe, but you will come back taller than before.

WE LIKE IT HERE

SEPTEMBER 1987

IT USED TO BE that when Midwesterners asked you where you were from and you answered "Dallas" or "California" or "New York," they were intimidated. Now they say, "We're sorry."

If home is where the heart is, then home is Midwest America, because that's where our heart is right now. Minneapolis has a city slogan. You can see it emblazoned across the ceiling of the giant sports dome above the good, clean basketball games: "We Like It Here." Some folks might say that's a pretty small-minded and defensive attitude. But people from Minneapolis don't care. They *do* like it there. (Nobody ever wrote "We like it here" about New York City.)

Dayton Hudson likes it there, too. Even Bloomingdale's likes it there. They go there for ideas, and their advertising agency is there. Imagine "the Coast" going all the way inland to place an ad. And now the Ghermazian brothers, who built the mega-mall of Edmonton, are putting up the largest mall in the world—859 stores—in Minnesota. There must be some good reasons.

Now take that other "apolis"—Indiana. "Back home in Indiana"—home of the Pan American Games and the reincarnation of Union Station as a mixed-use festival marketplace. Today there are 107 stores in the $50 million complex, as well as a 276-room hotel.

And nobody ever sings, "Why oh why oh who oh, why did I ever leave Ohio?" Because they don't. Hello, Columbus. The Limited Inc. likes it there. Occasionally the company sallies forth to buy up Bendel's in Sodom and Gomorrah. But they don't like it there, so they go back home. Lazarus, the prototype department store is there, and Big Daddy Federated oversees it from Cincinnati.

In St. Louis, they rescued their Union Station and glorified the original— adding lakes, beer gardens and a luxury hotel. It's an admirable synthesis of reverence for things past and modern creativity. The staff wears choo-choo T-shirts saying "Woo! Woo!" And downtown has been magnetized by the Rouse Company. First they had to do it in Boston, Baltimore and New York City, but now they're moving inland. They also galvanized downtown Milwaukee, creating a facade connection many diverse architectural elements. Milwaukeeans used to sing "I'm from Milwaukee, and I ought to know." Now they've unglued themselves from their smug, indifferent suburbs to promenade Grand Avenue downtown.

Detroit was recently dubbed the "rust" belt. Now it's the launching pad for Lee Iacocca management. The first American plants of Japanese car companies are all located in the Midwest. East and West are meeting there. This may start the revival of American manufacturing. (The best radio commercials heard this year all came from Doner Advertising in Detroit.)

Chicago, "a hell of a town," hosts the Retail Advertising Conference, a friendly, quality, excellent exchange held in January. Every now and then there's chat about moving the meeting somewhere warm and more "exciting" (Miami, Las Vegas, Dallas). And every time it stays in Chicago, where it's been for 35 years. (We like it there.)

Ed Debevic's, Chicago's hottest restaurant, is suddenly Beverly Hills' hottest restaurant as well. Sean Penn was spotted eating Midwest food there after his initial jail stint. Chicago also has the only U.S. store—Marshall Field—declaring total war on AIDS, while the leaders on either coast ignore this matter of life and death.

For over 100 years, people have met "under the clock" at Marshall Field. And many people (like my family from Milwaukee) know that Christmas isn't Christmas without a day at Marshall Field. They get on the train to experience the personal and family gasp. This is the Midwest mentality at its best.

On the subject of mentality, look at the Midwest's marketing attitude. McDonald's (in Oakbrook, Ill.) is the most Midwest of marketers and currently runs commercials about such things as families and love—little 30-second operas that can leave you smiling through your tears.

What is going on here? "My, my," as they say in the Midwest, "how things have changed." Five years ago, the Midwest was the seat of unemployment, failing manufacturing, dull, provincial, exit door to the sunbelt, a place to leave. Those who stayed were living a backward glance at Norman Rockwell. Cherry pie, a nice glass of milk under a nice big shade tree on a real nice summer day. Don't rock the boat, make waves or get "above your raising." And don't get critical. We like it here.

While the Midwest waited, the rest of the world got worse. Not too many years ago, we were all shocked by small-scale quiz-show scandals. Then Vietnam. Then Watergate. Now look at "the untrustables." They cover the earth. Goodbye, religion (Jim and Tammy Bakker). Farewell, Wall Street (Ivan Boesky). Goodbye, government (Iran-gate). Bye-bye, politicians (Gary Hart). It's even "*Arrivederci*, retail." Dishonesty. Disappointment. Distrust. Don't trust anyone over—or under—30. "In Nobody We Trust."

Then one day, the Midwest developed a sense of humor. The Midwest doesn't laugh at itself easily. But *Lake Wobegon Days* sold a lot of books around the country. It's a humorous look in the mirror; people elsewhere read the book and like it. (It's the best regional novel about the Midwest since Sinclair Lewis.) The Midwest was changing its image. It was beginning to build.

The most important change was the way other Americans were starting to feel about the Midwest. The times were right. We began to like it there.

The lasting morality of the Midwest connects with what we want today. We would love to meet an honest man, or be served by a friendly clerk. We yearn for honesty, sincerity, goodness and friendship. We want home cooking, home towns, home shopping, home fires and *Family Ties*. We want our factories Iacocca-ized, our relatives Keaton-ized, our mashed potatoes with gravy. (In fact, there is a sort of cultural exchange in food. Midwest restaurants that used to offer nightmares—like the chilled fork and the salad bar—now routinely serve up itty-bitty baby asparagus spears and San

Pellegrino water, while sophisticated coastal city restaurants feature mashed potatoes and gravy as a side dish costing $7.)

We want to shop the pages of the Land's End catalog. Their guarantee says, "Guaranteed. Period." And last year they had a 68-percent net profit increase. The freaks on the hot-shot coastal fringes are noticing.

California loves to be first, New York biggest, Boston, Miami, New Orleans, Dallas, L.A., San Francisco and Seattle are ethnic, idiosyncratic and special. But lately, the people who live there are reading books about fatherhood and watching game shows on television, grinning from ear to ear while nice women win refrigerators.

What's new and true in the Midwest? A lot of the best ideas, creativity and people in the country. Don't panic, though. The Midwest is not quick to change its values or its mind. You can still see some fairly amazing views of the old Midwest mentality. Midwesterners love expressing themselves in bumper stickers and T-shirts. I saw one bumper within a mile of the Indianapolis airport that read, "I'm in no hurry. I'm on my way to work." Sears sells a T-shirt inscribed: "Drink 'til you puke."

People in Midwestern malls still wear their hair in rollers. They're still getting ready for "later." And I actually witnessed a couple strolling in a Cleveland mall wearing T-shirts with one reading "Slave" and the other "Master."

Everything may not be up to date in Cleveland or Kansas City (as far as being fastest, trendiest and first), but there is a good and growing feeling that everything is right in Kansas City—whether it's up to date or not. Feeling good is more important that being first.

There are lots of places like Kansas City. Try Flint, Toledo, Fargo or Des Moines. Go visit their stores. Check out their video facilities. Stay in a very nice hotel. Eat good food. Read their papers. Watch television. Meet the people. You'll like them.

Why aren't these people and places in the news? They will be. Wait and see.

A WARNING TO NEW YORK CITY VISITORS

JANUARY 1989

NEW YORK has always been the fastest place in the country to find out what's going on. Yes, I've written many columns about New York. But this one will be different.

I've preached for years that it is an essential destination to experience the current and coming state of things. It is the idea center of fashion, finance, tourism, art, entertainment and the state of society.

Take retailing for instance. The speed of change is unparalleled. In the last few months, the best stores in New York have suddenly gotten much better. If you haven't seen Dean and DeLuca, Zona and Country Floors, you're behind. And Bergdorf is changing by the moment.

The rate of change is equal in almost every other field. And just as quickly, AIDS, crack and homelessness have gotten much worse. I've always said, "You won't believe how fast New York has changed." And now I say the same thing, but with sadness.

Two buyers were talking behind me in the airplane between Dallas and New York. "Take off your earrings and your watch. Put your purse inside your coat. Look both ways. Never, ever walk down a street that has nobody in it. Don't take the subway." True. In fact, it's now alarming to even take a taxi. Taxis are just like little yellow cars that have escaped from the subway. The drivers may be insane.

In the last year at my home, I have doubled the strength of the alarm system, covered the back of the building with barbed wire, installed 1,000 watts of light at night, wired every plant in the garden to the wall. And still we've had plants stolen, windows broken, graffiti sprayed on the walls, had to step over the homeless lying in the front door and interrupt a man who was urinating on the front window while he explained, "Hey man, it's just rock and roll."

I live three blocks from Lord & Taylor and three blocks from the Empire State Building. A woman in front of my house was stabbed. I counted 36 semi-conscious people lying in the street during a ten-minute walk one Sunday morning.

It's not just New York. I was told to lock the car doors driving through downtown Calgary after 6:00 p.m. A friend in Santa Fe has an alarm system fiercer than mine. A buyer from Temple, Texas, knows a family whose six-year-old was shot and killed in the crossfire in front of a crack house. The district manager for a chain of video stores in Baltimore knows of four children under the age of six who have been wounded or killed in the neighborhood this year. There are three crack houses within two blocks of one of her downtown stores. And have you ever been to Miami or Detroit?

War! We always think of war as something that takes place in some foreign country. What is the difference between New York and downtown Teheran? Just language.

A few months ago, Sam Dunn and I were walking home from a seminar dealing with the quality of life. We were both robbed, had our clothes torn off and were severely beaten up. My face swelled to twice its usual size. I canceled performances for the first time in 25 years and had surgery to reduce the damage done to my face.

What can you do when it happens to you? Well, you don't get much help from the police or the government. You must take matters into your own hands. You can put up even more protection for your home, but you can't take it with you every time you go out.

The least you can do is raise hell as publicly as possible. Awareness helps. Get others to protest. Together, we can make a difference. Sam and I wrote a letter and asked friends to duplicate and send it, spreading the alarm. Almost immediately, about 10,000 letters went out to those people we vote for and pay to protect us.

"This letter is an alarm and a demand for action. Peter Glen and Sam Dunn were robbed and severely beaten Saturday, October 15, at midnight on 36th Street, between Fifth Avenue and Madison. Three men attacked suddenly from a hidden position.

"The streets were completely deserted. Fortunately, a passing taxi stopped and the muggers ran away. One-half hour later after calling 911 twice, the police finally arrived at their house and told them that the attack had not happened in their precinct and that they had reported it to the wrong people. Under pressure, the police agreed to file a report which would be transferred to the right precinct within a week.

"You have been elected to protect us, and you are failing utterly. We are paying for protection, and we are not getting it. We elected you, and we pay.

"This letter requires an immediate response."

Those Dallas buyers were right. Take off your jewelry. Don't dress conspicuously. Don't carry a lot of cash. Don't walk down an empty block at any time in any neighborhood. Cross the street if you're approaching idlers. Look around and behind you. Don't walk alone. Take cabs from door to door. Talk to the driver as you get in, and if the driver is nuts, don't get in. If you've had too much to drink, get someone to accompany you home. Don't talk to anyone. Don't take candy from strangers.

Paranoid? Exaggerated? Don't wait to find out.

A trip to New York is still the fastest way to discover what's going on. It still has ideas, urgency and excitement. But it's also what the cover of *7 Days* (the latest magazine about New York City) proclaimed: "AIDS, Homelessness, Crack and the Public Life of Death."

That's what it's like right now in New York. Take my word for it. If you can make it there, you'll make it anywhere.

HELLO, COLUMBUS

OCTOBER 1990

COLUMBUS, OHIO, is the capital of the United States as far as the customer is concerned. Test marketers thrive there. Products that live or die in Columbus will live or die everywhere else shortly thereafter. Columbus is the pinnacle of customer acceptance, and therefore it is not strange that it is now becoming the capital of retailing as well.

Let's "test market" an idea. Read the following list: Houlihan's, Limited Express, Lane Bryant, El Torito, The Gap, Lerner's, Toys "R" Us, Kids "R" Us. Are these all national chains? Are these the success stories of American retailing today? Are all of these the essence of Columbus, Ohio? To each question, the answer is "yes," and they are all located on a city block of 34th Street in New York City. If you put a roof up over the entire block—including the two troubled department store anchors, Altman's and Macy's—you'd have a mall.

The micro-America, one-block-on-foot tour in New York City starts at the corner of 34th Street and Fifth Avenue. This short, smart, one-block walk from the former Altman's to Macy's shows you everything that's right and wrong about retailing today in one sharp snapshot. The extremes of success and failure stand side by side—going out of business or enjoying their best year ever.

You can stand in the smoking ruins of Altman's, an empty and depressing scow beached on the best piece of real estate in the city. You face the Empire State Building where the ground floor is occupied by two restaurants: Houlihan's, which is jammed, and El Torito, also jammed. The people inside are dressed by The Gap, which is virtually next door, and Limited Express, right across the street.

Stroll into Limited Express. There is as much sophistication in this Ohio-born store as there is in most of the stores in Paris, and it's a lot cleaner. It is, in fact, spotless.

Hurry in to be welcomed by an aggressive stack of the item of the day. This is likely to be representative of Express' brand of merchandising genius. It will be undebatable, acceptable, reasonable clothing that is presented in clever, new colors—the perfect no-risk blend of fashion and innovation. The theory seems to be "basic, but bright"—and it works. You'll smile at the giant, oversized "French-ish" props and designer-designer furniture without feeling threatened by the clothing. Even the radio station is French, but not the merchandise. The place is mobbed by males and females wearing great clothes at reasonable prices looking for more great clothes at reasonable prices, and then going to eat and drink at Houlihan's.

Next door is Lane Bryant. This company honors one quarter of the population—the one-half of the women who wear large-sized clothing. There's oversized furniture in the windows and oversized fixtures, all elements perfectly calibrated to target and please oversized customers in search of real fashion. But there is no service.

Two months ago, I hear Les Wexner tell his staff that the new 34th Street Lerner's was The Limited Inc.'s proudest store in New York. It is located next door to Lane Bryant. I asked the greeter-guard at Lane Bryant where Lerner's was. She said, "Say what?" I asked her again where Lerner's was. She said, "Beats me!"

I crossed a piece of clean New York pavement into a shockingly good store full of cheap, fashionable merchandise. I have not been in a Lerner's since learning to laugh at the very idea in high school. The customers looked as awed as I did. We all were drawn to the rear of the huge interior by the sound of live piano music. It turned out to be emanating from a man dressed in a dinner jacket playing a nine-foot ebony grand piano in the curve of an opulent staircase—which could have been borrowed from the Metropolitan Opera—that led up to another huge floor of fashionable, cheap merchandise.

The aspirations of Lerner's customers are vividly visualized in sight, sound and fashion. The rejuvenation will be enormously successful, and it will spread out quickly.

Outside Lerner's, a sidewalk vendor is making a killing selling "Black Bart" T-shirts. Here, the Columbus image breaks down. In Columbus, Ohio, high school principals are still fretting about white Bart Simpson merchandise.

Go into Herman's. Try to ignore the filthy awning, the dirty windows, the burnt-out light bulbs, the tattered displays, the out-dated graphics and the bad smell throughout the store. Herman's does carry "everything" in sporting goods, but none of it is located in any comprehensible order.

A feeling of general low-grade anger permeates the store. And then it suddenly breaks out. An enraged employee, furious and frustrated at the checkout counter, smashes her fist onto the computer and walks off the job, screaming on her way across the floor to the back office, "Fuck, man, I don't work for no NCR I don't get fuckin' paid for working for NCR!"

Don't pass up Conway's just because you may find its shopping bags revolting. You've seen hundreds of them already. There are 14 Conway's stores within a six-block radius of Macy's and the New York garment district. Two of them are in this block. The first one is typical, an uproarious mess crawling with customers. The idea is very clear and simple: They buy and sell everything the garment industry makes that doesn't sell. It is cheap. It gives arrogant New Yorkers a chance to smile down on the mobs who jam its premises and spend their money there.

These New York sniggerers might be as shocked as I was when I wandered two or three additional doors into a handsome cosmetics and beauty store so new it didn't yet have a sign up.

"What is this place?" I asked the guard, admiring the marble floors, good lights and good display.

"This is Conway's," the guard said. "This is our new look."

You pass a store saying, "Going out of Business!" You pass a toy store. It is forlorn and empty. If you look straight ahead to the intersection, you see a mammoth new banner flying from the facade of the disastrous Herald Center. The banner proclaims: "Coming Soon! Toys "R" Us! and Kids "R" Us!"

The introduction to Canadian begins with a chipped sidewalk and signs excusing the construction. Its windows are full of good outfits and signs saying, "Pardon our appearance." There are 27 people in one line waiting for one cashier. The women I walk in with say: "How many cashiers they got in this place?" "Looks like one to me" "Yeah, and she's a slow one, too."

Those women walk out again. I go to find a manager. I say, "Who can I talk to about the long line at the cashier?" The manager says, "Nobody." I say,

"Well, what do I do if I want to buy something?" He says, "You wait, like everybody else."

"That's not good enough," I say. But the manager is walking away. He says, "I don't need to talk to you."

Across the street, The Gap has seven cashiers, all enjoying their jobs, and their customers are happy. A lot of money is changing hands.

Macy's still stands on the main corner. The windows are full of puke-colored French knits, and many customers peering into the windows are discussing how ugly they are. Inside, the old Titanic is tired. The salespeople mosey from zero to zero. The guards radiate suspicion. Even the Cellar seems to be exhausted. All the clothes I saw on 34th Street are here at Macy's, too, but they seem to be slumping on their hangers. This morning's *New York Times* ad reads: "Take an additional 20 percent off our already discounted prices on all swimwear." And then, because it's 6 o'clock, Macy's closes. Another declining day comes to an end.

Meanwhile, back at The Gap the lights are turned up high and the store goes into its energetic evening business. Seven cashiers deal with seven lines of customers. The staff wears clean, neat Gap outfits. On my way out, the girl who is polishing the glass on the front door stops polishing and opens the door for me. "Thanks a lot," she says, ignoring the fact that I hadn't bought anything. "Have a nice evening."

So, you no longer need to go to Columbus, Ohio, to find out what works today. You can walk it on 34th Street, where you learn the things customers want from their stores right now: They want to get dressed easily in reasonable, fashionable, "undesigner" clothes; they want customer service; and they want to get on with their lives.

PART FOUR
RETAIL

SEVEN KINDS OF STORES

MAY 1984

THERE USED TO BE just three kinds of stores in the world, and each one knew what it was doing. Each one had its own sort of visual merchandising. Department stores were the perpetual "big deal" with budgets, plans, ideas and lots of display of one kind or another. Specialty stores and chains could get away with strange stuff—one-of-a-kind windows that didn't need to be approved by a dozen merchandise managers. Or the chains just sent our neat complete "packages" times the number of stores in the chain. And mass merchandisers did not do much of anything except duplicate neat stock keeping, maybe with plan-o-grams, never with imagination. Visual presentation usually amounted to resurrected garland installed after Thanksgiving.

So where's the store in 1984?

Certainly not in three neat types.

Following is a nice, clear exposition of the seven kinds of distribution channels (formerly called "stores") that now exist, with some hints of their individual strengths for visual merchandising.

1. The Department Stores. The good ones will survive. No store but the department store can hit the public with sheer, big scale. Only a department store could create Macy's new main floor in New York City, or Dayton's St. Paul re-make, or Parisian's laser gift-list print-outs, or Bloomingdale's getting 20,000 customers in the first hour at Valley View in Dallas. No other kind of store can get the massive impact of Ornamentalism at Marshall Field's, or Japan as staged by Filene's, Wanamaker's or Robinson's.

Only a department store can really launch a Ralph Lauren Home Fashion set-up thoroughly or turn a ton of fixture acreage into a wish-fulfilling Nordstrom. And it is visual merchandising people that do the department store job which sets it apart from other kinds of stores.

2. Chains. We all wish we owned The Limited or The Limited Express, and wish we'd thought up Casual Corner's multiplying-separates sales pieces. The Limited has proven that classy windows, signage, fixtures, total graphics, store identification and fashion impact (all the work of high-standard, uniform, continuous visual merchandising) can sell clothes in over 500 locations.

The trademark of the great chains is discipline, and if there is no room for individual display talent at each location, good. If you like the company, go work at headquarters and set the standards yourself. Don't mess around with the store.

Benetton, Crate & Barrel and Laura Ashley also have instantly recognizable presentation. The good ones will last.

3. Mass Merchandisers. If you never see Sears, Penney's, Target or a great new supermarket (Grand Union on 86th Street in New York City, or Ralph's at Oceanside), go soon. You're in for a shock. Penney's has Halston and Bergdorf's doesn't—but they've both managed to do it without losing any of their customers. So has Sears. So has Target. While Bloomingdale's has a swing shop called "Stars of the L.A. Freeway," new prototype Penney's stores have Marilyn Monroe with skirt swept up in what is actually a better display. Dayton's pillow-wall is a standard of excellence, but it is virtually identical to the new ones at Sears, Penney's and Target.

The biggies are coming back, and they're spending money on visual presentation.

4. Specialty Stores. The last remaining citadels of imagination, point-of-view and controversy, as well as strongholds of individuality: Barneys' 1983 Christmas windows; Norma Kamali's new store on 56th Street, New York City; lotsa stuff on Melrose Avenue; any store carrying Memphis furniture; Wilkes Bashford or Gump's (most of the time), both in San Francisco; Byerly's near Minneapolis; a single pizza-tool pushcart in Venice; and the best gift-with-purchase bit of all time—Cartier's Cabbage Patch Doll giveaway with any purchase over $1 million.

5. Catalogs. When is a store not a store? This all used to be called "direct marketing," and regular retailers ignored it. Now they try to do it. (What "normal store" does not have a second-rate catalog?) But now the real specialists—Spiegel, Sharper Image, Patagonia, Land's End, to name a few that are still great right now—are there and likely to stay there. In fact, Catalogia has opened a "store" in Richmond, Va. Every imaginable catalog and computer ordering device are right in the store. This is *not* great news for visual merchandisers, unless they go into print.

6. Catalog Retailers. These are a new breed. Eddie Bauer, cataloging since 1935, now has 28 stores. Brookstone does both. Crate & Barrel does both. Esprit, now with an amazing factory outlet, has opened a retail store in Hong Kong, with Los Angeles, New York City and Europe coming right along.

The catalog people who have opened real retail stores have no history of dumb display, and so they've made very exciting moves. They are presenting in many dimensions.

7. Off-Price-Discount-Membership-Factory-Outlet-You-Name-It. Whatever it's called, it's the gang that the big boys keep waiting for to go away, and it's not going away. There are all sorts: plain like Sym's, Marshall's or Wal-Mart; full service and entertainment like Kids "R" Us; glitzy like Club Mart of America two blocks from Macy's; clean and clear like Ross Stores California (where they all wear buttons saying, "Don't pay department store prices"); wildly successful like the Price-Club; and so on. So many images cloud predictions about visual merchandising.

There is no customer loyalty. The customer shops in not one, but four distribution channels per week. Nobody shops only and always at Altman's. You spot Broadway shopping bags schlepping through the Price Club every day. Brookstone customers order through the book and thrill in the stores.

The United States now has 146 percent of the retail space it needs. All seven of the above are going to have failures and successes, and soon.

All seven channels are "splintering"—Bamberger's is a department store, a catalog store and a discounter. Too many department stores are lousy discounters too often and real department stores too seldom. They perform two or more functions at once. This is confusing, but sometimes works.

Specialty stores are splintering. Charivari has five stores in New York, each one carrying different merchandise. Wilkes Bashford does it in San Francisco. Britches of Georgetown does it in Washington, D.C., and Atlanta.

Malls are splintering. There are regular malls, outlet malls, discount malls, strip malls—and all of them have "Muzak."

Even manufacturers are splintering—Ralph Lauren, Laura Ashley and many specialty stores carrying home furnishings, clothing and anything else that sells.

Diversification has hit and changed us permanently. Confusion is gaining over clarity.

Only the good ones will survive.

So where's the store in 1984?

All over the place, and the visual merchandisers are following all seven yellow brick roads....

LIFE WITHOUT HERBS

OCTOBER 1985

ARE WORDS VISUAL? Sure they are. There are stupid fashion ads to see in every magazine and newspaper and tens of millions of polluting signs to be read in every store in the world. There are department names only their authors understand, and there are pronouncements by fashion people that nobody can understand.

Most retail words take perfectly normal ideas and twist them beyond all human recognition—condescending to customers, making them laugh and leave.

America could just die of cuteness. In Michigan, there's a drive-in called "Honk 'N Holler." You're supposed to do just that. And there's a truck stop and diner in Tennessee called "Tank 'N Tummy." We all hate this sort of stuff. But what's the difference between that and Saks Fifth Avenue talking about "S'Fabulous" and "S'Fantastic," et cetera, et cetera. I think it's "S'Ftupid," and it makes me "S'Fick."

Bullock's has some real winners, like "Boulevard Dresses" and "B.W. Woman." Who knows what any of those mean? Bloomingdale's took some of its darling names to Texas where mystified cowpokes still are trying to figure out what is meant by "Sutton Sportswear" and "Beekman Dresses." How about "Y.E.S.?" Even New Yorkers wonder about that one.

Did anybody ever ask customers what they are looking for, write down the answers and then start putting up departmental signs?

The worst copy ever written came from Bonwit Teller a few years ago. It was a stab at describing a dress: "Hush! Can you hear the rustling whispers of taffeta upon the staircase?" It went on like that, except people reading it probably excused themselves to go to the bathroom.

And now something horrible is loose in the world this summer. The "fash-ionettes" are at it again. Dogged by poor sales, they have dusted off their thesauruses and screwed up the English language once more. The following ad messages came from one depressing month—July, 1985...

"I regret that I have but one life to give to my plaids."—Gimbel's

"If there is ever one absolute, 100 percent, don't-even-think-of-breaking-it-commandment, it is this: Get thyself a 7/8 length coat."—*Town & Country*

"Life without herbs is unthinkable..."—*Metropolitan Home*

The people who write such trash are sick. The people who allow it to be published are worse. This "miserabilia" used to appear dependably in every Altman's ad, but the virus was contained. However, it seems to have escaped in July and infected every merchandising copywriter in America. Does anyone think, even for one second, that this sort of verbal garbage will sell merchandise?

What about signs? American department stores put signs out over merchandise at the rate of about 15,000 per square acre. Consciously, there is no reason for this. Subconsciously, it is probably done to fill sign holders. Unconsciously, it is probably their way of apologizing for the fact that there are no salespeople.

These signs all say "New Arrivals," or "Price as Marked" (imagine that). Sometimes they say "New for Spring." They're all the verbal-visual equivalent of green leaves for spring and dead leaves for fall.

Come on, folks. Let's not bother to say that this pollution isn't visual and not your business. If it isn't your department, why don't you come up with the guts to *make* it your department? Customers see ads and signs before they buy, so it's all visual merchandising.

Fire the copywriters. They can complicate anything. Throw out your sign holders. Nobody will miss them. Strip those dumb department names right off the wall, and come up with some simple descriptions.

Most urgently, get rid of the people who think this way. They are the real source of the mess. Unfortunately, this will include most fashion coordinators (or directors or VP's of fashion, or whatever they're called). These people are responsible for finding out trends and giving them adorable little names that no human being could possibly understand. One great recent piece of copy was for a leather-trend story quite incredibly called "Hide and Chic." It's so horrible, I won't even identify the store.

Far worse though, and probably beyond our control, are the self-styled verbal pronouncers of fashion—those compulsive personalities who seem to have been chosen by God to make announcements through such purveyors of "news" in the fashion world, like many magazines and *WWD* and *W.* One of the embarrassing stupidities of all time was uttered this year in Paris and dutifully (almost gleefully) reported by *W:* One Marie-Helen de Rothschild emerged from an Yves St. Laurent couture show and said, "At last! We can live again."

If you can divorce yourself from your own defensive prejudices and look back at us from the outside (from the customer's point of view), you will see why we are so often ridiculed or even more often, ignored. We need to admire and emulate our customers, not abuse them. Right now, we must rebuild their shaken interest in us. The public already thinks fashion is boring as hell and showing disinterest in not buying it.

Real simple language was good enough for Shakespeare ("To be or not to be, that is the question") and for God ("Let there be light"). But that's all too simple for fashion people.

We are communicators. It is all we do. It doesn't matter whether it is spoken or printed or painted or sculpted in three dimensions. It all faces the customer. And the customer faces us all right back.

Today, the customer's saying the one idea that can't be argued with: "I don't care." That's *very* plain English.

P.S. Altman's is still doing it ... Bulletin from *The New York Times*, Thursday, August 8, 1985: "If enemy aliens from outer space cause all the knitting needles on Mother Earth to disappear into some ultra-sonic infundibulum whoosh! like that, 99 percent of the world's would-be best-dressed women would find themselves wearing nothing at all this fall."

P.P.S. As a service to our readers who may be too ignorant to understand Altman's copy, we provide the definition of the word "infundibulum" as stated in *Webster's Ninth New Collegiate Dictionary*: "any of various conical or dilated organs or parts."

A MESSAGE TO DEPARTMENT STORES

JANUARY 1986

DEPARTMENT STORES have lived through a lot, and the worst thing they ever lived through was the "boutique" trend followed by the "store snatcher" trend (manufacturers in search of keeping their identities), the "splintering" trend and other confusion that made them lose their grips. For many years, department stores have taken all those trends entirely too seriously. Boutiquing made so much money when it started that nobody realized big stores were going to pieces.

The department store started losing itself, its look, feel and image. It lost its own unique philosophy and shopping experience—everything that made it "that store" to the customer. The customer started drifting from store to store. Loyalty was a dead issue, and shopping lost its flavor. After customers tire of being trendy, they want a store that is their own lifetime companion. Yet as of January 1, 1986, the "trendy-visual" panic is still on.

Retailing thrives on change, and so does everything called fashion, but it needs a permanent skeleton to hold it together. That inner structure is called image.

Today, you can go to any city in the country and find a store identical to the one you just left by walking into the next one you come to. It can be a Federated, Associated, Cartered, Hawleyed or Haled, or any other store at all. It will have no image, or it will have too many. It will have 200 little "image-ettes," about 50 to a floor in a major branch. There will be lots of decoration, but no overall design, no harmony, continuity or unity. Therefore, the experience itself will also be imageless and fractured into thousands of incoherent little pieces.

"Retail as theater" has been misunderstood. It doesn't mean 500 amateur performers each performing for 30 seconds. This theater (which I've often praised and seen wholly misunderstood) needs a playwright, music, props, costumes and more. However, all of it—every bit of it—needs that governing hand of a director, and everyone must do what that director says. If the director is a genius, the store works and runs forever. If the director is an accountant, the show closes on the road.

So, in 1986 there are two kinds of department stores: those with no image and those with too much miscellaneous image. A brand new kind of department store of the future is needed. Yes, there are such stores here today, but not many. You can see them in New York City, and they may exist elsewhere, too.

It started at Saks (not a trendy store, perhaps). But it has been there a long, long time doing nicely. The rest of the country didn't pay much attention to what Saks started several years ago. This retailer, which has never sacrificed itself to any "current" look, solidified its attitude and started pouring money into making Saks look more like Saks than ever. Saks got clearer and clearer to the customer while everyone else diversified.

Then Macy's suddenly appeared and made so much money so fast that nobody really looked at the long-range image the retailer was planning. The good old store revealed itself as layer after layer of later looks was carefully pared away, exposing lofty pillars and simple floor plans while using every new visual technique. A new tradition was created that made a mix of the past and present.

Bergdorf Goodman closed every store but one, and made itself the concentrated temple of couture that it is today. Everyone missed this because they never went there in the first place.

During all this activity, the rest of the country writhed in the throes of every passing fad. They absorbed chrome and glass, high-tech, electronics, post-modernism, surrealism, neo-classicism, pre-punk, punk and post-punk warehouse and a dozen or so other little design ideas that came and went like lightning. Department stores became scrapbooks capturing the entire history of design.

Now, at last, the most copied store in the world is doing such a fundamental change that the audience might actually see the show and figure out what's going on. Everybody loves to hate Bloomingdale's, except their customers. You've heard that old song, "Nothing could be greater than to ride the escalator in Bloomingdale's...."

Five years ago, Bloomingdale's threw everybody off the track—including itself—by installing the trendiest main floor of all time. It was so wildly divergent from what anyone expected that it succeeded despite itself, exerting a kind of morbid fascination over customers and other retailers by creating crowds wanting to go in and see what would happen with such a grotesque design. It was a triumph of chaos and cosmetics over clarity. It wasn't even trendy; it was ugly and dark, and it worked.

That was five years ago. Today Bloomingdale's is putting its money into a very different kind of thinking, having decided it would kind of like to stick around for a while instead of being just the trendiest store on earth. There's nothing like bad business to wake you up. The main floor extravaganza started to bore even the "Bluppies" that hung in there. Bloomingdale's sent someone out into the world to look at Saks and Macy's and the customer—

the customer—who was standing in Bloomingdale's yawning.

Bloomingdale's is never boring for long, though. Go to the new, expensive, admirable fourth and sixth floors. You won't be shocked, amazed, uprooted, revolutionized, hyped, thrilled or flattered. You *will* be pleased. You'll probably buy something. You will want to come back again. Even the salespeople seem to have been slightly humanized.

All the labels and brands and designers are there and all with their own identities and signature logos and materials. On the fourth floor, you'll find Armani, La Prairie, Nipon, Polo, Tahari, Montana, Ellis, Klein, et cetera. On the sixth floor are Baccarat, Waterford, Wedgewood, Rosenthal, Mikasa and others that lead defined existences. The radical change is that even these big people are subordinated and integrated into a clear, overall design plan that is Bloomingdale's.

Please be careful to look at all of this slowly. It looks so "nice" that the big, underlying change is not immediately evident. You might be tempted to say, as visual people do, that there is nothing there you haven't seen before. You have to train yourself to see differently. If you're looking for flashy ideas of any kind, you'll miss the point.

It's easy to see Kamali, Charivari, Comme des Garcons and Susanne Bartsch. They look great. They have an image. They are small, though, and they should be like that.

Remember the ancient department store adage: "Everything under one roof." Well in the last ten years department stores should have been saying: "Everything under 1,200 different roofs, all in the same location. Come in, and you'll die of cuteness. You won't understand what you're doing because we don't either. Come share this experience. And good luck to you."

Now the time has come to put everything under one wonderful roof. It's virtually a new idea. Saks, Macy's and Bergdorf's have been around a long, long time. Their images may have been battered under various regimes and owners, but something vital stayed aloft the entire time. They changed along with their customers, but they never stopped being whatever they were to themselves.

There's a role for trends and experimentation in retailing—in small stores, not department stores: The small stores are always going to be the most exciting, newest, newsiest stores in the world. But the department stores are going to make the money—if they do it right.

Next year at this time, there will be far fewer big stores in business. Those left are going to be wonderful.

HOW DO YOU LIKE THEM TOMATOES?

MARCH 1986

ONCE UPON A TIME in Tunisia, just one person did it all. Just one person planted tomato seeds, grew tomatoes, threw a blanket over them against an unexpected frost, picked them when they were ripe, paddled them downriver to the market (it was only open Saturdays from 6 a.m. until noon), displayed them in triangular pyramids, sold them to customers and then went home. It was a one-person show with total control—expert, fun and successful. This has been going on for 2,000 years. And it's happening again right now. In fact, it's an unexpected and major revolution in retailing.

There is a brand new old kind of store that is run by vigilantes who have taken the law into their own hands. These outlaws are manufacturers, and they are staging a series of one-person shows that is passing traditional retailers right by. Every store sells only its own products, and each sells them only its own way—the new "company store." Gaze at this list of manufacturers all opening their very own stores. This list grows daily. Not one of these companies was a retailer until 20 minutes ago.

J.G. Hook: Mickey & Co., New York City
Merona: Pebble Beach, Calif.
L.L. Bean: Freeport, Maine
Benetton: worldwide
Aca Joe: U.S.
Inwear-Matinique: New York City
Parachute: Canada, U.S.
Esprit: Los Angeles, New Orleans, Hong Kong, Cologne
Ralph Lauren: London, New York City
Giorgio: Beverly Hills, New York City
Cotton Ginny: Canada, U.S.
The North Face: U.S.

Visually, these are the most daring stores in America. And every single owner is accused of egomania, ostentatious spending and not making a profit. Almost all of the accusers are traditional retailers.

L.L. Bean has been adamant about quality for years, not only of its products, but of the way those products are sold. That's why the company is a catalog first and foremost. But hordes of people have been finding their way to inconvenient Freeport for years, and the factory store there is reputed to have sales of $55 million per year.

Banana Republic and Eddie Bauer are two who have seen fit to leap from catalog into retail, but they do not design and make all their own merchandise. We're talking here about people who make their own stuff and sell it themselves. They get more sophisticated every day.

Fizazz, Mujani's Coca-Cola store, is nothing short of an entirely new approach to merchandising fashion that most people thought was dead. At Fizazz, the "sweats" are previewed on a bridge by the customer using interactive video that shows details on the small screen and also projects on the wall. Then the customer goes down to the cafeteria, gets a tray and picks stuff from colored pictures. The staff scrambles up the ladders to get what customers want. (This actually means they have to *serve* the customers— another new concept.) Nothing seems old. Sweats are not dead at the company store.

Ralph Lauren's Bond Street store in London is a perfect model of presentation. Plans have just been announced to triple its size. None of his other stores do it so completely, but he owns this one and nobody gets in his way. This month, we'll see what $12 million can do to an old castle on the corner of 72nd and Madison—his second company store.

Another company store, Inwear-Matinique, tries hard in SoHo to show how to put its products together. All fixtures coordinate and wheel around. They're more active than most of the staff who sleep there.

The Los Angeles Esprit store cost $15 million and is a stunning flagship for a manufacturer who is manic and absolute about image presentation from the swatch through to the final customer. This store has total control, and it looks it. Customers have been seen to walk in, gasp, wobble and sit down. It does *not* remind them of the last department store. Esprit's new company store in Cologne, designed with Ettore Sottsass, will open soon.

What are these new stores all about, and why is this happening? Well, they aren't "designer" stores. That gang (the Kenzo-Armani-Versace-Frizo mob) has been doing it their own way for years. They have always known what would happen to their merchandise if the big boys got their hands on it. It vanishes in the general haze of some "Designer Nook."

These new stores are not the discounters, outlets or direct mail folk either. And they're not the department stores. They're something entirely new to hate.

Five or six times this year, other vigilante/maverick/entrepreneurial manufacturers will get so fed up with diluted presentations of their messages that they will go for the radical visuals of the new retailing and open six or seven more ambitious new stores with their own names on them that will support and sell their own merchandise. The revolution is growing. We are returning to the full-cycle designer/manufacturer/seller/tomato person, only now it's called the freestanding, full-price, glamorous, manufacturer-owned-and-operated factory and company store.

The "factory store" used to be a cheerless manufacturer's back room selling overruns or "seconds." It was never a showcase. The plain pipe rack/no service format efficiently cleaned out the extras and seemed like a real value to the customer. Factory stores became factory outlets and then factory outlet malls. These were tour bus destinations and had some amenities, but they were still ugly.

Then the manufacturers started attacking normal retail channels. Frustrated and furious, they started trying to wedge their own identities into normal stores. Cosmetics people did it first and best. They supplied merchandise, but also had visual material and even architecture. Some of them even paid the salespeople. This was the beginning of the "shops within shops" and the dreaded "boutique" era that started the destruction of department stores. What was once a cosmetics island with identification all over it soon became the brand name epidemic that caused shoppers to neither know nor care where they did their shopping. And the manufacturers started opening their own company stores.

What will all this do to visual merchandising people? You probably know three talented people who have already left traditional stores to work for manufacturers. I'll bet you know 300 talented people who are stuck in stores battling manufacturers and their management who want to tell them how to do their jobs, or even do *their* work for them. I'll bet you know 3,000 customers who don't care who runs what store as long as the store excites and serves them fast.

The tomato genius in Tunisia and the new company store have a lot in common. They both sell horizontally, from seed to sale and from fabric swatch to checkout line. Neither one allows a store to put a wall between themselves and their customers. They both say everything: "This *is* my department." And they both sell a lot of tomatoes.

The future of retailing can be seen in this revolution. Tune in again in five more years. You'll see many more total operators like the tomato person in Tunisia. These daring new stores will succeed because they have seen the basic need to change the entire system, and they have the courage and the vision to go back, way back, to the future.

RALPH IS IN THE DETAILS

AUGUST 1986

HOW OBSERVANT ARE YOU? In what store can you see and experience the following details and many, many more?

Uncanceled antique European postage stamps on a desk in a country sitting room.

The only towel wall in the world that is as clear as every other towel wall in the world—but this one is curved.

Bonsai pines, because they are more interesting than regular pine trees.

The store auditioned various canaries for the tones of their voices so they would make harmonious chords when they sing together. (Breeds that fit the image are nuns' heads, cordon bleus and silver bills.)

As if that weren't enough, the two mop-topped canaries (names Paul and Ringo) each require one slice of red apple every day at 3:30 p.m.

A pair of roller skates that a staff member asked his mother to send down from upstate New York, where she had been saving them since he last wore them at age 11.

Candles that have been lighted and then snuffed out so they don't look unused.

Twenty-four-hour access to a theatrical workshop so midnight inspirations can be executed and installed by noon the next day.

A woman in tears on the staircase because one of the portraits reminds her of her deceased husband.

Red-striped $42 silk ties worn as belts around employees' waists—an affectation that might become a fashion statement.

Stainless steel dumbwaiters hidden behind discreet, fabric-covered doors delivering programmed snacks up and down five floors.

A bright red wool blanket thrown across a bed in an otherwise non-red room, with this explanatory quote from someone, "That makes it NOT Laura Ashley."

More quotes about caring enough to pick up a rubber band dropped on the floor or rearranging a toothbrush in a bathroom setting: "It's my baby. It's important."

Men working in Alterations, wearing neckties.

Elevators that didn't exist and were duplicated from the ones in the Paris store because they were right.

An elevator operator who mischievously calls out "Home Furnishings," knowing you know that's not what it is when you reach the floor that sells things for the home.

Windows that are "staged" with paper equivalents of props and merchandise, then lighted. The merchandise is placed, working from front to back—a hot and painstaking job.

Polo mallets used to adjust the lighting.

A staff of eight in the Creative Services Department, just for the New York store.

The real grass in the windows that is misted as often as the vegetables at Dean and DeLuca.

Genuine solid brass chains and locks that anchor the street-level flower boxes to the building so nobody steals them.

A handwritten hangtag on a teddy bear reading, "This is Casey. Casey loves chocolate ice cream, but only if it has chocolate sprinkles on top."

Solid mahogany boards inside bolts of furnishing fabric.

Cleaners carrying Windex and rags around in logo shopping bags.

Strawberries, raspberries and stuff like that served to customers from 3 to 5 p.m., then cocktails and canapes after 5 p.m.

Dinner catered free for creative service employees who work after 6 p.m.; lunch catered free to all employees—sample lunch menu: Soup—seafood bisque. Main course—devilled egg salad with pimento, avocado and alfalfa sprouts; sliced sirloin of beef with Alpenzeller; strawberry cream cheese on date nut bread. Salad—dilled potato salad; avocado stuffed with shrimp; tossed green salad with herbs. Desserts—fruit salad with cream; peach sherbet.

Old tapestry fragments recycled and made into cushions.

A young man's dressing room with a worn miniature leather wing chair, a worn miniature teddy bear and photos on the walls of grade-school polo teams.

Sober lighting for menswear, brighter lighting for womenswear, and lots of outdoor lighting for home furnishings.

A "staging calendar" to gradually move one season into the next; no "suddenly it's spring"—surprise, surprise—department store tactics here.

Props are not called props; they are "artifacts," they are real. The artifacts are *not* for sale, a fact that is grieving customers, who want it all.

No barbershop—yet.

Vivaldi and jazz in the morning, Frank Sinatra at 5 p.m., when the evening sun begins to go down.

Constant maintenance, not just because *Architectural Digest* is coming, but so that it looks just as good to the customers at 4 p.m. as it does to the first arrivals at 10 a.m.

All leather chairs in fine condition, but every one of them old.

Trouble in Paradise: a coordinating woman overheard informing a customer, "I'm not a salesgirl." This one used to work at Bloomingdale's. A nearby real live salesgirl snickered when she heard this unfortunate remark.

The most beautiful and astonishing flowers. They are all absolutely in the image, but extreme, exotic, magnified. They stop you every time you see them—not just the mammoth, extravagant arrangements, but the little incidental jugs of wildflowers related to every color in the wallpaper behind them.

The booklet issued with the opening says: "It is the embodiment of a way of living, a source of quality and tradition." Then it stops. There are 18 pages of remarkable photographs of real people wearing the merchandise, but NOT ONE WORD OF COPY. All advertising types should think this over.

This store teaches you to look more closely, seeing more than you might have done without it. Their conviction about detail is so absolute that yours improves with simple contact.

Don't plan any comparative shopping for the same day. The standards of every other store you encounter will make you angry, especially the oblivious Madison Avenue neighbors—all of those boring European outposts full of stunning, but stunned, sales types squinting at you from behind their Gauloises. A bomb has hit the neighborhood, and they don't know it yet. They're all still in there listening to modified rock and roll, pre-judging customers.

This store has no security bell on the locked front door enabling the staff inside to decide whether they want to let you in or not. This store has two doormen, and they open the door before you get to within spitting distance.

Maintaining all this excellence will be the test. It is possible, as many skeptics point out, that perfection is just there while the store steals the spotlight. Cynics will wait for them to join their snotty neighbors in forgetting to wipe the ashtrays clean after they empty them. They'll watch for somebody to tape some crummy note up on the wall by the sales desk. But as they already have the store looking as good each day at 4 p.m. as it was when it opened, they might also have it be just as good four years from now. And if they do, they will have raised the standards and kept them there for all of us.

Once again, we see what happens when a "manufacturer" wants to do the selling his way by becoming the retailer as well. The single best thing about this store is that it is not intimidating. Everyone is friendly and enthusiastic. They are knowledgeable; they care. This all makes customers care about buying the merchandise. The store is very grand and very expensive, but it is fun and exciting. It is hard to remember encountering this combination anywhere else in retailing. Most stores with half the class are twice as humiliating to ordinary people. The early sales reports are staggering, but not surprising; even at this level, there is no excuse for condescending to customers. They've got it right.

Who said, "God is in the detail"? —Mies van der Rohe.
Who said, "I will never be satisfied"? —Doug Tompkins.
Who said, "No detail is small"? —Me.

Of all the far-too-many stores in the world, which one comes closest to being perfect?
Ralph Lauren.

THE MORE THINGS CHANGE ...

DECEMBER 1986

MERGERMANIA. Leveraged buyouts. Retail acrobatics. Isn't it depressing? Every kind of company in America is getting everyone together in the company cafeteria and telling them they're not what they were, they're now something entirely new, they've merged, they've been sold. They say that everything is getting bigger, simpler and more profitable. "And before we forget, we'll need fewer people and here's the list of those who are fired ... with all best wishes."

It isn't just airlines that are merging, cutting, standardizing, homogenizing. Retailers—and especially department stores—are thrashing through reorganizations that show their panic to the world. Among the most critical casualties are the visual merchandisers at those stores. Gone are the days when department store visual executives came to the markets with ideas and authority of their own. Now, like the poor sportswear buyers, they come to execute someone else's orders. They can moan and wriggle and complain and argue very reasonably that their stores need image and individuality and that they are the ones who can do it, but they still have to buy and install whatever some geniuses doing the thinking for 16,000 stores tell them to do. "Think and feel whatever you like, kiddies, but then do what I tell you to do. Love, Hitler."

A few gruesome headlines:
- Bamberger's is no longer Bamberger's; it's called Macy's. Macy's already made its West Coast stores anonymous by demanding they all do just what New York tells them to do even though the West Coast is a totally different world.
- Wanamaker's is no longer Wanamaker's; it's for sale. Soon it'll be part of something else. More sameness.
- Gimbel's is nothing at all.
- Ayre's, Pogue's and Stewart's are no longer Ayre's, Pogue's and Stewart's; they're all just Ayre's. More sameness. In fact, the folks who own Ayre's and Pogue's and Stewart's aren't even Associated Dry Goods anymore; they're all just little toy soldiers at the May Company. More sameness.
- Dayton's used to be Dayton's, and Hudson used to be Hudson. Now they are one, and nobody cares.
- Rikes isn't Rikes and Shillito's isn't Shillito's and Lazarus isn't Lazarus. They're all just homogenized milk.

Will you live to see more of this? You betcha. Here's a picture of the new retail apocalypse. You've heard of generic products. America has invented some monsters. Take food, for instance. We live in an age where it is possible to be served something at breakfast called "fruit flavored jelly" and at lunch, you can have "mixed seafood parts." Could it be long before we shop at a place called "store?"

Ain't it a shame? Visual presentation used to be the fastest way for any store to communicate its identity to customers. It still is for specialty stores, national chains and mass merchandisers. They still know that they establish their differences through visual delights. But go to any mall and watch while customers shop, select, decide, approach the cashwrap, whip out their checkbooks and ask, "Who do I make it out to?"

Nowadays, customers don't even know or care what store they're shopping in. Those of you who still believe in customer loyalty have done a great job of deluding yourselves. Congratulations.

The ultimate standardization exists right now: Within two months, you can expect to walk into many major shopping centers and see three huge stores all owned by the May Company. Enjoy yourself while you lose your bearings moving amongst the same company, same management, same philosophy, same vendors, same buyers, same point of view, same objectives, and, of course, THE SAME MERCHANDISE PRESENTATION.

Maybe that anonymity doesn't matter if you're a Kmart, Wal-Mart or B. Dalton. Maybe the giant national chains benefit from standardization, and they *should* all be the same. They can't have 1,500 store managers all emoting display theories. But for department stores, their only decent reason for existing is their difference—their regional and individual point of view.

I know, the department stores all claim people love having everything under one roof—big selection, wonderful customer service. But you and I know customers don't believe for one minute that department stores ever provide any of those things. Customers do believe department stores still provide theater, scale, big ideas, unique merchandise, sheer excitement, show times, spectacles—all visual presentation. But now department stores are cutting all this out, their sole claim to image identification.

There is no difference between Wanamaker's and Woodies, and there is no help for the one big store called Burdines, Bloomingdale's, Bullock's, Belks, The Broadway and the Boston Store. In an age where individuality creates public heroes (Ueberroth, Iacocca, Reagan, Rambo, Dr. Ruth) and customers strive for personal style, the stores seeking to serve them are becoming blander and blander—more and more the same. And with every backward step, the accountants who run these stores are declaring lower and lower expenses, and therefore claiming success. It's a farce.

Department stores could use a Messiah. If I spot any saviors before you do, I'll surely let you know.

IN PRAISE OF SPECIALISTS

NOVEMBER 1989

IF YOU ARE GOING to work in a store between now and the year 2000, you'd better hope you're a specialty store or a catalog. Everyone else is buried in financing and re-financing, real estate deals, mergers and acquisitions. Meanwhile, their stores are unclear and unfocused about marketing, merchandising and customer service.

Most "in-store" stores are also doing badly. The customer is tired of trying to figure them out and would rather stay home by the fireside than face the Estee Lauder rep at a department store or trudge through the anesthetic experience of Kmart.

So much for the excitement of visual presentation, customer service and product knowledge. Shopping has become a chore. Shoppers ordered about $30 billion in merchandise from catalogs last year. That's 88 million Americans who shopped by mail or phone instead of schlepping through "real" stores expecting display, ideas and service. Don't you think those catalog operations could be called "specialists?" Have you seen their catalogs? They feature plenty of visual presentation, plenty of excitement, faithful and accurate customer service—and you don't need to put up with actually going out to be disappointed.

The great qualities of retailing have all survived. It's just that they've been translated into print. Who says Americans aren't literate? They can certainly respond to pictures and write checks. And they do it entirely at their own convenience.

Land's End? Spiegel? Smith & Hawken? They're the best of the best without the hassle of having to leave home. But there are stores worth dropping L.L. Bean on the floor by your recliner for, and those stores are even worth the travel, the parking and the gas. They're the specialists—people who know what they're doing and who care about it, people who keep their jobs for more than six months. If only such a dream could be believed, the bored millions who have stopped shopping (sometimes called "customers") the "in-store experience" might get up the excitement to visit the specialist.

A specialist can have a large store or a small one, a national chain or a single location, but the intensity of vision must travel to the furthest corner of the furthest store if it is to truly specialize. A specialist is a person as well as a store.

Great specialists are opinionated, editorial, theatrical, innovative, risk-taking, aggressive, eccentric and, ultimately, passionate and caring—certainly about their business and possibly even about customers. They are detail maniacs, motivators, curious searchers of the world, and enamored of whatever is new that fits into their image.

There are 15 qualities specialty stores can offer customers:

• Point of view. Specialists don't drag the whole world in by the hair and throw it all down in front of their customers. They pre-shop the world and bring back the parts they want their customers to buy. It's what they leave out that matters. They buy that way, display that way, and advertise that way. They give direction. They do the customers' work for them.

• Limited selection. The Sock Shop sells socks. Get it? The same company is going to open The Tie Shop soon. Get it? The Disney Store sells Disney, not everything. Customers don't want *everything*. They want Disney.

• Theater. Free entertainment, education, artistic pleasure, design, taste, fun, ideas, the new, the unknown.

• Consistency. We all know exactly what to expect when we go to McDonald's. That's reassuring when you're starved and you're standing in downtown Taipei and it works for your family. Now, compare the consistency you feel about McDonald's to what you feel when confronted with prices in department stores.

• Art. Drifting through Zona (New York City) is complete in every sense. What you see, hear, smell and touch add up to making the store a comprehensive work of art. And, better than museums, you can experience it. You can even buy it. That's what they're all standing there hoping you'll do.

• Authenticity. Tiffany, Baccarat, Burberry's. You could not possibly make a mistake in any of those stores. The greatest desire of most human beings is to be safe, to fit in, to blend, and these stores have mastered reassuring people. Want to be safe and tasteful? Want quality, tradition? Hurry, hurry to these establishments. They specialize in tasteful safety, self-assurance and only moderate label-consciousness.

• Authority. Do you get the feeling the people who serve you at Disneyland have some idea of what they're talking about? Those people have been trained. They're practically Japanese in their relentless cheerfulness. And they look at patrons as reasons for being their best.

• An unspoiled place. People would do anything today to find an unspoiled place—an unpolluted beach, a beautiful church. A good specialist can provide that "unspoiled" experience. Anyone who has ever grocery shopped at Stew Leonard's knows that there is excellence in the air. You can feel it the instant you hit the parking lot. And Disney should design our cities. We'd live longer.

- Courage. No store sells what anybody needs. There isn't a store in the world we couldn't get along without, so it takes guts to have one. Customers can sense this courage during every visit. It makes them happy.

- Imagination. The difference between one store (and one person) and another is imagination. Doesn't that mean that a specialist is, above all things, imaginative?

- Clarity. Wal-Mart is not a specialty shop, but oh boy, is it a specialist—and the most profitable store of all. Wal-Mart is totally clear to its suppliers, its employees and its customers. The nicest person in the remotest Wal-Mart can tell you all you need to know about the company. So can any manufacturer.

- Style. Laura Ashley, Ralph Lauren, Pierre Deux—all sell a single, integrated style. Everything goes with everything. You either like the style or you don't. Either way, it's easy to understand what's going on inside, which is the first of a series of steps leading to customers buying merchandise. And if stores have more than one style to sell, like Bergdorf's, they keep all of them separate. Style includes not only the merchandise, but every accessory, prop, display and graphic in the store.

- Image. More than style, image is the accumulated impact of every component in the company—from architecture to tissue paper. All specialists have it. If the image is strong enough, it can be re-visioned by customers in the mind's eye.

- Service. Everyone knows and is thoroughly tired of hearing how service is the single biggest route to profits and prosperity, but no one has ever provided it. Specialty stores can do it. First, they give their employees less to know, and they make them know it. This means that the employees can sell. They may even like their jobs. They may even like customers.

Whoever said it was easy to run a store? More people now than ever before are finding out how hard it is. They are the unclear, mediocre, timid "joiners" who pass their own uncertainty right on to the customers. Customers pick that up quickly. They go elsewhere. That's what's wrong with retailing.

If you're not a specialist, think about becoming one fast, or get out of retailing before the year 2000 gets to you.

It's not just your job. It's your life.

DO THE BEST YOU CAN

MAY 1990

NO ONE could ever have imagined the chaos and uncertainty of these crazy days. Our businesses are being run by bankruptcy judges, which is even worse than being run by real estate developers and bankers. Unfortunately, financial celebrities don't know much about merchandise or how to run a store, and the federal folks don't know a mannequin from a staple gun.

Mergers, acquisitions, lawsuits, retailers and manufacturers going out of business, unemployment—we've got it all, and it will get worse. David Glass, the president of Wal-Mart (a store for which these are the best of times) said to a group of investment bankers in New York City: "Half the stores in business today will be gone within ten years."

We whine and wait for a genuine merchant to come and lead us to peace and prosperity. But at the same time, no one could ever have imagined the global events of the last two months—in a world where country after country is run by the people for the people. Freedom is breaking out around the world. (China is ominously silent.) Poland? Rumania? East Germany? Hungary? Czechoslovakia? South Africa? Is that enough news for you? Any one of those alone would ordinarily last the news people for six months. Germany could be reunited within one year. Preposterous? Absurd? Impossible? Stay tuned.

The rate of change has left us all astounded. In Moscow's Red Square, the lines at McDonald's are now longer than the lines at Lenin's tomb. Who would have predicted that Melvin Simon would open malls in Europe, that a Disneyland would open in France and that the biggest news in Hong Kong is a mammoth Toys "R" Us.

Back home we wipe up oil spills with paper towels. Isn't it an ironic switch—new communist countries are run by free citizens, while our stores are run by government officials. And what about the fact that Japan, Britain and Canada own so much of the United States? A wit on the radio claimed, "We won't have a war with Japan next time. They'll just evict us!"

Of course, we have a new kind of freedom here, too—the freedom that being fired brings, the freedom that will be caused by creative people who realize now, more than ever, that they are their own responsibility and no one else's. No one can count on anybody to remain employed, creative and happy. In fact, in most stores, everybody is as terrified as everybody else of being out of a job. Working in a field that is creative has never been a safe way of life.

Retail needs creativity right this minute more than it ever has before. And it needs creative people so brave that they will be able to pick stores right out of the fire that's consuming them. This is a time for visionaries with guts, not "creative" complainers. And visionaries with guts will be doing their most creative work.

There's only one thing to do—make the best of bad times. This is good advice because if David Glass' figures are true, only the best will still be employed ten years from now. We shouldn't need any more convincing. It should be clear by now that things are terrible. We *do* need to acknowledge that fact, and then drop it. It's time to concentrate on doing the best we can under the circumstances.

If you lose your job, do something else. This could be your best chance to become yourself, if you aren't going after another job like the one you just got fired from. This could improve your life. Of course you have to eat, but I have never met a human being whose only method of survival was to have a job in a department store. Or any kind of store, for that matter. Or any job at all.

Why bother? What do you get for bravery of doing the best you can? What difference does it make? The answer is, you get to be the best you can be. That's all. There are no guarantees that doing the best you can will get you anything at all, except to fortify your own opinion of yourself.

Life is to be used, not just endured. You are your own responsibility. Nobody does anything for you. No one gives you a nickel or a hug for every step you take. You take each step alone. Each step is entirely a risk on your part, an investment in the chance that it might get you somewhere. We don't even know what we're climbing toward with every step, and yet we seem to feel we should be going forward.

There are no definite answers. The next step might get you creativity, money, happiness and love. But you'll never know until you take the risk of trying. What difference does it make? None, to anyone else. Everything to you. And since it is up to you to find your personal creative freedom, even if you begin by being fired, why don't you resolve to do the best you can— whatever you do—and live these times as if they really mattered. Live day by day, filling the present with effort and affection.

No matter where we find bliss, in the little world of retailing or anywhere on the altering planet, let's all do the best we can.

LES IS MORE

ON THE MORNING of May 22, 1990, the ballroom of the Marriott Marquis in New York City was shaking with cheering, screaming, shouting, flag-waving costumes and laughter. It was the kind of emotional display that the retail business had not seen in a long, long time.

Groups of The Limited Inc.'s "partners" (a small part of the more than 60 percent of Limited employees who are stockholders) were organized into company sections, and many were wearing costumes for the event. The Lane Bryant contingent was wearing "Dream Team" T-shirts. The Brylane group (Limited's catalog division for Lerner, Roaman's and Lane Bryant Fifth Avenue) wore outfits inscribed with "The Sky's The Limited!" Hosts and ushers sported lapel badges reading "Absolutely nothing happens until she says, 'I'll take it!'"

Limited Founder Les Wexner began by telling the 2,000 partners that it is the clear intention of the corporation to achieve sales of over $10 billion per year, and an after-tax profit of ten percent by the middle of the nineties. More cheering. Then he told how the company would achieve those dreams in two ways:

1. Associated partnership—More than 60 percent of employees are partners now, with some divisions boasting participation as high as 99 percent. This triggers shared vision and common goals for all 63,000 employees, each of whom thinks of customers one at a time and is encouraged to take risks in every aspect of the business.

2. Thinking small as the business grows larger—Divisions are self-sustaining units with independent responsibilities and the ability to be nimble in their operations. Remarkably, the "central group" of support executives in Columbus numbers only 60 people, the equivalent of less than one for every 1,000 employees.

Les introduced every president and praised them all. Then each division president spoke briefly (always to loud cheers) with remarkable unity of theme. The title of the meeting and the annual report was "Re-inventing Specialty Stores." That prefix "re" was heard many times in the talks: rebirth, reformat, remodeling, recasting, repositioning, rewrite, refounded— verbal tributes to The Limited's perpetual dissatisfaction with the status quo and genuine lust for change and growth. New stores, new products, new

10 YEARS OF PETER GLEN
132

companies and new strategies were all announced: Express is selling menswear ("Structure"); The Limited is opening Limited Too for kids; Victoria's Secret is opening bath shops, and Cacique stores selling fine French lingerie will be opening.

This year, the company will add the equivalent of 60 football fields of selling space, backed up by 50 football fields for distribution. C. Lee Johnson, the company's president of distribution services, announced "These projects will be accomplished on budget and ahead of time!"

Not one of the division presidents talked about the past. They only talked about what to do next. Most referred to the idea that playing it safe is "death" and that mistakes are not just tolerated, but encouraged, feeding experimentation and innovation. Howard Gross, president of Victoria's Secret, said, "The message at Victoria's Secret is to try new things and don't be afraid to fail. Our customer is more forward-thinking, more educated and more worldly than 99 percent of the retailers in America give her credit for."

There were many more memorable quotes: "Retail is detail"; "We hear our customer say she wants new ideas"; "Businesses that don't change are the ones that die"; "Every day our opportunity gets even larger than I previously thought"; "Our customer is the only one who can determine if we're successful." And Les was heard to say that he hoped he would be remembered as "a great sweater buyer." That was back in the days before the money types took over and ruined so many stores by talking about money instead of sweaters.

It is heartening to see that Les is still talking about great sweaters and great sweater buyers. Meanwhile, the money guys talk about bankruptcy, and Les and his partners have all the money.

The meeting was a joyous demonstration of the possibilities of retailing, and it was a vastly reassuring event compared to the grim annual meetings that have been taking place over the last two years. There were 2,000 people cheering in the darkness at the Marriott, while another 61,000 Limited employees were busy opening stores and greeting customers in 3,405 locations. The cheering seemed reasonable and justified. The Limited seems to be the best example of the blend of realism and idealism that makes a lot of money even today.

The meeting was not perfect, though. It was too long and featured too much ordinary rock-and-roll and too much ordinary audio-visual commotion. If that was because the visual talent of The Limited was busy entertaining customers in stores instead, good. That's where the creativity belongs first.

Les encouraged us all to visit the new Lerner's on 34th Street as soon as possible. He then consulted his watch and said that the next annual meeting would probably make medical history for kidney control. He charged us all to go out and evangelize. And then he finished by making an announcement which said he hoped would make the audience and the other partners of The Limited happy. He said that the Board of Directors of The Limited Inc. had approved a two-for-one stock split.

There was instant pandemonium and a total standing ovation. Reporters rushed to the banks of telephones Les had thoughtfully provided outside the ballroom. Most stayed to cheer. The cheers were real, and so were the occasional tears. In the ballroom of the Marriott on that sunny spring morning, the retail industry was celebrating its own hope.

CHEAP THRILLS

AUGUST 1991

ONE EVENING about two months ago I had an apocalyptic shopping experience. Before this conversion I was in danger of killing myself because I had been agreeing with everyone else in this industry that our business was failing, had never been so bad and could not be worse. Our self-esteem as well as the opinions of our customers were at an all-time low. We were also doing a better-than-ever job of announcing our own doom and then acting on it.

On the night that marked the beginning of my mystical revelation, I was attending one of those "industry" dinners where potent executives in costly suits get together to indulge in fine wines and self-pity. On that evening the complaining was particularly plentiful, and we were working ourselves into a really excellent fury until the senior vice president from American Express shared his shopping story. This renegade was running from table to table telling it over and over again, amazing the ranks of the higher, upper, major and even "top" executives. This man may well earn $300,000 or $400,000 a year, but he was talking about bargains. (In fact, there is probably no group of people in this world who loves CHEAP more than rich people. That may even explain how they get rich in the first place.)

The executive had just returned from a Florida vacation which included what he surely thought would be a deadly trip to a mall. But this was no ordinary mall; it was a mill—Sawgrass Mills, one of the huge new successful discount/factory outlet/brand name very successful malls. It was CHEAP. He had suffered his own apocalypse when he found and bought (and was wearing now and was telling us gleefully) the most exciting purchase he'd made in years—a genuine Pierre Cardin dress shirt for $4.

Shock waves rocked the paneled dining room. Could I feel *Vogue* and *Bazaar* fainting in the background? Here was an industry insider praising the virtue of CHEAP! Was this betrayal? Anti-fashion? Treason? Was this the sound of a rich man getting cheap and loving it?

Here was a successful consumer shopping in a successful mall, right in the middle of the current recession/depression/confession. I listened to this rich man wallowing in the new-found joys of cheapness and realized I'd heard that song before. I was delinquent and dated and a snob for ignoring it. It had been so long since I'd heard cheerfulness about retailing that I decided to investigate.

So I set out on a new adventure. I went in search of stores that work. I went discount shopping.

Dropping *WWD* on the floor, ignoring *The New York Times*, canceling my subscriptions to 70 or 80 fashion magazines, and putting on my cheap running shoes, I headed for Daffy's. I had never been to Daffy's, although a lot of smart and even fashionable people had been talking about it more and more. Daffy's is sensational. On the very threshold, they hand you a flyer outlining the arrival dates of shipments of your favorite designer so you can rush right in and grab the right kind of garments, Daffy's does not have a "complete selection" or piped-in Mozart or spacious dressing rooms attended by "fashion consultants." But they do have the goods—every name you ever cared about when reading the fashion rags—and it's CHEAP. And it's crowded. And the customers are grinning. It's FUN.

This is not news. A lot of people got there before me. But I never heard a word about Daffy's in the fashion press, which is their fault and my fault, and a big part of the problem.

Next I rushed to Dollar Bill's. Dollar Bill's has no dressing rooms at all (although you can bring anything back), and when I arrived the manager was on the microphone thanking customers for buying out his inventory and telling them to come back and why. I couldn't try on the raspberry Versace suit that was hanging there in my size, but I had tried it on before, up in the Versace Madison Avenue store where it sells for $1,400. I didn't buy it then. This time, though, I certainly bought it. Well, wouldn't you? I bought that

$1,400 suit for $299.99 CHEAP. I felt as giddy as the rich tycoon from American Express who found Pierre Cardin at Sawgrass. And I was having FUN.

Dollar Bill's is a hoot. And successful. Why didn't I experience this before? Wake up, Peter, and smell the coffee.

I hurried over to Conway's and found that they now have 14 locations. Inside every door is a rack of the kinds of casual clothes that people wear very day—$3.99, $2.99 and often $1.99. Now there's big new glamorous Conway's Third Avenue, halfway to Bloomingdale's. And "A Real New York Bargain" recently opened at Fifth Avenue and 36th Street, two blocks from Lord & Taylor.

At Century 21, the racks were jammed with designer merchandise, both European and American. I found Jean Paul Gaultier, Thierry Mugler, Charlotte Neuville, Rebecca Moses and Gordon Henderson. The *Times* wrote the store up under the heading "Designer Discounts" and concluded, "Paying full price is one thing that really seems to be out of style."

Customers are getting cheap. So am I. I hope I never again pay $1,400 for a suit if I know I can get it for $299. My snobbery is not worth the $1,001 difference. This may not be loyal to the antiquated standards of the business, but it is very loyal to a customer's intelligence. I must put myself on the customer's side. It is my mission statement.

Some of the mainstream is waking up. The Limited Inc.'s enormous emphasis on Lerner's New York is the best example with the best hope for the future. Lerner's always had low-end customers, but now the store is adding rich customers and the folks who used to be rich but aren't right now because of the recession/depression/confession. The store's getting a load of former snobs because the clothes are good and the atmosphere is extremely pleasant and the merchandise is CHEAP. A lot of people love that word. That word made Sam Walton a $12 billion fortune.

Thus began my recent retail re-education. And that's just the beginning. There will be more. Look for it in your own life. I'm on my way to see the rest of the country It's full of surprises, successes and fun. I hear the voice of Harry Truman saying, "It's what you learn after you know it all that really counts!"

WHERE THE SHOPPERS ARE

JUNE 1992

DON'T BELIEVE all the bad news you hear. Shopping is thriving right now—in stores you may not hear much about. The American consumer has changed locations, and we must find out where if we want to keep on eating.

The Price Club (good name) is a huge success. So are Costco, Home Depot and most of the other category killers because they do what they say they are going to do. They don't mess around with snivelling sidelines. They offer what the customer wants—price—and they thrive.

An excellent ad for Loehmann's announced: "A fashion victim is anyone who pays retail." And the Daffy's store in Philadelphia (which used to be a Bonwit Teller) ran a full-page photo of a turkey the day after Thanksgiving that said if you shop at department stores, "You are what you eat." Now Daffy's is running some very effective bus shelter ads showing two exquisite mannequins standing side by side, both wearing identical outfits. The price tag on one outfit says $515 and the other is $150. The headline asks, "Which dummy looks smarter?"

Dillon, Colorado, is a freeway interchange 70 miles from Denver. That's as close to the Denver Nordstrom as the developers of the Silverthorne Factory Outlets were allowed. These isn't much else out there except some taco stands, but the mall parking lot is jammed. There are handsome stores and—surprise—excellent service. At most stores you can return anything at any time for any reason—pleasantly. There's Geoffrey Beene, Nike, Liz Claiborne, Royal Doulton and dozens of other manufacturer's outlets.

Hordes of visitors now drive up to Sedona, Arizona, to see the red rocks and get introduced to energy vortexes and other New Age activities. But nowadays, the buses pull off the road before they get to Sedona so everyone can go to the Oak Creek Factory Stores. This outlet mall is not ugly. In fact, it's downright adobe—in keeping with the Arizona architecture the visitors ostensibly come to see. They rush at Anne Klein, Van Heusen, Harve Benard, and nobody can tell the difference between that mall and the big distressed malls back in Phoenix—except that this outlet mall isn't closed in and doesn't have a center court with some lousy art show or a bunch of fountains which usually don't work. These customers are happy snapping up the name-brand bargains. The energy there is often as close as the customers get to the New Age tourist attractions.

The same scene goes on in a big way at Sawgrass Mills, Potomac Mills and all the other "mills" across the country. At these huge developments, some with satellite shuttle parking lots and internal transportation systems, families spend whole days and millions of dollars behaving just like they're at Disneyland. Husbands grow old waiting for their wives. Children get more exercise than they do at school; in fact, this may even be their education.

What's the difference between all these mills and malls? There is no difference—same people, same brands, same hopes and fears and shopping desires, even the same "entertainment." There's no difference at all except the price, except the price, except the price.

I went to a meeting of furniture manufacturing executives and found that more than half of them had never visited an IKEA store. I know there are department store executives who have never set foot in a Daffy's or a Price Club or a Costco. These folks are practicing "denial," and it's every bit as bad for their health and the health of their companies as disregarding lung cancer is to those who smoke four packs of cigarettes a day. (I saw a T-shirt that said, "Denial is not just a river in Egypt.")

Do you think the late Sam Walton ever visited a Price Club, an IKEA, Crate & Barrel, Vons, Smith's, Daffy's, Sawgrass Mills? There are executives in every branch of retail who never leave their offices and who never even see their own stores.

One day last August an elderly gent walked into a Wal-Mart in a remote Texas town. After a few minutes he asked to see the manager. The manager appeared, and the gent explained he was Sam Walton. He noted that the store was dirty, and told the manager to close and clean up. And while the manager followed those instructions, Sam Walton stood outside in the parking lot talking to customers, explaining why they had to wait and how welcome they would be as soon as the store was ready to receive them.

Don't you think 30,000 Wal-Mart employees heard this story within a couple of days? Do you imagine that the local manager cleaned the store and cleaned it quickly while he kept one eye on Sam standing out front chit-chatting with his customers?

If we still sit whimpering about traditional stores, then reality has passed us by. It is the customer once again who leads the way, blazing new paths with money and creating success. And if we do not go where our customers go, we will not know what drives them until later when we sit outside the stadium listening to somebody else's team win the Super Bowl.

QUIVERING WITH HAPPINESS

ON THE 13th of December, Macy's sent to me a catalog filled with Christmas merchandise to be ordered by telephone.

On the 14th of December, I called Macy's Teleservice.

After waiting 20 minutes on hold, I was told that the last date I could order anything for Christmas delivery had been December 7!

Teleservice said to me, "Do you want to order or not? All I can do is take your order. Your order will be delivered within four weeks. If you're so mad about waiting 20 minutes, you should have read the catalog better. It says no Christmas delivery after December 7."

A supervisor told me, "All we do is take phone orders. If you have anything else to say, say it to customer service. They handle complaints like this." Click. She hung up.

On the 15th day of December, I called Bloomingdale's and they said they had many plans for "worry-free delivery." I could have all my packages delivered inexpensively the same day within Manhattan (free delivery to hotels within 20 blocks of the store); or I could have any in-stock merchandise delivered in the local tri-state area within four business days; or I could order with Federal Express as late as December 23rd for guaranteed December 24th delivery.

But I couldn't go to Bloomingdale's because a rainstorm with hurricane-force winds attacked New York. I sat trapped at home during the worst winter storm in 50 years, while everything in the city—including shopping—suddenly stopped completely. The television was telling me that because of this storm, merchants would lose $150 million worth of Christmas shopping revenue because customers would never buy the incidental impulse items they would only have bought that day.

And Home Shopping Network on television was telling me I could shop with them. They spun me a Christmas dream. It seemed to say: "Here comes the Miracle Piano. You are about to have a genuine mystical revelation when you see this Miracle Piano. We tried to find a stronger word than 'miracle' for this piano, but the dictionary didn't do it for us. This piano is not even a piano; an amoeba can play it. Anyone can play it. It is so easy to play that you don't even have to know how to play to play it. It does it all, baby. That's the *real* miracle folks, you don't have to breathe in or out, just give it a glance to activate its left hand, punch in a tempo, such as FAST or SLOW or

CHA CHA, 128 sound effects, lots of speakers, and in less than ten seconds and without even getting up from where you are lying right now, about as long as it takes you to charge this to any credit card on earth, in ten seconds with Miracle Piano, you go from lying in a coma on your couch to a triumphant debut onstage at Carnegie Hall. You don't have to do squat, George, not one thing but dig down deep into those pants right now and bring up a credit card—the miracle-simple, easy-order, easy-unbox, easy-play Miracle Piano is yours. It's now just $474, the flash-board is flashing, hurry, join us, George, participate, the cathedral is running low on miracles, fall on your knees, believe it, you can have Christmas without experiencing it at all...."

And then they were showing me how simple stereo could be. The remote control they were offering was the simplest I've ever seen, and that pleased me. It was a whole sound system, couldn't have been simpler, relieving me from having to even think. The customer on the call-in telephone just couldn't describe the excitement she had felt when she found out how simple it had been to get the system out of the box when it arrived. It was just *so* simple. And 50 million viewers nodded, saying, "Simple, yes, I like that. Easy to take it out of the box."

The dream flowed on as the camera panned the simple stereo. The manicured fingernails pointed out the meaningless details, while America drowsed along, spending the better part of many evenings sending money to the folks at Home Shopping Network who made it so simple.

Not one word was uttered about the quality of the sound. Not once did a salesperson or a swooning telephone customer even mention the subject of sound. They weren't selling sound. They were selling easiness.

Most wonderfully, HSC supports charitable causes, such as those who search for missing children. The "Bring Them Home, America" campaign is heartfelt and effective. I am certain that after customers do unto themselves, they are prompt (and prompted) to do unto others.

Soon the familiar 50-channel cable box will bring us 500 channels. In December, Barry Diller, who built the Fox Network, invested $25 million in QVC (another home shopping channel) after crunching numbers and seeing Diane von Furstenburg sell more than $1.2 million of silk garments in two hours.

Already, day after day, night after night, most call-in customers are quivering with happiness. One caller testified, "I keep it on 24 hours a day." There are possibly many of these relationships. While they iron, bathe, cook, clean, fix lunches, and otherwise enjoy the moments of their lives, these customers share their lives with a constant companion who never stops talking about merchandise. It works because it has achieved the greatest shopping simplification of all.

WOW! A STATE OF SHOCK

OCTOBER 1993

STEW LEONARD'S MOTTO has always been, "You have to make the customer say 'Wow!'"

Well, he's done it again and done it good.

Some time has now gone by since the news that Stew Leonard was defrauding his customers and the government, and I still don't know what to think about it. I've already been asked 80 times what I think about the news from Stew's.

And I don't know.

One of the best—one of the few, rare, very best in all our profession—a model, example, paragon, inspiration, even friend, has committed a major crime, conspiring to defraud the federal government of taxes on more than $17 million.

It's the largest criminal tax case in the history of Connecticut. He has done it squarely in the face of the people who made him rich: his customers. Customer service is the foundation of the Stew Leonard's supermarket legend, and those he has offended most are the same folks who made him rich—his customers.

It's not news that retailers break the law. Food Lion supermarkets are accused of bleaching old fish and putting it out again for sale. Crazy Eddie finally went to jail. Joseph Brooks and his son were busted at JFK Airport for smuggling watches through customs for sale at Ann Taylor. Sloan's Supermarket officers pleaded guilty to operating a coupon scam that defrauded manufacturers out of at least $3.5 million over ten years.

But Stew Leonard? Messiah of customer service?

I *do* know how I feel.

It is as if, at the age of 40, you just found out that Walt Disney strangled pets. Or that your mother is a hooker.

I am shocked.

I still think Stew Leonard devised and installed the best customer service I've ever experienced in an American retail business. I've learned more on each visit to his stores than I learn in a year prowling the halls of the mediocre. And at this moment his endorsement of me is the headline across the cover of every copy of my book *It's Not My Department!*

Greed, greed, oh greed. It's the easy answer to every kind of money crime today. Charles Keating, Michael Milken, and good old Leona Helmsley got it started. Leona despised the little people who pay taxes. Stew loved his customers, but he might as well have despised them. There's more to this than simple greed; that is the shocking part. Like Charles and Michael and Leona, this man had plenty of money. And money was not enough.

The details are movie-mythical: Stopped at JFK with $80,000 cash, four times. The fraudulent software recipe inside a hollowed-out copy of the *1982 Business Directory of New England.* Two in-laws and a general manager who stashed the cash in their rec rooms, $500,000 at a time. The oddly customer-inconvenient system of getting cash from customers for gift certificates. Small-scale but complex subterfuges. One can scarcely imagine the jolly family dinners at which these plots were hatched. The sweet naivete of the belief that family is a trustworthy concept, when every day the newspapers tell us nobody should trust anybody, even when they're honest. Fat with packs of cash stashed in the carry-on at JFK.

Stew's famous service philosophies come back turned inside-out now, and the effect is much different. "Rule No. 1: The Customer is always right. Rule No. 2: If the Customer is ever wrong, re-read Rule No. 1."

Not a word in the news about the children, who all work in the store. Stew Jr., Beth and Tom—none of them are named in the proceedings. Could they be saved by this generation gap? Or will this affect their frequent, popular, effective speaking engagements at $10,000 each?

And Mrs. Leonard, who is virtually behind the scenes except for her soups and sauces marketed in the stores. Whose side is she on? Sheer speculation, but sad, whatever the answer.

Sometimes I almost feel guilty writing about this because the Leonards are friends, and I admire them. But the notion persists that if I understand this I will find a constructive reaction to the news.

I must get it out, both the disappointment and the admiration.

COME WITH ME TO THE CASBAH

NOVEMBER 1993

ONE EVENING RECENTLY I was walking down Revolcadero Beach in Acapulco with a man who owns 11 franchised running shoe stores in Mexico City. His stores are suffering. His business is being gulped down whole by a voracious competitor whom nobody knows.

The most explosive global marketing force in the world today is unrecognized. It is not on the agendas of international conferences. Management does not make mixed-media presentations from podiums in air-conditioned ballrooms. There are no verifiable statistics about it, no data, no tracking, no research, no forecast, no cover stories, headlines, by-words, footnotes, not even a bite on CNN. In fact, except for customers—and in spite of all the grown-ups hyping global marketing—this force remains unrecognized. Only the customer knows.

It is the phenomenon of informal markets.

Street markets, transient vendors, garden markets, straw markets, flea markets. And as my friend talked, I had a sunset epiphany on the beach, because he made it clear to me this taken-for-granted, been-around-forever phenomenon is suddenly as fierce as volcanic Mt. Pinatubo. It demands attention.

Informal markets in Mexico have always been there, as they have been elsewhere, back to the time of the Aztecs and the Maya, and probably before. In ancient Greece it was the agora—the marketplace and commercial, social, political and cultural center of the city. And now, as the millennium approaches, these markets are exploding because of the global recession.

Nobody knows for sure, but my friend estimates that three years ago the businesses of the informal markets in Mexico were doing about $10 billion a year.

Now brace yourself: The government estimates that in 1993 the total amount of business in informal markets in Mexico will be $45 billion.

Customers have always loved informal markets. Ever since Hollywood started improving on reality, mysterious figures have appeared in black and white, beckoning and luring you to COME WITH ME TO THE CASBAH!— seemingly an unmistakable invitation to adventure, but really just another way to saying LET'S GO TO THE MALL!

I have been to The Casbah. I have willingly gotten lost in the labyrinthine souks of Fez and Marrakesh, dazzled by the scorching white walls and unexpected turnings, intricate mosaics, blue tiles, splashing fountains, secret vistas, iridescent fabrics, burnished metals and the smell of the spice piles; by the energy, action and money changing hands. I have smelled the camel market in Sousse, Tunisia, open only on Sundays from 5 a.m. until noon. The activity of a normal week of retail is compressed into seven hours of locomotive energy, all devoted to selling, waving one rug at a time until every rug is gone.

I have ventured at dawn to the markets of Papeete, French Polynesia. The sellers there all wear crowns of fresh gardenias, picked and woven at sunrise by the reef. Now they sell mountains of watermelons and 14 kinds of bananas. They sing. They dance and act up all day long, all in the name of selling. I have poked through the junk on London's Portobello Road on rainy Saturday mornings hunting treasure. And I've snaked up and down the mountainside streets of Kowloon in Hong Kong where thousands of vendors compete for attention, each under an umbrella, with displays of rodent and root and finch and ordinary housewares. Unknown objects and unfamiliar substances, all for sale.

I know how to "out-fashion fashion" by searching the flea market in Paris, just as soon as the designers do. And I can find the carts behind the Cathedral in Florence where the merchants sell the same clothes that cost ten times as much three blocks away on the Via Tornabuoni. These are all indelible selling experiences, creative, imaginative, urgent and powerful. And I also know why I feel constricted, short of breath and tranquilized by every mall in America. There is no action compared to the action in the markets.

These markets are full of stolen goods, legitimate goods, black-market goods, fakes and copies. Those who require the assurance that Gucci means Gucci and that Hard Rock Cafe is the real thing will not find happiness in the informal markets. But Mexico (and all the world) is experiencing a long, deep and seeming-to-be-permanent recession. And the demand for "designer label" diminishes in direct proportion to vanishing expendable income. Poverty, recession and fear of the future have caused the informal markets of the world to explode with violent impact.

My friend's stores are in ten of Mexico City's "best" mall shopping centers. The stores are doing badly, as are the malls. This man has done two things derived from his in-person experience of the city's informal markets: His eleventh store is not in the city center and not in a mall. It stands alone in a rich suburb, and it is working. He has hired two new employees right out of the informal markets, because they can sell.

Lord, can they sell! There is more and better selling in the informal markets of this world than there is in all the sluggish shopping centers. Informal market merchants know how to sell because of the only reliable motivator: hunger. If you are a nine-year-old who makes 38 cents a day, every moment matters and every sale counts.

Imagine a million or more employees around the world, all selling their hearts out—and this without a trace of training, or goals or quotas or contests or national meetings or district or regional managers. No research, no advertising, no sales promotion, none of the avalanche of complications that cost us money and slow us down. Nothing but selling, just selling.

What about the *cost* of selling this merchandise? Merchants are supposed to pay rent. And taxes. In the informal markets the vital matters of rent and taxes are debatable. The Mexican government is rushing to build concrete shells to house a million little carts and stands. They want the taxes on $45 billion worth of merchandise, but this will not be easy. Informal market merchants don't like rent and taxes.

Many selling costs do not exist at all: no credit, charge cards, gift certificates, personnel, administration, finance, insurance, warehousing, distribution, information systems, real estate divisions, training departments. No display delivery or diaper changing rooms. This saves a lot of money.

Back home we're still putting on center-court boat shows and mimes and Mother's Day specials and Kinderfoto and Ear Piercing Pagoda and wondering why it doesn't work. And it *doesn't* work. Even the International Council of Shopping centers admits mall shopping is drying up. The customer who spent 120 hours a year in malls in 1985 is now investing only 42 hours! The customer who entered 3.6 stores per mall visit in 1982 now goes to only 2.6 stores. The 1982 average visit of 90 minutes is now down to 72 minutes. Total retail sales in 1988 were $817 billion. Guess what? Total retail sales in 1992 were down to $788 billion. Where did the time, the interest, the money and the customers go?

There are no answers, because nobody is bothering to calculate the vast, sweaty retail underground. They are all waiting for somebody to close down The Casbah.

I think not. Right here in the USA there are flourishing marketplaces. Even here, some pay rent, some don't. Some are at tag sales, garage sales, yard sales, bake sales, swap meets, auctions, thrift stores and re-sale shops. In New York City the people lining up at Seventh Avenue showrooms on Saturdays have virtually destroyed the retail bridal industry. The green-market in Union Square sells out, and the supermarkets are full of rotting iceburg lettuce. Every street has fast collapsible sidewalk tables so the Cartier watches can be snatched away before the cops can catch them.

Kmart and Wal-Mart and other global marketers are going to be very surprised to find out who their competition is as they invade Mexico and other distant destinations. Their competition is not each other, but the informal markets of the world—and their computers and their research companies aren't going to tell their planners one single thing that matters. Kmart and Wal-Mart don't go low enough to compete. Even Wal-Mart's selling costs are infinitely higher than those of the street vendors.

On the beach in Mexico, I bought two remarkable Taxco silver bracelets, one with an amethyst. Together, they cost $140. These two bracelets would have been expensive in New York City or almost anywhere at retail, and the bracelets would be no more beautiful.

I have been to the floating markets, the klongs, of Bangkok, and seen the best displays of tomatoes under a tree in Tanzania. I have not yet visited the bazaar at Istanbul or the sulphurous market mazes of India. But I don't think I'll need to travel so far to see so much market activity now. One of these days I will drift in and out of the bustling casbahs of Cleveland, or Birmingham, give in to the siren songs of sellers in the souks of Oklahoma City. And I expect to find among the bargain-hungry throngs one or two adventurous scouts from Wal-Mart or Costco, studying the competition and understanding it.

ELEVEN WAYS TO WHIP THE WAL*

* Or Toys "R" Us or Barnes & Noble Superstore, Payless Drug Stores, Kmart, Price Club, BIZMART, Home Depot, The Incredible Universe or Bed Bath & Beyond

WAL-MART IS COMING to town!

You have three choices: play victim, fight to stop them or fight to improve your business and thrive.

Eleven scenarios:

1. Vote them out. A town in Iowa sued Wal-Mart to stop them from coming, but they lost. Then the whole town of Westford, Mass., in feisty New England, fought Wal-Mart in Westford. Now Greenfield, Mass., and North Olmsted, Ohio, have also stopped Wal-Mart. But this is eventually as futile as trying to stop Japan from making automobiles that work and selling them to us. That whole New England effort could have been directed at strengthening local stores instead of stopping Wal-Mart. Now they're left just where they were before—rusting. Just like Detroit.

2. Go out of business. There are too many stores anyway, so why bother? Unless you were just born to be a retailer—if that's the case, this will be your best test ever. Going out of business, like divorce, is sometimes the best idea. You won't begin your next enterprise without truly loving it.

3. Go into a new business. Bonnie of Bonnie's Fabrics in Viroqua, Wisconsin, went to the nearest Wal-Mart 200 miles away when she heard that Wal-Mart was coming to Viroqua. She came back determined to quit the fabric business completely. And then she opened Bonnie's Bridal Shop after clearing out the fabrics. There isn't another bridal shop within 400 miles. She has a new business, a new attitude and was smart enough to call CBS. They put her on the national news.

4. Raise the spirit of the neighborhood. You can't start while everyone else is depressed and feeling sorry for themselves. Your business is not alone; this is a hurricane that's coming for everyone. Get going. Call a meeting. Sound the alarm. Raise hell. Get people together. Present the facts. Present the

prospects. Give the wake-up call. When everyone is mobilized, you can begin.

5. Take a good look at your own place. Many of the merchants who go out of business when Wal-Mart arrives deserve it. They haven't spent one nickel or forged one new idea since the fatal day they decided they had no competition and went right on sleeping. So face it, and begin. Clean. Paint. Make your store look like someone still lives there, before you expect anyone to come in to shop. The physical shopping experience is as important as price and location and service. Fresh paint communicates action in a hurry; it's the fastest, cheapest, biggest thing you can do to announce survival.

6. Market and promote and sell. Shakespeare & Co., an old, established Upper West Side bookstore in New York City, was almost shocked out of existence by arrival of the Barnes & Noble Superstore one block away. But they're organizing more readings and promotions, printing T-shirts and producing pens, magnets and aprons bearing the names of recent titles. Nobody knows if this will work, but it will work better than trying to stop Barnes & Noble!

7. Create parking. The town of Winter Park, Florida, has a charming set of downtown shops, all suffering from shopping center and superstore competition. But the merchants association refuses to build a parking lot. They just can't agree on it. Meanwhile, there is no place to park, so nobody parks. Sales are terrible.

8. Turn the town into a museum. An aggressive, rich widow transformed the near ghost town of Winthrop, Washington, into an authentic Western Restoration. Today there are satellite parking lots one mile away with shuttle bus service. Other towns are making things quaint, luring antique stores, florists and design studios, but this only seems to work where quaintness counts more than merchandise selection or saving money. In many places it has been a costly disaster.

9. Buy only merchandise Wal-Mart *doesn't* carry. Or develop your own. Then tell customers about it. A toy store on Cape Cod is thriving even in the age of Toys "R" Us. They guarantee their customers that nothing they sell can be found at Toys "R" Us. Charming Shoppes designs its own merchandise and manufactures it around the world. Their next step is to make Charming

Shoppes a fabric converter. Today they make 70 percent of the merchandise they sell.

10. Launch a customer campaign. Locals formed the Bath Business Association in Maine. Shopping in downtown's 100 stores used to be uneventful. Now the area boasts weekly outdoor concerts, street dances, a Thanksgiving parade, extended store hours and TV advertising. They're behaving as if they were a shopping center. Members' sales are up. They're even taking the show on the road to teach other towns how to fight instead of die.

11. Customer service. Wal-Mart has a greeter at the door, but you're on your own after that. In the beginning, the superstores did not have service, but they're catching on. Now Home Depot has such good service, staff, seminars and knowledge, it'll be hard to compete. But for those who bend over backwards, care enough to remember your name and your needs, send birthday cards or thank-you notes, and go the extra mile to find the extra item, there are customers who will respond with loyalty and money. It's a lot better and healthier for you than going to court.

Wal-Mart is coming to town! And so are Toys "R" Us and Barnes & Noble Superstores, Payless Drug Stores, Kmart, Price Club, BIZMART, Home Depot, The Incredible Universe and Bed Bath & Beyond.

You decide—you can play victim, try to stop them, or improve your business and thrive!

THE STANDARDIZATION OF THE PLANET

MAY 1994

I GOT A PHONE CALL from an old friend at Steiger's, a New England department store company that recently celebrated its 100th year as a family business.

I visited them a few years ago to conduct sales training and service seminars. During this phone call I flashed back to the executive office hall—portraits of family lined the wood-paneled walls and offices and board room. I remember thinking even then: This is what department stores once were—grand, impressive. I thought the slightly ritualistic formality brought out the best in people; I liked it. The family was running the store, as it always had, which is what gave it personality and point of view and a good sense of people. I thought there weren't many like this left, that possibly its days (and its successors) were numbered.

Don Klein said, "I called to say goodbye. We're going out of business. The May Company just bought us."

Then he said, "I've worked here thirty years. I never made a resume until last week."

We have heard this story before—and *often* lately—and it hurts every time. No doubt The May Company will bring economies of scale and standardized procedures, and probably make more money than Steiger's. But the fun and the formality and the family will all be gone.

I know that nine out of ten department stores are now called Dillard's and that you cannot tell from inside any May Company store whether you are in Massachusetts or Madagascar. Twenty-two hours after you leave Los Angeles, you get out at Singapore, and 15 minutes after that you are shopping in a mall identical to the Glendale Galleria.

Plane-loads of Japanese shoppers sit rolled up like sushi all the way from Tokyo to Minneapolis to buy handbags in stores identical to those at home. Dillard's and The May Company and Mel Simon have anonymized the planet. The stores in the mall outside the controlled historic district of Santa Fe are out there because it's cheaper to be anonymous. And now customers trained to be blind to every consideration but price won't care. And the controller will be happy to be free of anything as lead-footed as local architecture or 10,000 years of style.

I know that Goldwater's was all Southwest and therefore indigenous. But now Goldwater's is not Goldwater's, nor is it Southwestern in any way—

except its zip code and its customers. I cannot actually remember whether it is now a Dillard's or a May Company.

Where are all the architects? Architects of genius have built us churches, homes, museums, restaurants, resorts and corporate monuments. But where the people shop, you cannot name a store designed by any major architect. Instead we shudder in the bargain basement known as "retail architecture" or "mall architecture"—big, practical boxes with excellent engineering.

Some say these faceless boxes are the best empty stage for individual stores. They claim identifiable architecture distracts ... you know the line. It's the absence of vision speaking, even more than the absence of money. It's as though the Vatican hired Michelangelo to paint the Sistine Chapel but first got the cheapest guy in Rome to build St. Peter's.

There are some stabs at identity. Many of The Rouse Company's revitalization projects (Riverwalk, Harborplace, Quincy Marketplace, South Street Seaport) at least have the grace to honor what was there before. And a few old railway stations now exist as shopping malls.

But how about a new store or shopping center that is an attraction in its *own* right? Horton Plaza in San Diego—there's one. Superstition Springs Mall near Phoenix is round and uniquely landscaped. Name another.

We used to build Empire State Buildings—unmistakable, aspiring, instant landmarks. Now we build buildings as vacuous as any skyscraper in Houston. Every city looks like Houston. Every country looks like Houston. We build in an everlasting non-style that cancels time and place and ends up empty.

Retail management is standardizing, too. This hurts even more; it is the standardization of people. Even if Don Klein stays at The May Company, even at the same desk, some of his heart will have gone out the door as The May Company came in. The new broom will bring in clean-outs and corporate philosophy and mission statements and images revised. It's "re-engineering," the hottest possible new temporary business concept.

If Don Klein moves to get a new job, it won't be at Steiger's. It doesn't much matter where he works next, because the new place will be the same as any other place. There was a lot of New England individuality about Steiger's woody halls. Steiger's is not New England anymore. But neither is New England. It too looks like everywhere else and even *more* like no place in particular. Customers everywhere stand at cash registers asking, "Who do I make the check out to?" It doesn't much matter to customers. They don't know; they don't much care where they are!

If there are any other Steiger's now, they're probably having lunch with

Dillard's and The May Company Tuesday noon. Hey, it works for McDonald's! The plaintive voice of the customer is growing even dimmer than the memory of the family ancestors taken off the walls at Steiger's. We are coming very close to a final facelessness in which it does not matter who shops where or who works where, because there is no "there" wherever you are. One price, one merchandise, one store, one personality, one mall. It's a dull world, shoppers.

This week I got Don's resume. All may be well, or even challenging. But for Don Klein, those 30 Steiger's years are gone—wiped away as clean as a sand castle on a beach in a high wind, gone with just one wave, goodbye.

PART FIVE
OPENINGS

BULLETIN FROM BARNEYS

ON SEPTEMBER 2, 1986, a large ocean liner and a tiled swimming pool collided at the corner of Seventh Avenue and 17th Street in New York City. The mammoth cruise ship was wrenched into almost unrecognizable shapes, scattering mosaic tiles all over.

I visited Barneys' new women's store on its second night, September 3. So did everyone else in retailing. Nobody was running the stores back home. Our world had barely recovered from Ralph Lauren and now, it was happening again. Except it didn't. We all arrived with great anticipation, hoping for a massive hit that wasn't.

The New York Times reported that sales reaches $200,000 on opening day, so nobody was sneezing at anything. The women's store has all the merchandise imaginable, but many stores have fine merchandise. Nowadays, we can all say with pride that visual presentation makes a store. At Barneys, the visual presentation disappoints.

The store is far from finished, but it is open. And it does show its architecture and attitude. Barneys has always been an architectural rabbit warren. There was always an air of faded pea green wallpaper and commissioned salespeople trying to make up their minds if you were worth waiting on or not.

That changed. Barneys grabbed a certain emerging youth market. The designer floors for men were actually designed by somebody, and they had the merchandise available. If you could put up with the confusion, you could find anything. Then the Penthouse blossomed, and women's wear appeared. The space was chic, expensive and exhilarating. It had great merchandise. Unlike the men's store, it was concise and clear. People said that if Barneys ever got serious about women's wear, they'd want to see it.

It's a risky idea. The world doesn't exactly need another women's store. Menswear is a different matter. There was always plenty of room for Barneys, even in a town with Paul Stuart, Charivari, Brooks Brothers, Bijan, Saks and more. People went to Chelsea to find Barneys even before anyone had ever heard of Chelsea. But they could buy women's wear everywhere.

Not too long ago, Barneys started becoming famous for its window displays—adult fairy tales and lots of other good things. Then, this July 4th, the store had a series of windows that shook the city.

Everyone in New York City was doing something about the Fourth of July, saluting the Statue one way or another. Bloomingdale's put down a bright red

10 YEARS OF PETER GLEN

carpet studded with stars. Everyone had an idea—ONE idea. That's where Barneys started, with a single idea that, before the windows ever got done, was the best idea of all.

Barneys understood what Liberty is and put it into the windows. Liberty is whatever it is to whoever is feeling it. The store commissioned almost 100 artists from every field to do whatever they wanted to do as long as it portrayed the Statue of Liberty. Why didn't anyone else think of this? A couple hundred people stood in front of the windows every night. Some made several visits to walk back and forth absorbing the melting pot itself—an immense variety of individual approaches to the Statue. America is a combination of Kamali, Hermes, Warhol and 250 million other individuals. Barneys caught the notion and put it into the windows.

Meanwhile, the endlessly publicized opening of Barneys' mammoth new women's store was being delayed for the third or fourth time. The combination of the best windows and the longest delays eve only fueled the blaze of conjecture about Barneys. Expectation was tremendous.

The merchandise matters, and it is marvelous at Barneys. All the good designers are there, including lots of fascinating new ones. The boring traditionalists are thankfully absent.

There are four clever display spots: an ancient refrigerated display case for chocolates; an extravagant painting over the buffet of rich people dining; the fantasy valance in the kids department; and several opulent cases like the one in the lower-level hall that showed a peplum coast so well it made the trend intelligible. And there is one clever idea on the main floor—fake windows with fake vistas. But the "views" themselves are uninspired, and when you look down at them from the upstairs windows, you can see they are fake, propped up with two-by-fours.

Visually, physically, literally, there is no overall style to Barneys. First the architecture: It is as if a brace of architects battled it out and everybody won. It could have used an absolute ceo. They did try to provide a sense of occasion at the entrance on 17th Street. You'd think running right into the foot of a six-story marble staircase would do it every time. Except this time. Barneys managed to deflate the moment by simply not lighting the area and by putting am uncivil, timid girl behind a huge desk with a vase of very ordinary flowers.

The monumental staircase is six floors of circling glass and marble that should be ceremonial and thrilling—but there are some odd features. The staircase isn't exactly curved or symmetrical and doesn't ascend in a circling rhythm. Little angles and side trips make it look more bent than curved.

All six floors open off this staircase, and the walls of every floor are a bright shiny white, clashing with the little huddles of expensive furniture someone put here and there to demarcate departments. And these walls simply don't work with the gray, tan and metal looks of everything else.

The whole store has a very surprising grayish, greenish sort of gloom. There are no brights and no darks, no punctuation nor contrast anywhere. The lighting is very odd. Cosmetics, for instance, has very bright ceilings with no lights near showcases. Salespeople, makeup artists and customers are left in a vaguely gray/green twilight. And illuminated barrel arches in the main floor arcade leave the merchandise below in comparative darkness.

The arcade, with its not particularly graceful pillars, leads off to the Co-op, the new young women's store. Accessory and home furnishing shops (really cubicles with visible air conditioning ducts) open off this arcade. Once you are geared up for an elegant promenade down this main aisle, its non-existence is a let-down. The entire center of the aisle has been dug out to provide a big hole with a restaurant at the bottom.

Down in Le Cafe, the swimming pool is deep and wildly tiled. Barneys is famous for its service, but in Le Cafe there were seven customers and nine staff, and the staff people were leaning against the walls talking as if they'd been there for years. It was remarked that the one good thing about Le Cafe was that you could look up women's dresses on the balcony above and that they women already know it, so that's why they stand there. A new retail tradition is born.

Another bent staircase takes you down past light fixtures with bulbs exposed from above to a sort of pool-within-a-poolside patio area. This pool has ordinary plants, dirty water and frog fountains that weren't operating.

There is very little lightheartedness at Barneys. The entire enterprise has been taken very seriously. The kids boutique is cute, more or less, and the Co-op, which opened while I stood there, was instantly mobbed. But it was so unfinished that it was impossible to tell what it's supposed to look like.

So, everyone went and everyone milled and everyone murmured and remembered Saks and Bloomingdale's fourth floor. The merchandise got raves, from the linens to the hot new designers upstairs. But there was very little commentary about the store itself—the store that everyone had hoped and expected to be stunned and thrilled by.

There was one ugly remark overheard, but it wasn't intended to be nasty, just thoughtful: "Maybe," a fashionable woman said to her friend, "they should just sell menswear."

GIORGIO GOES DOWNTOWN

JUNE 1989

WHAT IS GOING ON with menswear? I know that women's wear is not selling, but there must be a better reason than that for the avalanche of new, expensive men's stores opening every hour in New York City.

Giorgio Armani has now opened a resoundingly mediocre new store, Emporio Armani, in New York City's Flatiron district. This is a self-conscious artistic store with many flaws. Its opening was celebrated in *Daily News Record, Women's Wear Daily, The New York Times, New York* magazine and every other publication—all raving about every infinitesimal detail.

The store obviously cost a lot of money and is designed not to be trendy, and therefore never outdated. But the most telling tidbit in all the reviews was that Giorgio Armani himself had not actually seen the store. One hopes he would have been disappointed. There are no lights in the windows. The showcases are too deep and also have no lights so that the costly little watches and caps are all but invisible to the naked eye. There aren't enough dressing rooms for the waiting try-on artists who jam the premises, and the salespeople are so taken with their own personal grandeur that they have passed beyond speaking to customers. Instead, they stand picturesquely posed around the floor in pretty good imitations of the models in the catalogs.

I was in the store for 20 minutes without being approached by anyone on any subject. When I asked a girl for an address card of the new store, she said there weren't any, and she didn't know the address or phone number of the store. She said, while desperately searching for a pen to write the store address on a piece of paper, "I've only been here two days. I don't know anything."

There was one nice touch—big outdoor boxes of tulips blooming in front of the store. All the rest, as someone once said, is "deja vu all over again." Much is being made of the fake wood sculptured shirts and jackets that ornament the walls and fixtures; the Armani-logoed, wing-shaped ceiling; and the costly wood counters. But there's nothing you couldn't see in a SoHo side-street gallery. The human element consists of the usual hostile door guards, rackety jazz music and other elements of good taste for which Armani is known.

Right next door to Emporio Armani is Paul Smith, by now a venerable ancestor in the neighborhood. Bloomingdale's has redone its whole menswear operation, while Louis of Boston holds forth two blocks away.

Bergdorf has announced massive plans for Fifth Avenue and 59th Street. Barneys has a branch in the World Trade Center, and the Gap (both men's and women's) has opened almost as many new stores as Sock Shop International.

Every one of these stores appears to have come from exactly the same architects and designers. They all have the same materials, shopping bags, understatement, wood mixed with concrete and a cumulative air of sobriety which is better at inducing somnolence than sales. But they all make little gestures toward amusement by stocking a few weird socks and a few antique watches. The salespeople are more remote than ever, the suits are more and more conservative. In fact, the merchandise is so conservative that it it's still hanging there two years from now, it will still look good. This makes a lot of sense if what the world needs now is tasteful, permanent clothing. And that has always been successful in menswear. However, now the question is whether or not the world really needs 45 clones of Paul Stuart or one Paul Stuart is enough.

The fashion industry was built on innovation and change, on the appeal of new replacement clothes. Now it seems that all this new equipment will last as a matter of style until the garments wear out.

There still seem to be armies of men and women who still like pawing through the costly racks of similarity, and who still get adrenaline rushes from waiting to get into dressing rooms to try on more of what they came into the store already wearing. I saw those aspiring folks waiting in line with Louis and Paul Smith opened, and recently at Emporio Armani. I'm sure they'll all get dressed again when Bergdorf unveils a no-doubt tasteful, adult menswear store across the street from its present tasteful adult premises.

So, congratulations to the people designing all those stores, taking all those pictures starring all those models doing all those poses in all those tasteful locations at great expense. One of the reviews said that Emporio Armani is the best thing that's happened since Ralph Lauren opened his castle at Madison and 72nd. Oh no it's not! Or if it is, it certainly doesn't compete with the vision or the romance of shopping at Maison Ralph.

I think Giorgio Armani missed more than his own New York store opening. He seems to have also missed the concept, the design, the materials, the merchandise and the staff out here in the Colonies.

If anyone was going to put a store into a neighborhood of vibrant possibilities, they would put it down on Fifth Avenue this afternoon. And, God knows, the world is still full of people who believe that the entire clue to retail is "Location, Location, Location."

If that's all there is, then Emporio Armani is a hit. But if there's more to retail than real estate, Giorgio Armani should get on Alitalia as soon as possible and add some excitement to his brand new store in New York City.

BREATHLESS AT BERGDORF'S

NOVEMBER 1990

AT 10 a.m., Aug. 29, 1990, Bergdorf Goodman Men, a new $20 million store, began its first hour of life. It was a glorious morning. New York City at its infrequent best—perfect weather, brisk, exhilarating, snatched between the choking days of August and the brand new hope of autumn. A perfect opening day.

There were still workmen attacking some stubborn hinges on the front Fifth Avenue doors. The restaurant wasn't ready, the haircutter wasn't open, the shoe shiner wasn't shining shoes yet and the elevators didn't work—although there were hordes of dressed-up helpers to escort you to the escalator. In the midst of it all ran Angela Patterson, Bergdorf's vice president of store planning and design. Her speed implied she had a vicious punch list of not less than 3,000 details that were not yet perfect. But everything was close to perfect.

The first person I saw when I walked through the front door at 10 a.m. was retailer Harry Rosen from Toronto. I suddenly remembered that Harry Rosen had also been the first person I had seen on the opening morning of Barneys' big addition a few years ago. There were other retailers standing around as well.

There were Bergdorf executives looking nervous and excited. Bergdorf's Chair and CEO Ira Neimark strolled back and forth, stopping to peer at possible dust motes in otherwise perfect displays. He was trailed by a group of well-dressed flutterers who responded vibrantly to his every utterance. Staring at a less-than-conservative jacket, Neimark chuckled and said, "Someday, I'll wear something like that." And one of the flutterers gushed, "Oh, Ira, I love you in bright colors!" A little later, a woman suddenly rushed him, saying "Ira, you look like a star." But another acolyte interrupted her, speaking as if she were making a statement to the press, "He always looks like a star."

There were lots of staffers standing everywhere, most of them in careful, angular attitudes. I had the impression that everyone who worked there had gotten a haircut within the last three days and had definitely though about what they were going to wear for opening day. There was pride in the occasion and excitement. It was a genuine event.

The customer amenities at the new store are wonderful. They include the best telephones and toilets in any store in New York City. The actual customer service, however, in its human form, could use a few more rehearsals. By 10:15, the salespeople were already ignoring customers behind the Fifth Avenue entrance. There are lots of salespeople. There were four behind one counter, and they were testing and spraying and sniffing each other's scent applications. I jiggled a Penhaligon's tester and sprayed some on one wrist. One of the chatterers broke away from the pack to come over. He shook my hand and said, "You have my taste."

Upstairs on three, a mixed group of executives and salespeople were gathered around a tie display at a major intersection. There were discussing a loud tie and their supervisor. "Oh Maurice, it's you!" one squealed quietly. "You must buy it."

A young man with extraordinary hair skittered down the main aisle, saying over and over, to no one in particular, "This key does not fit this stockroom. This key does not fit this stockroom."

Two salespeople on tour were gasping for air. "You just can't take it all in at one time," one confided.

On the third floor, I was approached again. I was deep in the Issey Miyake outpost examining costly goods when a salesperson roared up behind me and "Dolce and Gabbana! Dolce and Gabbana! Oh God, I'm sorry, sir. I thought you were someone else." And I was even approached a third time. A department-managerish woman said to me. "I love your trousers. Whose are they?" I said, "They're mine." She looked quite astonished.

Time magazine says we are beginning an era of "hunkering down" as customers. Customers are starting to prefer excellent French's mustard to the excesses of Grey Poupon. They know that Smucker's jams and preserves are excellent. The Gap sells far more Polo shirts than Polo, and there are no apologies for any of this.

Bergdorf Goodman disagrees, and it does so with passion and determination. If anybody gets the retail rich business, it's probably going to be Bergdorf Goodman.

The building itself now crowns the neighborhood.Coming just after the completed renovations of Grand Army Plaza, the Plaza Hotel and its own original building, the new store helps make this majestic intersection one of the fine urban ensembles of the world. Now if only Ira Neimark could get rid of the hideous General Motors building, the achievement would be complete.

Inside, Bergdorf Goodman Men is a triumph of visual presentation. You should get on an airplane and go see it. It is a synthesis of the main objective of retailing: to give a clear, consistent image throughout in physical terms; to show the merchandise clearly and with excitement; and to create an atmosphere that persuades people to buy things.

Three floors radiate out from a stately central rotunda, using lively materials and intriguing ornament—and enough surprises to demonstrate that good taste does not need to be boring. This is a store that whispers, but the whisper carries.

The directory tells the merchandise story. Three floors of the best and most expensive clothing available from everywhere make up what must be the world's only "department store" of men's couture. If you are rich and you care what you look like, you will probably shop in this store.

Each presentation in each department is completely and clearly differentiated from all of the adjacent departments, yet the overall impression remains consistent Bergdorf Goodman. Take the Ralph Lauren section, for example. The white marble floor is a fine, "Bergdorfy" statement that is right for the store and also give Ralph Lauren a new twist that works for him. I doubt that even Ralph himself has so far installed white marble to show off his stuff, but here it is.

There are dozens more intriguing details—the intense rugs in Turnbull and Asser, good music, splendid lighting without one bulb hitting you in the eyes, deco ornamentation that summarizes the neighborhood.

At about 10:45, way back in a tasteful corner on the first floor, a tasteful—but intense—scene was going on. Several seasoned salespeople were standing behind their precious counters watching Angela Patterson displaying a mania for detail. And that is why the store is as good as it is—because huge scenes are made about details. Angela wanted a light bulb refocuses, and it wasn't happening. "Change the bulb," she commanded. "Get a ladder." There was a pause while the workman considered. "Do it now," said Angela. "Hurry. Use my name. Do what you have to. Do it."

The workman decided to do it and sped off. Angela raced upstairs to the next emergency, and the salespeople were left behind their counters discussing her. They summed Angela up with, "That's why this place is called

Pattersonopolis."

I asked Angela what she was going to do next. "

Vermont," she said, "three days of total isolation. But then I'm coming back to work. Be sure to come in next week and see what we're doing to the old store."

By now it was after 11 a.m. A horde or rich people had just come in. The second hour in the life of the new store had started.

A TALE OF TWO LANDMARKS

JUNE 1991

TWO NEGLECTED LANDMARK buildings in New York City have just been vivified—one well, one badly—and the two opposing treatments make good study. Both are stores.

The triumph is Henri Bendel which gobbled up the old Rizzoli location and the store next door. That store had been ignored for 40 years, despite the fact there were always rumors of buried treasures—including genuine Lalique windows and other splendors—underneath the perpetually going-out-of-business electronics and table linen hawkers squatting on the old disheveled premises.

Late in February, the new Bendel's opened during a war and a depression proclaiming: "There are no rules for personal style. But there is a new address." The new store is more than the sum of its past. The architects honored history, cleaned it and improved it. Bendel's and Fifth Avenue and the rejuvenated treasure all look better than ever. And a couple of million customers showed up to admire it and spend money, too—something Bendel's had never made much of, in spite of its reputation for forward fashion.

The disaster is the Flatiron building, a national treasure of great historic importance—the first skyscraper ever built. The structure was so doubtful in 1920 that people camped out around it in tents, wanting to be present when it fell down. Now it has. It's been brought down by some Italian garment manufacturers who wanted to establish a presence in New York City with their new store in the Flatiron building. This they have done and done it badly, for all to see. They have destroyed the building by contradicting it instead of making more of it by finding points of synchronization.

Architectural contradiction can be effective opposing an existing building. It has been done by I.M. Pei, who put a startling glass pyramid in the central courtyard of the Palais du Louvre museum in Paris. The palace and the pyramid are entirely distinct from one another. The two buildings each have different materials, shapes, proportions, rhythms, ornaments, scales and differing ambitions. Each is strong enough to exist on its own, creating a new and fascinating play between the two. Both buildings gain new life.

It is true that no one will ever again experience the Louvre again the way its original architect intended. Luckily, though, the new pyramid is a beautiful thing itself and would have been complete on its own in another location, just as the Louvre has occupied its rightful place for the last few hundred years. It is a new marriage that throws off some valid sparks of excitement.

No such sparks have happened at the Flatiron building. There is plenty of opposition, but every aspect of the renovation seems to have been done to obliterate the original. It is so blunt that it must have been a deliberate intention, as though the architects were insecure enough to have to demolish the original instead of daring to enhance it.

The Landmarks Commission is paid by taxpayers to preserve great buildings and to supervise their redesign. The opening publicity brouhaha made much of the fact that the owners of the new store had contributed heavily to the commission. One wouldn't want to think this accounted for the commission's absence of conscience. But the commission didn't do its job.

Both the owners and architects can't claim ignorance of their inheritance. In fact, adding insult to injury, they ran a series of two-page ads in *The New York Times* featuring this hypocritical announcement: "This store represents the first step toward restoration of the building which, in turn, for 90 years has borne witness to the things in which we believe. Something which was beautiful yesterday and will be beautiful tomorrow. An original form but yet in harmony with its use. Something different but which appears familiar. From today, our garments will live in the house of an American friend."

What has been done? They call it "deconstructivist" design. The inevitable triangular corner space which forms the climax of the building has simply disappeared, converted to a stockroom, closed to customers. It can't be reached. The sidewalk-to-ceiling 20-foot windows have been eliminated and blocked completely by new interior walls. This is, admittedly, a very difficult space to use, but so is the courtyard of the Louvre. The ugly new walls are visible from the street and inexplicably constructed of gray steel highway barricades.

The interior fittings and furnishings are made of more of the same highway blinders, or else they're fabricated of equally irrelevant, vaguely Scandinavian blond woods. Plain old "sale" tables are littered with "art" books. The clothing is hung in no particular order, and you can get the same merchandise three blocks away at The Gap for less.

A sarcastic little acknowledgement to the Flatiron building is made on the ceiling. Someone has saluted the original ornamental plasterwork by calling attention to it with violent colors. In all the space there is not one gesture, not one material, not one use of space, and not one furnishing that synchronizes with the building it inhabits.

To top it all off, the new store is equipped with nasty salespeople who seem to have come down from Madison Avenue and brought their attitudes with them. A friend of mine went to visit the new store and was unapproached while she wandered around. She was about to leave when suddenly a salesperson materialized and said to her: "If you give me your name and address, you can be on our mailing list." My friend said, "No, thanks." But the salesperson had the last word. She stared at my friend and said, "It figures."

The Flatiron building will never be the same, and time and customers will tell what's going to happen to this new store. As Mark Twain said, "The public is the only critic whose opinion matters at all."

RISING SUN, SETTING SUN

DECEMBER 1993

IF I WERE investing $100 million in retailing today, I'd go for the brains at Home Depot.

Customers need and want what Home Depot sells. Home Depot sells it better than anyone else; their service is better than anyone else's; and they make money.

After losing money for two years in Japan, Isetan, the Japanese department store group, has built a $100 million dollar store on Madison Avenue in New York City. And hired the Pressman family to run it. Barneys' customers do not really need what Barneys sells, and less and less of them want it. In their $100 million citadel, they present this moda better than Bergdorf's.

On opening day at Barneys, a customer was jumping up and down and yelling at a saleswoman.

"Eight floors of black dresses! I ask you to show me something to wear to my son's wedding, and you show me black dresses! He isn't dead! He's getting married! I already have five black dresses! Everybody has five black dresses! If I wanted black dresses, I could have stayed home!"

Eight floors of black. Barneys is playing it safe.

The store itself is beautiful, but not extremely so. It is tasteful but not daring, perfect but not fun. Every chair is carefully selected, set, and so is every fitting, every fixture, every light and every lacquered lamp. But none of it is thrilling. Barneys has built a great big ice cream sundae — with no cherry on top.

Every real artistic effort needs a central, identifying focal point that lifts the entire enterprise ten percent higher.

There is a restaurant in the hills near St. Tropez that is in every way perfect. I cannot remember what we had to eat—although it was perfect. It was the explosion of 500 peonies in the middle of the room that symbolized the place for me.

I have loved visiting the Louvre, every mile of it, but it was the Winged Victory at the top of the staircase that made me gasp.

It is in this area—visual presentation, the thrill of seeing—that Barneys plays it safe again, but here they'll probably be sorry. I longed for an identifying punctuation mark. There is no logo violet shop-ping bag, no rose, no mouse ears, golden arches, Statue of Liberty. For $100 million, I want a cherry on my sundae.

I didn't get it at Barneys.

There are a lot of questions. Why did Isetan do this? Is it because they wanted a palace on Madison Avenue? Where else could they go, now that Rodeo Drive is a ghost town?

Didn't Isetan want to make money? The Japanese retailer made its $250 million investment in Barneys (for Madison Avenue and other stores) just before the global recession hit Japan. The chief executive at the time was then removed from his job. Isetan was becoming like so many other companies who went on managing the eighties into the nineties.

Ten years before, Japan did everything right. While we weren't looking, they took the lead in world banking, automobiles, electronics, real estate, record companies, movie studios and even fashion. They shook us all up while we scrambled to learn new names. Yohji, Kanzai, Yamamoto, Issey, Mitsukoshi, Miyake, Matsuda de Garcon! We gasped while they shredded garments, charged more money and plunged the insecure fashion world into blackness from head to foot.

Japan had fashion, but they've never really had a great store in America. Mitsukoshi is minor on its 57th Street corner—seven garments and a restaurant downstairs. Matsuda is squeezed between two other shops on lower Fifth. Felissimo is just adorable, but small. Takashimaya is a stupendous store of sorts, but it's much smaller and a different sort than Barneys.

Is this just more of the leftover prestige that Ralph Lauren and Giorgio Armani wanted when they built palaces? Is this Bergdorf Goodman again, blowing $20 million on their Fifth Avenue chateau?

Let's get to the point: Money.

Ralph Lauren makes money. But Ralph is a person of his times, and his stores are still wanted and needed. They sell a single look to people who want a single look. His new Madison Avenue sport store is twice as theatrical and five times more fun than Barneys.

One day one newspaper quotes a Pressman projecting annual sales of $200 million for Barneys' new store. The next day the "quote" is $150 million. That careless $50 million difference, give or take, is more than the biggest branch of a department store will do all year. Even the lower quote brings us the prospect of a store that must do $417,000 per day. That's a lot of frocks.

Are we seeing the Rising Sun setting over Madison Avenue?

On Barneys' opening day, just one block away, New Yorkers were being treated to the surprises they long for. Admiring crowds were gathering around a vast bronze cat set down in the planting on Park Avenue. Seven other corpulent Botero sculptures—bloated, but somehow lovable—were also attracting attention. "Customers" were stopped in their tracks, cooing over these big, funny, sweet instant landmarks. Indelible, memorable, everything that Barneys isn't.

In six weeks the big Boteros will be hauled away and Barneys will still be straddling Madison Avenue. In six weeks they'll have to be doing $417,000 per day (or more, depending on which report you fancy). And maybe they will. Maybe we underestimate the energy of fashion, or the power of black garments, or the money of the Japanese or the genius of the Pressman family.

But if not, the Pressman family—all of them—can convert the store into a condo and live in it. The folks from Isetan can stay there when they come to New York.

Barneys will be the most expensive, most tasteful private condominium apartment building in New York.

WHAT'S UP, DOC?

APRIL 1994

A COUPLE OF MONTHS before Christmas a gigantic rabbit appeared at the otherwise sober intersection of Fifth Avenue and 57th Street. This apparition loomed unexpectedly between the stony eminence of Bergdorf Goodman on one side and the permanent fortress of Tiffany's on another.

Something strange is going on in New York City. This will come as no surprise to those who think that everything that happens in New York is always strange.

This rabbit raised eyebrows at uneasy neighbors like Chanel and Galeries Lafayette, but the eyebrows of Chanel and Galeries Lafayette are always raised, so nobody noticed. Customers were checking the progress inside, behind the giant rabbit, waiting for the scaffolding to come down so they could get into the store.

By the first of December the Warner Bros. store was open for all to see, and all came to see it. By December 10 the lines tripled up and stretched around the corner, making it hard for customers to get into Chanel.

Superman pushes up the elevator and it is jammed, too. This is an adult entertainment store, selling more smart jackets and original cartoon cels than sightseers' souvenirs, and it has recharged the whole area.

Two blocks south—a 20-second walk—the Coca-Cola store is packed.

But that's not all. Three blocks south, Takashimaya has opened the only Japanese store in America that really matters; it is an austere, magnificent emporium that sells fine things at highly exalted prices and then gift wraps them in a way that makes it all seem worthwhile. At Christmas time the gasp-making five-story entry well was hung with chandeliers whose many lampshades glowed with, of all things, pasted-on intense red amaryllis petals. Gasp. More entertainment.

And that's not all. One block west of Takashimaya the lines form early for hamburgers at another kind of shrine, the Harley Davidson Cafe. This is the successor to the Hard Rock and Planet Hollywood, but it's centered around a great American product as permanent as Levi's. Riders, would-be riders, and vicarious riders are jamming the 20,000-square-foot space to eat and drink and stare and shop in the shop. Whoever answered the phone lied to me. She said there wasn't more than a ten-minute wait. When I got there, the doorman said, "Ninety minutes at least."

There's more. One block east of Fifth, on Madison at 56th, a super-hyper-cybernetic Sony store is interacting with the throng. Entertainment.

And more. Four blocks north at 62nd and Madison looms Barneys.

None of this was there one year ago.

What's happening?

All this innovation is taking place at one of the world's great crossroads. This is not a neighborhood, like SoHo or Tribeca or Madison or Columbus Avenue. This is the heart of the city, where establishment is long and inno-vation is rare. Bergdorf's and Tiffany's and FAO Schwarz and Burberry's and Chanel and all the rest all the way down to Saks seem to have always been there. And they have now been shocked into the kind of attention that may lead even them to be innovative or be gone.

Downtown nowadays is hard to find.

Most U.S. city centers have disappeared. Los Angeles never had a center, and now even Rodeo Drive in Beverly Hills is all for rent and nobody is rent-ing. Chicago never could decide whether it centered on State Street or Michigan Avenue. San Francisco is losing its Union Square center where the dowagers Saks and Magnin now languish.

Many great cities still have centers: think of Paris, London, Hong Kong. Nobody goes to Istanbul to visit the suburbs. The city is an attraction. The climax of their civilizations can be seen on certain corners just as surely as the centers of other cities can be found in their ancient marketplaces.

This is nobody's fault and nobody's responsibility, but even if it only depends on blind luck, New York City is lucky because its center is being revived.

This Christmastime I was shopping my brother around town, and as we approached the corner of Fifth Avenue and 57th Street the crowds increased. We could see the giant snowflake suspended above the intersection as we aimed for Warner Bros., Takashimaya and Harley Davidson. Even the regulars seemed to be reviving: the five-story interior Christmas tree at Bendel's, made entirely of spices and dried flowers, caused astonishment. Tiffany's windows seemed better than ever. Only the sad Trump Tower Atrium seemed to be dead back in the eighties.

As we rounded the corner onto Fifth Avenue, a great wave of people surged about under the snowflake. Bells rang. Lights winked merrily. People were dressed for the occasion. People were cheerful in dozens of languages. We were temporarily transported out of crime and war and hunger and sickness and all the other detritus of current events. There wasn't much of the reality of the evening news in view at the corner of Fifth and 57th, but there was hope and excitement and beauty and imagination and rejuvenation, as if something new were trying to be born, a real city Christmas.

My brother looked at the spectacle and said, "This is a throng!"

There is only one way to face the future constructively, and that is to invent it. It's part of the "or else" we're facing. Business is reinventing itself right now—or else. Management techniques and even business education are changing themselves—or else. If we reinvent our educational system, we may be able to reinvent ourselves. Or else.

I do not mean that pitching a huge electric snowflake or running a big rabbit up the wall will save us, but the first step in creating the future is to set forth a new appearance.

New York is, as usual, the best and the worst of everything. This Christmas it seemed more interested in presenting the best than regurgitating the worst. We do not need to be convinced that everything is awful. We need instead to be persuaded that what is good needs to be magnified. By some serendipitous Christmas coincidence, New York decided to present its hopes instead of its fears to an unsuspecting public who had merely come shopping. The people who created Warner Bros. and Takashimaya and Harley Davidson and Barneys could have saved their hope and their money by waiting for evidence of better times.

But they didn't. They armed themselves with courage and moved directly from hope into action. They independently put their dreams into architecture and turned on all the lights. They seemed to know that New York is the place to demonstrate that the best way to face forward is, as all great merchants know, to imagine the future and then act on it.

Hopeful, isn't it? The only odd note in the 57th Street revival is that old Warner Bros. slogan, "That's all, folks!"

Oh no it's not!

PART SIX
IMPROVEMENT

SIGNS AND SAYNGS

AUGUST 1984

SOME OF THE BEST SIGNS I've seen are not in stores. They are in offices in stores, or in employee lunchrooms. These "signs" are very personal. They are not something sent out by marketing departments to thrill customers. Instead, they are signs that people have put up to talk about and stimulate themselves and others.

One of the best (and biggest) of these signs I've seen was about 12 feet long, on the wall behind the chair of the chairman of a store in New Orleans. As long as you were looking at him, you were also looking at his message—"Assume Nothing." It clearly made its point.

Why do great quotes work so well?

1. They are telegrams—urgent, brief and to the point.

2. They are small enough to remember or carry around as reminders of what we wish we were doing better.

3. They are small seeds that can be handed out at meetings where they then grow into sermons, speeches and systems of thought.

4. They spark agreements or disagreements, thereby lighting new fires.

5. They are quotable, said by people who know how to express things well.

These sayings, slogans, aphorisms, quotes, et cetera, also tell a lot about the person who put them up. Here is my own collection of quotes. They mean a lot to me because some of them are signs to live by.

- I've been rich, and I've been poor. Rich is better. — Mae West
- Mediocre people are always at their best. — Somerset Maugham
- And the end of our exploration is that we return to the place we started from and see it for the first time. — T.S. Eliot
- 'Tis better to drink life in one flaming hour and reel across the sun, than to sip pale years and cower before oblivion. — Walt Whitman
- Show me a good loser, and I'll show you a loser. — Vince Lombardi
- I always try to see more in people than they see in themselves. — Alethea Mattingly
- The test of leadership is not to put greatness into humanity, but to elicit it, for the greatness is already there. — James Buchanan
- Every man with a new idea is considered to be a crank, until his new idea succeeds. — Thomas Edison
- What you can do, or dream you can, begin it; boldness has genius, power and magic in it. — Goethe

- If you aren't fired with enthusiasm, you will be fired with enthusiasm. — Vince Lombardi
- When you get to the top of the mountain, keep right on climbing. — a nine-year-old blind girl
- Every job is a self portrait of the person who did it. Autograph your work with excellence. — unknown

I RESOLVE

JANUARY 1985

"I AM a great visual merchant. I have the imagination, power, authority and money to do whatever I want to do to prove again and again that visual merchandising sells merchandise." You do believe that, don't you?

It is January. As the year changes, so do you. Here are the changes that I see:

1984 and Before
  Technology
  Machinery
  Manufacturing
  Amplified Sound
  Rock and Punk
  Jet Speed
  Quantity
  Short Term
  Possessions
  The Economy
  Leveling Mountains
  Criticism
  Having
  Things
  Thoughts
  The Body
  Self, Self, Self
  Me

1985 and After
Touch
Hands
Services/Ideas
The Human Voice
Grand Opera
Walking
Quality
Long Term
Earth, Water, Air
The Environment
Climbing Them
Praise
Giving
People
Feelings
The Spirit
Other People
You

Now, I resolve to act. I resolve...

• To know and experience more, because I know that ideas come from experience, and I've never learned everything. I may not be the first man in Ohio to wear a skirt, or even two watches, but I will know about them first. I got my own GoBot for Christmas, and I will travel down the Nile before this year is over. Then I might be able to come up with something a little less stupid than "Back to School." As the Red Queen in *Through the Looking Glass* says, "It takes all the running you can do to keep in the same place. If you want to get somewhere else, you must run at least twice as fast as that."

• To make my store more "high-touch" than "tech," because I know that if we are going to stay in business, it will be by luring customers with experiences they cannot get more efficiently from a machine. They can order by the numbers at home, but they will leave all of that and travel great distances if I can promise them adventure and excitement.

• To clarify my store's image, stick to it and fight for it. I will counter every manufacturer's attack with an image of my own and work towards a fascinating partnership.

• To shuffle splintered trends because today my customer is interesting and diversified, and wants every choice in the world—without confusion. So

I must learn to juggle 17 attitudes at once and lay them out coherently, all on the same floors, on the same day, at the same time. I resolve to discipline my work so I can make decisions for the customer, saving her from chaos and endearing my store to her.

- To murder Mother's Day and Father's Day and Back to School and Spring and Summer and Fall and Winter, which are just a few of the myriad dumb cliches we all use everyday. I will invent new words and images before my customers expire from all the sameness I bestow on them, and I will force this issue—through war if necessary—until originality and innovation are reborn. My customer is alert, alive and ready for anything new in August, and I call it "Back to School." I will stop this nonsense now and treat my customers and my own brain with respect.

- To broaden my knowledge of the competition: first, by knowing that it is everything for which money is paid, whether it goes to *Dune*, Disneyland or the District of Columbia; and second, by never forgetting ever that every store in the world wants every customer's dollar as much as I do. For they, too, will do anything to get it. Only by knowing what everyone else is doing as soon as possible can I get to the same place first.

- To criticize, raise hell in restaurants, stores and airports until the standards rise, and I get what I want and deserve. I will try everyday to never say, "What difference does it make," remembering that no detail is small. I want to tolerate less mediocrity, laziness, incompetence, excuses, lateness, lousy execution, relaxation, uninspired efforts, punishments, rewards. I want better meals, rooms, seats and service, and I will never think that one person cannot achieve a change.

- To maintain excellence even if I'm lucky enough to hit it, because I know that excellence is fast and fragile, that the target moves, that the world revolves, and that staying there is infinitely more difficult than getting there just once.

- To battle sameness wherever I see it (everywhere) and to develop difference instead. The purpose of knowing what other people are doing, even when it's right, is to find out quickly how to do it otherwise, whether it is a prop, a mannequin, an item, a system, color, a sound, lettering, a landscape or lunch. I will listen to Frank Sinatra sing "I Did It My Way" often, with the volume high. I will play it to my management in their sleep.

- To become a master marketer. Once we were called "display." Then, finally, we got to be "visual merchants," and since that time, some of us have been satisfied. I want more, and that means more than "visual merchant." It means Marketer, the only complete, comprehensive, total ambition of a brilliant store. I want to be a Master Marketer. I want it all.

• To take myself less seriously and my job more seriously, and not to confuse the two. That way, I will be able to laugh at myself and join the human race, and plow all my energy into the work, where it belongs.

• To honor my people more because I have that privilege, and I know this is what they work for. I know that their work lives only briefly. I will tighten up two things in my administration: discipline and recognition, achieving perfect balance between these two different necessities. I will see more in my people than they see in themselves, and make them rise to their own possibilities.

Finally I resolve to know that visual merchandising is more than just my job. It is my means of self-expression—to influence others and to use my talent and my courage together to express what I believe and to make it beautiful.

All things are possible. Pass the word.

THE USE AND ABUSE OF THE STATUE OF LIBERTY

JULY 1985

WHAT ARE YOU going to do about the Statue of Liberty? Ignore it? Some of you will. Some of you even ignored the Olympics. Not one major Los Angeles department store did anything at all about the Olympics. What were these retailers waiting for? A bigger event?

The country is into patriotism and the Statue of Liberty. Some of the marketing efforts are Quality and, of course, some are trash.

Miller Brewing Company implies that drinking its beer makes you American. If you don't, you're not American. "American Tuna" (a new brand) is "the only brand of tuna packed exclusively in the continental United States by a national tuna company."

Some efforts are a bit more serious. American Airlines gives added mileage credit to frequent flyers for $100 contributions. Macy's is being picketed by "Buy American" marchers. Old Grandad, since printing a patriotic ad, has been deluged with 10,000 orders for reprints. Wal-Mart's "Buy American" program includes the cancellation of merchandise worth some hundreds of millions of dollars, to be replaced by American-made merchandise. Sam Walton "has a leadership role in American retailing," says Walter

Loeb, industry analyst at Morgan Stanley.

The general manager of J. Walter Thompson sums it up: "If you can incorporate the new patriotic feeling into a campaign that fits your product, there's no question it will have appeal." He figures the patriotic sell will be around as long as people in the United States continue to feel good about their country.

So, the whole country is behind it—both because of opportunism or good marketing or even, occasionally, genuine patriotism. It's time to ask how retailers—those lovable current events mavens—are responding.

As of now, there is a list of 61 retailers and shopping centers planning retail promotions registered with the Statue of Liberty-Ellis Island Foundation Inc. The list is interesting—and horrifying. The promotion is good enough for the likes of Tiffany, Saks, Bloomingdale's, Steuben Glass, Henri Bendel, Lord & Taylor as well as the Rouse Company and Melvin Simon, both mall developers. But evidently, it's not good enough for stores like Famous-Barr, The Broadway, Meier & Frank, Sakowitz, Nieman-Marcus and others. Or maybe they're waiting like they did for the Olympics.

Of all 61 promotions planned though, only eight are taking place in stores west of the Mississippi. Apparently, the notion of liberty hasn't hit them out there. Yet at the same time, the governors of all 50 states are declaring "Liberty Week." What does this mean? The citizens care, but retailers do not?

Here's what some of the 61 stores (and some unregistered stores) are doing...

• Proffitt's, Knoxville, Tennessee, sent the Statue of Liberty the world's largest valentine early this year.

• Tippecanoe Mall, Lafayette, Indiana, bought a 32-foot, cold air, inflatable balloon replica of the Statue and transported it to the mall, where it unfolded all wrinkled and slowly filled with air for amazed customers. The mall also had a 32-square-foot puzzled of the "Lady" to be worked out by shoppers.

• Barneys, New York City, had a silver flatware window with forks propping up the scaffolding on the Statue.

• Casual Corner has nationwide windows about the Statue right now.

• Godchaux's, Baton Rouge, Louisiana, has a 12-foot Statue of Liberty head.

• Wilkes Bashford has a chic Statue head wearing yellow sunglasses.

One inspired idea—a really big one—is in the works already. Early this year, a very distinguished group of New York visual merchants assembled (you know all their names). They wanted to plan together before setting out to be their own isolated, inimitable selves. They shouldn't worry about imitation. They'll all keep their creativity if they're good enough. And because they started together, they hatched an idea with impact. Each will remain entirely individual in execution, yet form a coalition of "United Artists" around a single issue, on a single date. They'll also scoop the rest of you with a brilliant piece of timing.

While others wait until next year, here's their big idea...

October 28, 1985—the Statue of Liberty's 99th Birthday! This should be great. And if these folks are as good as they sound, they'll do this and then do something more in 1986, just as the joy reaches its height.

So get on with it. We're all going to get to see the Lady used in a big variety of ways—some great, some terrible. It is an important (I almost said "sacred") project, and these few words might help to stop some of the cheap, unnecessary things that might happen.

Every retailer must join in. But here is a warning: Don't trash the Statue. It's only a matter of moments until some markdown maniac comes up with a value-bargain-trash promotion about "life, liberty and the pursuit of sales." This will be fairly disgusting.

Remember, the repair of the Statue is symbolic, not just literal. It coincides with the reconstruction of our national thinking on matters we have allowed to rust—pride, quality of products and services and the American quality of life.

How are you going to come up with your brilliant, sincere idea?

• Start with the right attitude. This is not merely a gimmick for raising funds to save a statue. If you're really ambitious, you'll be finding ways to raise our consciousness about the idea of liberty itself.

• Do some work. Study. You'll find out fascinating things, like the fact that the index finger of the Statue is eight feet long. You can explain this at your next major dinner party.

• Read your history. Art. Sculpture. Patriotism. America. The more you learn, the better your idea will be.

• Make it good. The public will tire fast unless the presentation gets stronger and clearer with every repeat.

• Don't think it's a trite subject and, therefore, not worthy of your talents. Think again. "Religion" is a "trite" subject. So are "family" and "life" and "death." Liberty is not an entirely unworthy subject.

This is your chance, visual merchants. You ask for it all the time. You want recognition, respect, dignity, praise, power and real reaction. You—

and everyone else in your profession—are going to *have* to go at this one. You'll be compared with the best and the worst. It's going to be a great big "Do Ms. Liberty" display contest. Do it. And do it right.

The Statue's real name is "Liberty Enlightening the World." I hope that includes retailing.

THE MAN WHO COULD HAVE BEEN GOOD

NOVEMBER 1985

"For what shall it profit a man, if he shall gain the whole world and lose his own soul? Or what shall a man give in exchange for his own soul?"
— *The Bible*, Mark 9: 36-37

HAVE YOU lost your creativity? How much does it matter to you? How frustrated are you? Are you ploddingly engaged in doing floor plans, choosing colors, fixing wigs and filling windows? Are you carrying out in fear what should be done with energy? You disfigure the face of creativity to do your job without joy. What are you going to do about it?

Many people employed in stores are always complaining. They go to coffee, lunch and dinner and gripe about their bosses. They are, according to themselves, misunderstood, abused, ignored, shot down and frustrated. If it weren't for their bosses, they would each be Michelangelo.

Of course some of their moaning is just state-of-the-art complaining. But some of it is true. Some folks do work in a corporate dictatorship. And that is death to creativity. This essay is dedicated to anyone who works fro a frustrating boss, and there are lots of them. Such dictators/egomaniacs use power to abuse people. Horror stories abound.

What do you think of a manager who demands that his employees play it his way—and only his way—if they want to keep their jobs? He allows certain suppliers and prohibits others. Particular people can't be spoken to in public. Attendance at certain trade shows is forbidden.

Such a man may be very talented, though. However, he's got the "power-gone-wrong" syndrome. And that's sad, because power can be used for good. Consider what he does to others, what others do to themselves by staying and what he does to himself in the long run.

Working for this kind of man would be like joining a cult. Those entering must sacrifice themselves and subscribe to the master. It gratifies the boss the same way the worldwide publicity probably gratified Jim Jones in Guyana. The pity is that many people who work for this "leader" do not have the guts to do anything about it. It all works well to keep them in their jobs, but it costs them their souls. They will suffer by failing to use their talents. But the fate of the man who uses his power this way is surely far, far worse— he will always know that he could have been good.

Great bosses are ones who see more in others than they see in themselves. They drive employees hard, but they drive them outward in the employees' own directions, not in theirs.

Great employees are not victims. They fight for their souls. They have more than talent; they have guts. They don't underrate themselves or allow themselves to be underrated.

So what do you do when you find yourself in a job that does not develop your abilities? Well, your boss may be a miserable egotist, but nobody is responsible for what happens to you, except you. The privilege of working in a creative field is that it gives you exercise of self-expression. This is your most precious possession. If someone takes this away from you or you allow it to be snatched and you don't mind, fine, stay where you are. But if you're unhappy, you're in trouble. You must decide either to do something or else prepare to go on groveling forever.

There are three kinds of people in the world: leaders, joiners and followers. If you want to be a follower, go work for an egomaniac. If you are a joiner, join a mediocre company that may let you do whatever you like. If you want to be a leader, you have to get into a organization that wants you to thrive. You can't thrive in a place that stops your abilities. A corporation with a strong image *does* have its discipline. If it is humanely operated, it demands many individual contributions within that structure. If you are stifled and you stay, there is a major danger. Left unused, your talents will rust. If you ever later get to use them, you will find them weakened. Creativity needs exercise, though, or it will waste away.

Why do followers and joiners stay? There are many answers from this "immoral majority."

1. "It's a great store, great prestige."
2. "We've got great power in the market."
3. "I've only got 15 years to go."
4. "To tell you the truth, I'm just too lazy to get out."

5. "The boss isn't so bad."

6. Fear of change.

7. Fear of failure.

8. Fear of being blackballed by the boss.

9. Low self-esteem.

10. Attracted to self-destructive situation.

11. Lack of guts. No courage.

Courage is the single indispensable key to action. It is rarer than talent. And think of the talent that is lost for lack of a little courage. Without it, you don't belong in the corporate world. Just think what it will be like in 20 years when you are still spending your coffee break complaining.

Your options:

1. Stay there. You may be successful if you play it right.

2. Depart. You may find joy painting very small paintings on your own. Vermeer did, and he was close to perfection, although I don't know how you'll eat or whether you are actually another Vermeer.

3. Stay and fight. Do something so dazzling that everybody notices, and then demand an audience with whomever is over your boss. Tell the top the truth. You may get to take over.

4. Quit. Take a risk. Become yourself. This is not for everybody. Don't do it unless you feel it is inevitable. But if you desire freedom more than jail and your present job is jail, if your creativity means more to you than security, and if you have the courage, quit and save yourself. Start over. You stand a chance of living your life according to your blessed creativity. You can gain the world and keep your soul. Start soon. Remember, you are rusting. Get on with it.

Finally, to the dictators/egomaniacs out there—*you* can be good. You have the power. You are industry leaders. You can influence everyone to grow. You still have the power, but you might have the satisfaction of knowing that those who follow you also like themselves—and maybe even you. Think of all the energy it takes to be a jerk, when that energy can be used instead to be a benefactor. The highest form of creativity is helping people grow.

THE LES AND SAM SHOW

JUNE 1986

ONCE UPON A TIME, in a land where everything was possible, two men did better than everyone else. Their names are Les and Sam. Sam is the richest man in the whole land, even though he is a retailer, which is not how most people get rich. Les is not as rich as Sam, but he isn't exactly dirt poor—and he did make the cover of *New York* magazine as the land's "most eligible bachelor."

Les and Sam are so famous that all sorts of stories about them go around. Some are not true. For instance, it's not true that Les was buying General Motors and General Foods. Nor was it true that Sam was taking vows of poverty and retiring from the world. But some of the stories are true. Les bought Lerner's and Lane Bryant and Bendel's. He plans to open Bendel's everywhere across the land, and he danced up and down Madison Avenue, which he partly owns. Sam danced too—in a hula skirt on Wall Street, fulfilling a promise he made to his employees when they made a big fat profit. He explained to the press that he was very cold, but very rich.

Les lives in Columbus, Ohio, and Sam lives in Bentonville, Ark., but they both go to New York when they have big news to announce or when they feel like dancing.

Les opened a basilica on Madison Avenue, putting together a lot of his different stores together in one location. You can see every level from every other level, and every level is crammed with people buying merchandise. On a clear day, you can see as far as Bendel's.

Sam drives a beat-up pickup truck and holds pep rallies every Saturday morning in Arkansas.

Les is bringing Italy (Krizia) and Japan (Kenzo) to the masses and producing the most successful private label clothing in the land (Forenza). Sam canceled $300 million of imported goods and is buying American.

Les and Sam are remarkably different people, but they have certain things in common. Both have one-syllable first names, and both are called by them. People at Federated are not called by their first names, ever: "It ain't fittin'."

Les and Sam both "invented" their companies and have run them since they began. That's where the consistency comes from. It's rare. You can see such continuity at Saks, Mervyn's or Nordstrom's. But most stores change presidents, and therefore policies, every Tuesday afternoon.

Les and Sam devised and stuck to clear and consistent images in each and every store. It is this clarity that makes both of them clear to their customers. It is this consistency that makes their customers buy the merchandise that makes them rich.

Right now, Les and Sam are at the top of the heap and could be expected to live there happily ever after—if they weren't in retailing.

Beware of becoming an expert. Beware of success. It leads to repetition, self-assurance, smugness. It makes you fat, but not sleek. The risks you've taken begin to become recollections instead of actions.

Remember Harry S. Truman? (He could have run The Limited and Wal-Mart, couldn't he?) He said, "It's what you learn after you know it all that really counts."

Remember Sakowitz? Gimbel's? Alexander's? Montgomery Ward?

Every time Goliath falls, there is some risk-taking David in the field with a slingshot. Who will be the next Les or Sam?

I would be slightly nervous if I were Les or Sam. I'd look up long enough from my buying to realize that other retailers have learned from me and are stealing ideas. Stores are learning their image-differentiation lesson, and some are actually coming up with clear images of their own.

Take a look at what's happened to The Gap and its little brother, Banana Republic. They have clarified and strengthened their images in every "limited" way; in architecture, print, photography and merchandising—all the joys of visual presentation and quite an achievement for a company everybody doubted two years ago.

And while other stores' identities are being forged, a certain disease is hitting The Limited: Toxic Creeping Sameness. Could it be that Les Wexner is beginning to confuse being the best with being the biggest? He is the man who has fostered the clearest marketing images in retailing. The Limited is The Limited, and Hunter's Run, Forenza and Kenzo are each completely clear in the minds of all his customers. This is a marketing achievement of singular importance, and we all admire the accomplishment.

These singular hits are all beginning to blur, though. For the first time, The Limited looks like Lane Bryant when you stroll by. Lerner's reminds you ever so vaguely of The Limited with its piles of knitwear on tables in doorways.

Take that famous front door table, for instance. Sure, one good idea can be transferred to another. And, God knows, the fixed item gift-with-purchase table inside the front door of The Limited was a visual and commercial smash hit. But now that table stands in the front door of The Limited, The Limited Express, Lane Bryant, Victoria's Secret and Lerner's. That's the same front door in five stores in every mall. And at South Coast Plaza in Costa Mesa,

California, where The Limited appears to be *unlimited*, there are two Limiteds. That's at least seven of the self-same tables in just one mall.

So suddenly, all across the land of Les, that's a total of about 50,000 tables inside 50,000 front doors. One even expects a table right inside the front door of Bendel's. Of course it would be something chic, like a free white oxford button-down shirt with every $2,400 Jean Muir dress.

Les needs a new idea. Duplication is not the same thing as innovation. That standardization works better for Sam than it does for Les. Wal-Marts are all supposed to be the same. So are Sam's Wholesale Clubs. But then one doesn't find 20 of them side-by-side in the same mall.

For now, though, the Les and Sam show goes on and on while other retailers whimper and wait for them to slow down so they can catch up. They snarl and snip, "Yea, yeah, but will they be able to keep it up?" Les and Sam probably think about this question even more than the competition. So does Doug Tompkins. So does Marvin Traub. It is in the nature of good people to be perpetually dissatisfied.

Les and Sam deserve their own dissatisfaction and their successes and our admiration, as much as anyone in retailing. They lift us up.

Not everyone is complaining, not The Gap, not IKEA. They are genuine, adult enemies. These enemies haven't yet stopped playing "store" to start playing "buy." It is possible that one of these days The Gap will forget The Gap and start thinking about IBM and Associated Dry Goods. The Gap, too, might start merging ideas as well as properties and catch the creeping sameness virus that is infesting our malls. So maybe next week Les should take a break from buying Benetton and Melville to take a walk through a mall to see if he can tell his stores apart. And Sam, who personally visits hundreds of his stores each year to keep in touch with what's going on, might stay home in Bentonville instead and concentrate on buying General Motors. Or Les and Sam might be tempted to relax. Maybe they'll read their old reviews just once too often or take things for granted or forget to take risks.

So, look behind you, Les and Sam. There could be trouble in your land. What will happen next?

Don't pay any attention at all to the rumor that Les Wexner just bought Sears. It's not true. Everyone knows that he's not interested in selling home repair items. He's a fashion merchant. Although he may, in fact, be writing a check for the entire Asian continent so that he can get better deliveries. If you want to worry about something, worry about that.

And it's absolutely untrue that Sam was just writing out a check for The Limited when he ran into Les, who was writing out a check to buy Wal-Mart.

This is ridiculous and should not even be imagined. The only way those two would ever come together is on a split ticket for the nomination for President of the United States.

Just picture it: Les will have a sale table inside the front door of every home in America, and Sam will have a small Statue of Liberty night-light in every child's bedroom. Who says life isn't advertising?

Sam and Les should stop reading their checkbooks and go talk to their customers. They should go to a mall, unannounced and see what customers see. When they get there, they will probably see U.S. Shoe and Kmart and Dayton-Hudson trying to buy up Brookstone, Laura Ashley and The Rouse Company.

It is far harder to maintain excellence than it is to expand it. Les and Sam no longer need to worry about getting rich. They need to worry about staying that way. If they do, their customers will continue to be grateful and to buy things, and the Les and Sam show will become a long-running hit instead of a fad. Then Les and Sam and their customers all across the land will all live the way people in fairy tales ought to—happily every after.

RISK AND OTHER FOUR-LETTER WORDS

JULY 1986

LACKING PRACTICE, the notion of risk-taking starts to dim. Little by little, the world of possibilities recedes. The thrill of taking risks gives way to the comfort of security.

What is the most exciting thing you ever did? I'll bet it involved taking a risk—not knowing the outcome, but going ahead anyway. We all take some kinds of risks. Getting up in the morning is a risk for some people; they'd rather stay in bed forever. There are people so timid that it is a risk for them to even bother breathing in and out.

The artists of the world are risk-takers. They create. Because of them, the world is a more exciting place.

Most people don't take risks. Fear works better for them. The fearful people are necessary. They do the work the artists dream up. But for the real individuals, life does not get going until they use all of their abilities. They are the blessed few, and they are definitely worth considering. They are not just painters, conquerors and astronauts; they can be found everywhere.

They change the world just by occupying it. They dare. They act with passion. They are not afraid.

The main reasons people don't take risks is that risks can fail. We have just lived through a risk that slowed us all down—the catastrophic end of the Space Shuttle Challenger. But that same kind of risk made us walk across the face of the moon. And because we are a nation entirely founded on risk, we will certainly try it again.

Risk-taking is an absolute requirement for astronauts. Most of us are never tested so severely. We worry about risking the wrong remark or an impolitic move or designing a store that would stun instead of soothe the public. Many, many of us prefer to play it safe on the good old straight and narrow. "What if it doesn't work?" "What if they won't let me?" We end up keeping our jobs and risking little.

Later, it's too late. Age and experience are the enemies of courage. The litany of excuses grows defensive. "It could be worse." "It's not that bad." "What difference does it make?" "I've only got ten years to go."

Lacking practice, the notion of risk-taking starts to dim. Little by little, the world of possibilities recedes. The thrill of taking risks gives way to the comfort of security. It drops away and then one day, you find yourself suspended out in space, looking back at what you might have done in the nostalgic distance. How small you've become, how fragile. But you're secure, and your whole little world has never been threatened. You're safe from the fear of inspiration, safe from failing—never making mistakes, never being hurt or attacked or even being noticed.

No matter how serene it all is, your soul will know. You won't be taking risks, but you won't be seeing your dreams fulfilled.

Well then, what about risk and retail? Since risk is probably the only thing that distinguishes one store from another (and one person from another), it is a vital ingredient in visual merchandising. Anything you do that comes before the public eye is probably invisible if it doesn't have an element of risk. There's too much nothing to look at. Customers admire and respond to guts, and they ignore the products of insecurity. Nobody remembers "adequate" visual merchandising. Try to imagine Brooks Brothers or the Christmas decor in the run-of-the-mall.

Somebody once did a nice but normal table setting at Macy's. Everything about it was correct. It had a table and chairs and knives and forks and spoons and cups and saucers. The cups even had coffee in them. When it was done, it was good. But it was boring. The visual merchandiser decided to take a risk. For two days and nights he stapled and glued and rigged and wired and then hung the whole thing sideways in midair. What had been acceptable, instantly became great, and customers stopped and stared and bought the merchandise.

Once before Christmas, in the same store, some major monumental vice president made his annual pre-Christmas tour of the Christmas shops. He made his Royal Progress from one end of the floor to the other, noting that each shop was good. Dozens of display people and merchants followed him at a respectful distance, listening to every vice-presidential word.

When he came to the end, he turned to the crowd and said, "It is good. Everything is fine." Relief waved through the crowd. But he was not finished. He then said an amazing thing. He said, "Do it better." This was a great thing to say, and it had a great effect. The people who had worked so hard to be accurate immediately got the message. They got angry, enthusiastic, energized. They swept across the floor, doing it again, and this time their only option was to take risks. They pushed the entire floor from adequacy into excellence. It became inspired.

Right now, risk is a good word. The time is right, since we have too many stores, and too much sameness and apathy to compound the felony.

Risk is taking the risk of becoming the cleverest word since "excellence" and could, like excellence, lose all its meaning. Walter B. Wriston just published a book called *Risk and Other Four Letter Words*. It's good. So is the whole idea. Hurry, hurry, before it's too cute.

The risk is the whole person. It is not just your work, it is you. It's a shame that more of us do not practice risk-taking, because to take a risk is to risk living fully.

IN NOBODY WE TRUST

NOVEMBER, 1987

HERE'S THE MOST CONSTRUCTIVE marketing idea for 1988: Restore the customer's confidence. Every dollar and every coin a customer brings into your store is inscribed "In God We Trust." But today, the customer knows you are not God. Today, we trust in nobody. This may not be a crime against humanity, but it sure is bad for business.

We don't trust baseball players. Major Leaguers are often caught filing down balls with emery boards and sandpaper in their mitts.

We don't trust car manufacturers. Chrysler admitted to setting odometers back to zero after using the cars for testing, then selling them, as unused.

We don't trust airlines. They're not always ready when we are, and the skies just aren't as friendly these days.

We don't trust Wall Street. Would you give your savings to Ivan Boesky?

We don't trust politicians. How do you feel about Hart, Meese, Reagan, and that lot?

We don't trust religion. Tammy Faye and Jim Bakker have now become our very own Ferdinand and Imelda Marcos. What's to stop us from worrying about every other televangelist and fund raiser using the name of God to get themselves gold bathroom fixtures?

Do retailers escape the serious charges facing evangelists, politicians, financiers, airlines, sports stars? Most retailers are not perceived as dishonest. Or are they? Do you think any customer is fooled by "50-percent-off garbage" that masquerades as a real deal? Do you think customers trust or believe in "Sale Sale Sale?"

Retailers, like everyone else, are misleading, shifty and vague. But at least the customer always has the choice of going somewhere else immediately. And although retailers may never stop price wars, they could build customer trust by building customer service—not just talking about it.

Would you trust a store? We do trust The Limited where "No sale is ever final." We trust Land's End where everything's "Guaranteed. Period." We trust Sears with its "Satisfaction guaranteed or your money back." We trust Stew Leonard's grocery store where a 6,000-lb. rock stands in the entrance way. You have to walk around it to get into the store. A cemetery stone carver inscribed the famous slogan, "Rule No. 1: The customer is always right. Rule No. 2: If the customer is wrong, re-read Rule No. 1." We trust L.L.

Bean when they say that if you request a replacement button after 23 years, they'll send you one free. We trust Nordstrom where it's actually possible to still expect—and get—good customer service.

That's a very short list. Do people trust other stores? One thing is certain, they don't trust customer service. Ask anyone in any mall. They'll probably tell you that stores are indifferent, sloppy, shiftless, boring, apathetic and all the same. They'll say the same things to describe employees—maybe with the addition of careless, rude and unenthusiastic.

Stores do not serve anybody anything. Customers are just unwelcome interruptions of accounting procedures. They're bargain-hunting pests who steal merchandise and irritate little managers and might even demand to see "an officer of the company." Poor customers! They will spend four or five depressing minutes with a person who long ago stopped working for them and now spends his declining years somewhere "upstairs" holding long, unnecessary meetings about markdowns.

A long time ago, Texaco used to advertise, "You can trust your car to the man who wears the star." And customers believed it. Today, Texaco is bringing back trust. A new Texaco ad just appeared with a twist on its memorable old slogan. The word "trust" appears in it three times: "Texaco...working to keep your trust after 84 years... Trust Texaco lubricants... Since 1965, hydraulic pump operators have trusted Texaco Brand Oils..."

Trust may be the big lip service corporate hobby horse for the next year. Some don't need to say it. Many will say it, but they won't actually do anything to deserve it. And many will do nothing, which is what they always do best. But some will realize that the time has come to restore consumer confidence in something.

We've all got our work cut out for us. The customer is in a state of general disinterest, depression and very low expectations. The smart retailers will start today, no matter how long it takes, no matter how extremely difficult it's going to be to get customers back and interested.

If government, religion, the airlines, hotels, the space program, nuclear power plants, Wall street, ad infinitum need to clean up their messes, then surely little old retail must do it too.

Or consider the alternative—"In God We Trust," but not much else.

DRESSING FOR STRESS

JULY 1988

WE USED TO DRESS for success. Now we dress for stress. If you live in the late eighties, you live with stress. The caring nineties haven't kicked in yet. The biggest problem facing all of us who work right now is stress—experiencing it, facing it, and learning to deal with it.

• *Newsweek* cover story, "Stress On the Job" (April 25, 1988): "Our jobs are killing us... Twenty-five years ago we had a chance to bounce back before another crisis. Today we have chronic, unremitting stress. Our bodies have eroded... It's hurting morale and the bottom line."

• *Business Week*, "Stress: The Test Americans Are Failing" (April 8, 1988): The article claims that stress is the most costly and unattended problem in American business today. "When J.C. Penney announced it was moving its headquarters from New York City to Plano, Texas, employees were so upset that the company expanded its counseling staff from one to 12." Stress-related problems currently cost $150 billion annually in health insurance and disability claims.

• *Wall Street Journal*, "Biggest Test for 1988: Surviving Stress" (February 1, 1988): "Stress is reaching such unhealthy levels at a growing number of companies that productivity and loyalty to the company suffer."

• *USA Today* (April 25, 1988): "If you doubt that stress affects you, think again. It affects everyone."

• NBC Television, "Stressed to Kill" (April 25, 1988): "Severe stress, on the rise in America, can be fatal."

Imagine how department stores will love this stress stuff. They can all sell "Dresses for Stress." Lord & Taylor can run one of its pithy dress ads—"Say yes to stress"—with cocktail stresses, daytime stressing, moderate and better stress, not to mention (although not at L&T) budget stresses. And we all know about designer stresses; we rely on *Women's Wear Daily* to update us. Imagine taking an assistant stress buyer to lunch.

Test yourself and see if you have any of the following symptoms: intestinal distress, rapid pulse, frequent illness, insomnia, persistent fatigue, irritability, nail biting, lack of concentration, increased use of alcohol or drugs, hunger for sweets, takeover jitters. Stress is the biggest—just coming to light—problem in American business. And retailers are certainly worse than others when you consider the seismic shenanigans going on in our stores.

You don't have to work for Penney's, Federated, Allied or Macy's to get the news. Anyone half-aware is aware of suffering from stress—lots of it, and it's not imaginary. Probably never before has retailing been so besieged with the kind of change that drives people nuts. Add to that the fact that retailers are notably uncertain in the first place, and you have the vision of a massive home-like institution for deranged retailers, with a waiting list to get in.

Omens are coming fast in the visual merchandising field. Every day one hears that entire visual departments have suddenly been eliminated. Company images are changing so rapidly that a creative person doesn't have any clear direction on what to do in the first place. The gigantic mergers have created an epidemic of sameness from store to store that surpasses anything we've seen before.

Everyone lives in fear of being fired. And you don't need to be neurotic to feel paranoid these days. Every time the phone rings, you could have just been merged, acquired, terminated, phased out, golden-parachuted or just plain fired. Imagine coming to work next week to discover that you do not work there. This will not stretch your imagination. You could list 20 associates who became ex-associates within the last three months. If people earning $800,000 per year were fired last week, how essential do you feel you are going to be when the raiders turn the lights on in your room?

What can you do about stress? The best idea, although not everyone can afford it, is to move to the Bel-Air Hotel in Beverly Hills. It is safe to say there is no stress ever at the Bel-Air—if you can get past paying for it. If Robert Campeau wanted to relieve his stress, he would move there immediately. A rapid calculation shows that a single room for a year, no meals or tips, would run about $485,000. So what else can you do?

• Maintain a sense of humor. Laughter is good for your health.

• Meditate. You can do this in meetings with your latest CEO who won't last anyway, so it doesn't matter what is said.

• Get a massage. This works, but it doesn't cure you.

• Exercise regularly. You'll look great on the beach, and you'll feel good.

• Eat more sensibly. You are what you eat. It is still a shock to watch people eat what they get on the airplane.

• Limit intake of alcohol and caffeine and other less-legal methods of elevating the spirit. Drugs are great until you crash.

• Take refuge in family and friends. Couch potatoes know that's what VCR's are for.

• Delegate responsibility. Don't just get stress—give it.

• Stand up to the boss. But hurry. The boss is on the way out and so are you.

• Take charge of your life. Elizabeth Taylor did. So can you. It is harder to get a reservation at the Betty Ford Clinic than at the Rainbow Room, but you feel better when you get out.

• Quit. Cut your losses. Move to Petaluma and grow sunflowers.

In a very famous and gruesome case history, a certain island in the Chesapeake Bay was inhabited by a species of deer that found itself getting more and more crowded and more and more stressed as the population increased. Suddenly, one half of the population of deer died. The only explanation for this is some awesome safety mechanism in nature came to the rescue of the deer by killing half of them. I certainly hope this doesn't happen to retailers.

THE FAX OF LIFE

MARCH 1989

I DON'T HAVE A FAX machine. I don't even *want* a fax machine. I sit here banging away on a typewriter. It's not even a word processor—although it is electric. It can perform a dozen things I don't want it to do. I used to have an even better typewriter. It was a real finger-banger that produced huge, grade-school letters. I loved it, but it finally broke down, and they don't make them anymore.

I suppose I've missed out on a lot of things. I never had an electric peanut-butter maker, a popcorn popper, a yogurt maker, an electric pants presser or a solar-operated tie rack. I'm not a gold card carrying member of The Sharper Image. I admire the way they run their business, and I'm sorry that fax machines have cut into their success. But Fed Ex-ing, like faxing, gives people another excuse for not doing things on time.

People used to say, "Have a nice day." Now they just say, "I'll fax it to you." Fax is already practiced by 45 million Americans, although we're way behind the Japanese. More than half of Japanese telephone calls from Japan to the United States are to fax machines. And who says the fax is just high-tech? Peter Max is faxing art. Peter Max is very high-touch. Isn't it? Well, anyway, it gave him another new career.

Listeners send WNEW-FM faxed song requests 24 hours a day. Bloomingdale's advertises "Fax Fashion"—whatever that is. The cover of

New York magazine trumpets "Fax Mania." An expedition climbing Mt. Everest sent back progress reports by fax. Donald Trump has fax machines in his car and on his boat.

I'm probably the only person in the world without a fax machine. I know I'm not keeping up. I'm just like the railroads, which didn't look up to notice that the sky was full of airplanes. I know that David Sarnoff was wrong, wrong when asked about the future of television. (He replied, "Television is a scientific and technological impossibility.")

Each day, the postman brings me less and less real mail. The Fed Ex bills mount up. My correspondence dwindles. My phone rings less and less. I am a faxless human being. I get embarrassed because people are always telling me they're about to fax me, and I have to tell them not to. "Retrograde." They shout: "You, who talk about change! Faxless? You're not saving time!" I haven't even got time to get a fax machine to save time.

I want to register a complaint. In ancient times—pre-fax—people did things in a timely manner, getting their work done through good planning and careful communications. Sometimes in an emergency they used special delivery, which cost a dollar extra. Then came Federal Express, which costs $14 a letter instead of 25 cents. All pre-fax trash! Now nobody has to do anything on time. Everything can be an emergency. All you need to do is mosey over to the fax at the very last second and do it. And you get more free time!

Here I am, as reclusive as an organist in Wyoming, and I just love to bother to do things "live." I still bother to actually go to trade shows and conferences, which means I undertake fax-less journeys wrapped up in parkas and boots. I suffer every inadequate airport and eat the toxic food. Then I ride in filthy taxis into real downtowns, check into duplicative faxed hotels, unpack, and get ready to experience life in person. I enter ballrooms and showrooms hoping for ideas and inspiration and to see and hear imaginative people presenting ideas to an audience in person—even though it could all be faxed instead.

For those who bother to make real journeys, our experiences are real—not copies. I like live performances better than television; real musical instruments that require sawing, plucking and blowing more than synthesizers; pictures more than computer graphics; and mashed potatoes better than micro-nuked Tater Tots. Nothing can replace the human voice unamplified, the handwritten valentine, or the joy of getting things done with self-assurance—and on time.

Imagine the future. Typists will apply for disability. Messengers will join the unemployed. Postmen will deliver nothing except Mother's Day cards to fax-less old ladies. We'll buy our merchandise from television. We'll never leave home. All of life's transactions will be faxed in and out of airless office environments. There will be no lunches, no meetings, no parties, no dates and no love affairs. Imagine hearing, "The check is in the fax." Imagine singing, "I'm going to sit right down and fax myself a letter." You'll need a fax from your doctor is you miss a day of school. We will swell along in high electronic bliss, faxed out of human interchange.

While I sit here longing for the horse-and-buggy days of typewriters and telephones, I know that if I had a fax I'd have much more time. I know that as each new electric miracle occurs, I will have less and less to do. And finally I will be free to lead a facsimile life. But I don't want a facsimile life.

Oh, maybe I'll get a fax machine. Maybe I won't. If I do, I hope I'll use the time I earn to better use my life.

DON'T WORRY, BE HAPPY

MAY 1989

BOBBY McFERRIN'S simple-minded lyric, "Don't worry, be happy," is the best example of wish-fulfillment we've had in a long time. It's such a nice sounding little idea—as if that's all there is to changing the world. And he's so appealing that this song wins every award in the music business.

We can learn a lot from stores that aren't worrying. They aren't worrying at Sock Shop International or The Gap or Land's End or Stew Leonard's or the Disney stores. They're too busy working to worry. Visual presentation is not on hold whenever you find successful retailing.

There's plenty of worrying going on, though, if you work at Zayre's or Sears or any number of department stores. And in many stores, visual presentation seems to be on hold. A day trip throughout New York City shows less that's new or imaginative than at any time in recent years. A car tour of Los Angeles, ordinarily a gold mine of novelty and innovation, shows that Melrose Avenue is following Columbus Avenue into boredom, and it's "The Day The Earth Stood Still" in many shopping centers. San Francisco has a walloping new Nordstrom, and very little else that's new or even changing.

The list of stores not to be missed in Chicago has not had to be reprinted in a year, except for Bloomingdale's.

So much visual direction has always come from the fashion industry, but that industry is enduring its longest standstill in many years. People are not buying clothes because they are confused, bored and shocked by prices. So the stores stand still in presenting merchandise that does not move. All is not well in the fashion halls of America.

People are buying electronics. (Just wait until high-definition TV; your fax machine will be a memory.) People are traveling and going on cruises and paying $7 to get lost in "The Wooz," a Japanese-invented labyrinth in "Vacaville," California. People are skiing and scuba diving, and now, suddenly, snowboarding. All these activities cost money, and customers are spending plenty. So look there for visual inspiration.

It's time to change the way we look for ideas, and the places we look for them. Try going to a billiard parlor or the hot new restaurants for inspiration. You'll come out with far, far more than you will from visiting spring fashion openings and mall promotions. Visual inspiration is thriving on MTV, in the design of new hotels, and on radical TV commercials.

A clue to the roots of transferred inspiration can be found, once again, at Disney. The company didn't look at current retail design to find out how to put together its new stores. Disney looked into its own entertainment business for visual ignition and customer service. It simply moved its great success with entertainment into a great new success in stores.

Compare smiles, for instance. The old seventies smile reappeared very suddenly at Acid House, a London rock joint that combines the influence of drugs with the last throes of fashion. The smile reappears as an ironic comment on our current worldwide lack of "smilingness." Bloomingdale's put in a now-you-see-it, now-you-don't swing shop to catch the smile.

Then along comes good old wildly successful Walt Disney Enterprises, putting in shops selling happiness all over the map, complete with bright blue carpets into which are woven dozens and dozens of non-sarcastic smiles. It makes you smile. Your feet follow the smiles as they carry you from wish to wish and on to the cash register.

So, which smile would you study for inspiration in visual presentation as you plot your survival for 1989? You have this odd choice: the ten-minute smile of a drugfest or the everlasting smiles of substantial Walt Disney.

There is another great smile abroad in the world. It is the logo of the Darling Point shopping center development in Sydney, Australia. The smile smiles toothily out of cards, flags and shopping bags. People all over Sydney are carrying toothy grins from Darling Point. It's the cheeriest logo in years, and you want to believe in it.

Suddenly the world is full of odd, assorted smiles, ranging from the uncertain to the genuine. How can you put this to work in your work? Start off in front of the mirror in the morning. Simple a this may sound, you may be surprised in what you actually look like before you present your face (or your ideas) to the waiting world.

There is more to be done in visual presentation than ever before, and fewer people are doing it less happily. This bound to affect your work. Your work will affect customers. Customers will affect sales. And you see the current results.

There is a corny slogan over the employee entrance to Stew Leonard's dairy store in Norwalk, Connecticut. It says, "If you see someone without a smile, give them one of yours!" This implies that you have one to give away. Check your mirror. If you are not smiling, quit this afternoon and get a different job.

If you are not happy with what you're doing, you won't be able to communicate it to your audience, and you won't be very good at it. If you are happy, then you can move on to cause someone else—and even some customers— to flash a bright, sincere smile right back at you.

TELEPHONE VICTIMS

AUGUST 1989

TELEPHONES were invented so that people could communicate. Today they're used for abuse instead of communication.

There are various kinds of telephone abuse practiced by pretensious people. The most frequent is putting you "on hold." By now, you may spend as much as 20 percent of your day on hold. And who has dared to decide that I must listen to Def Leppard or "Claire de Lune" while I sit there aging and waiting?

There is a hotel chain that instructed its operators to say, whenever they gave you the extension you asked for, "It is a pleasure to connect you." Bonwit Teller tried something like that once. Every person answering a phone at Bonwit was required to say, "Bonwit Teller. Have a nice day." But because most of those people worked in New York where the phones were busy all the time and people tended to be unpleasant, it usually came out as a garbled hostile snarl—"Bonwitellerhaveaniceday—hold!"

I hate the messages that companies use before condemning me to "hold." "All of our agents are busy serving other customers. At the first available moment, we will be here to provide you with the same outstanding customer service we are currently providing someone else." Nobody believes that for one second.

If I have to be on hold, why doesn't someone just tell me and then shut up so I can get on with my filing or finishing my new novel. Can the music.

Phone mail is the latest execu-toy. It's not exactly like hold, but it starts the same way—with a great big "no" the minute your call is answered. For as much as five minutes you have to absorb a crash course in button-pushing from the synthetic computer-generated voice which always sounds drugged. Listen closely. If, God forbid, you forget which button to push or go past it to the next set of instructions, you've got to start all over again—possibly long distance—and psych yourself up to punch exactly what it tells you to punch exactly when you're told to punch the next time. In any case, even if you graduate with honors, all you've really done is leave a message on a machine, and you still haven't spoken to anyone.

Metro-North, the railroad company that provides commuter service between Manhattan and the suburbs north of New York City, uses one of those automated attendants. The voice tells you to press the first four letters of the rail line you want to take. But maybe you don't know that there is a Harlem division and a New Haven Line. It tells you to press the first four letters of the station you want to go to. Maybe you want to go to Stamford, but you'd go to Greenwich if there was an earlier train.

Maybe you're calling Sears, which also uses those systems in its New York area stores, and you want to find out about vacuum cleaner bags. Is it hardware ("press four") or appliances and home furnishings ("press five")? By the time you reason it out in your mind, the voice is telling you about the credit department and catalog pickup. It's a technical fix to a problem of relationships with customers. This system actually makes it more difficult to do business.

The answering machine has turned the telephone into entertainment. The curious sentence, "We are unable to come to the phone right now," has become our new pledge of allegiance. What does it mean? That you have been hit by a truck and are at this moment being treated for skull fracture in the emergency room at Bellevue?

I have a friend who wins the interruptive-cuteness award for giving a different irritating musical history fact every day. "Hi, this is George Crutcher's machine. On this date in Paris in 1752, Christoff Willibald Von Gluck premiered his opera *Iphigenia in Tauride*. I'm not able to answer your message right now..."

One day I called a very concise friend of mine, and her machine said, "Leave a message." I thought that was just great, so I tried it. Within three days, 11 people told me I was being rude. Now I record, "This is Peter Glen's machine. Tell us as much as you can, and we will call you right back." I always get lots of information from people that way—and I always call back.

If you are so fortunate as to ever reach a living person, you will be abused in the form of insults to your intelligence. "I'll see if he's in" drives me crazy. Doesn't he or she know if he's in or not? You get the feeling that this secretary is going to put on a backpack and a pair of hiking boots and get out a compass, call out the dogs and sled, and go and find this individual down in the cafeteria. It think it's cheap. It's not good service.

There also has to be another way of saying, "What's this in reference to?" If I wanted to tell a stranger the results of my CAT scan, I would do so.

The worst of all telephoning sins is not returning calls. It's rude, and it's frequent, and it's inexcusable. It is a cheap, fake way of acting powerful. It means somebody didn't answer your message because they think you're not important. It happens every day. Calvin Klein is so good at this, that it got into a story in *The Wall Street Journal* (April 12, 1989). Deborah Burns, the new president of the company that owns Calvin Klein Cosmetics, was trying to get in touch with Calvin Klein himself. According to *The Wall Street Journal*, "It took Ms. Burns ten weeks to get her first appointment with the designer (Calvin Klein). Mr. Klein's business manager ... didn't return her calls. Finally she got her foot in the door by inviting Mr. Klein's assistant Kelly Rector (now his wife) to lunch."

Calvin Klein's attitude and that of his organization are typical of the constant need for insecure people to demonstrate their power. It is especially typical of the fashion industry, a gang not known for decency or sincerity on *any* subject.

After ten weeks of this ridiculous nonsense, the article continued, "Ms. Burns won the designer's confidence by telling him she needed his help. 'She always says the right thing to everyone,' Mr. Klein gushes. 'She's really an extraordinary woman.' "

Can you believe that? Calvin Klein has decided that Deborah Burns is "an extraordinary woman" because she doesn't mind begging, then having the whole squalid dialogue publicized.

I once made 37 calls to Ralph Lauren's offices—not even to Ralph himself—trying to enlist their help for an AIDS benefit. I wouldn't have put up with the humiliation for any other reason.

Here's the best-ever story about getting someone to talk to you. A friend of mine is a wardrobe designer for a major soap opera. Every store in New York City loans clothes in exchange for credit on the show. Only one of New York's top-snot stores wouldn't even answer her calls. She wanted to borrow clothes from that retailer, but mainly she was offended that she could not get an answer from the owner—a one-time A&S buyer who now runs a small empire of very fine clothing stores.

After she had left 27 unanswered messages, she finally got angry. She sent this world-famous, no-phone-answering fashion person a box containing $275 worth of flawless red roses and a note. The note said: "Dear Madame, I have called you 27 times. You have not called back, not even to say 'no.' Enjoy the roses. Next time I'm sending a bomb."

Madame called back within ten minutes. And she said "Yes," by the way. I guess she was motivated.

Try calling Stew Leonard's grocery store sometime. I did. Most supermarkets don't even have a listed number. The don't want to hear from you. I dialed the number of the store, and a voice said, "Stew Leonard's. This is Jodie" (real person, real name). I asked if I could talk to Stew, Jr. Jodie said, "Sure." And within ten seconds I was talking to Stew Leonard.

That's communication—and great customer service.

RESOLUTIONS FOR THE NEW REALITIES

MARCH 1991

FOR THOSE OF US who always see danger in a crisis, this is clearly a threatening time. But for those who find opportunity in every turning point, this will be a time of combat, change and growth.

The retail business is always fragile, dependent on the current climate. And right now, our work is all uncertainty. Our customers have departed from the easy days of idle shopping because they're facing other issues. Half the stores in America will close within ten years. Half the people working there will have to find employment somewhere else. These are not imaginings; they are the new realities of retail life. And they'll also affect our suppliers and their suppliers, too—all the way back to the sheep who supply the wool to make the yarn that converts to the cloth that designers sell and deliver into the hands of people like you who hope to sell to your customers.

I believe that anything can be improved, no matter how dire the circumstances. It is our privilege—indeed, it is our responsibility—to do the best we can. And that is even our highest response to life.

We must improve if we wish to continue to be employed. These times require the clearest thinking and the strongest resolutions. We must begin to form the changes in thought and action that face us all. Here are ten resolutions for the difficult days ahead:

1. We must resolve to stop creating bad news. This year, the media did more than its share to murder the retail business. So did the retail business itself, with its loudest mouths shouting dire predictions and premature announcements of disaster. We must remember that optimism is contagious, too, and a good attitude can make the best of it.

2. We must resolve to study the new realities of marketing until we understand the times. Customers face the new realities by shifting quickly from Grey Poupon to good old French's, and they're satisfied. Or they march out of all the old department stores and into the Gap, and they're satisfied. We must keep up with customers, derive our new ideas and forge new creativities based on understanding what is going on. Marketing people are, above all, people of their times, and these are the times that keep them alive.

3. We must resolve to restore our merchants to merchandising, pulling them out of the banks and the credit meetings and putting them back into the stores where the only truth resides. Mark Twain said, "The public is the only critic whose opinion matters at all."

4. We must resolve to practice quality until we achieve it. We cannot survive too many days like the one in which President Bush gave the Malcolm Baldridge Quality Award to Cadillac in the morning, then in the afternoon General Motors recalled 580,000 of those automobiles.

5. We must resolve to expect the worst of everything as fervently as possible, until we check and double-check and check again and again. This would save us from familiar humiliations like the unchecked $1.7 billion Hubble Telescope embarrassment, and could restore our faith in NASA and the future of our space program.

6. We who value creative freedom must resolve to battle censorship and fight for the right which is given to us by the Constitution. Senator Jesse Helms and others like him have decided to interrupt democracy and redefine it for us. Now we must fight for funding and for freedom.

7. We must resolve to love our work. Those who don't are self-destructive. Not loving what you do is a lot like not loving yourself, and that is excess baggage. In these times, people are fortunate just to have a job and the sooner they stop complaining, the sooner they can devote their energy to improvement.

8. We must resolve to find new people to admire. We could find a few who tell the truth instead of lying—Milli Vanilli, Pete Rose, Marion Barry. We could rise above greed by abandoning our emulations of Donald Trump, Michael Milken, Charles Keating and Leona Helmsley. We could aim our brains a little higher than Roseanne Barr and the underachieving Simpsons. Surely we could do better, and surely we must.

9. We must resolve to fight in the combat zones right here in America instead of everywhere else. We are now the 23rd most literate country in the world. We have a sick economy with worried citizens, pollution, drugs, homelessness, disease.... Anyone younger than 22 has never lived to see us do great things. It has been 23 years since we landed a man on the moon. We need to fight here at home before we bleed to save the rest of the world.

10. We must resolve to value our health enough to honor it. Health is a gift which has been granted to us, and we are responsible for giving it love and maintenance. It is irresponsible not to eat well, exercise and practice the health of the mind before engaging the body in any of these improvements— or any of your own.

In its 1990 review-of-the-year editorial, *Life* magazine concluded with the words: "We must resolve to do better." Oh, how I agree. I think that's just what we need to do—and quickly.

We, as individuals, must resolve to do better regardless of our jobs, the economy, the assortment of wars, pollution, illiteracy, homelessness, greed, debt and lack of focus. We must do the best we can. If bad times bring out the best in people, these times are going to be spectacular.

In an interview shortly before his death, Sir Laurence Olivier was asked to explain what made him the world's greatest living actor. Sir Laurence replied, "One does the best one can. One cannot do more. One must not do less." We are not doing the best we can.

Sometimes we feel that salvation is beyond our control, that we are too insignificant to make a difference. And so we do not do the best we can. But I agree with *Life* magazine—Let us resolve to do better. We must not do less. And we must do it gladly.

REALITY MARKETING—WHAT IS IT?

APRIL 1991

Part I:

AS THE CLEANING CREWS at stores worked late mopping up after this year's Christmas bloodbath, a great many retailers already knew that is wasn't Santa Claus who had visited them. It was, instead, something called reality.

A new reality has come to stay for this season and perhaps for many seasons to come. Some retailers even realize that the world as they had previously known it has changed fundamentally—and forever. What this means is that most retailers will have to change themselves to adapt to the new reality or face the alternative of an even more rapid decline. Many will not survive.

We do not like this. For years we have earned a hefty living selling fantasy. And so we sit, moribund, hoping that recession won't become depression. Our reactions are all too pale. We are not facing the tiger, and the tiger is staring us right in the face.

The customer's mind is no longer in the mall. It's elsewhere. People buy things when they feel good about themselves. They don't enjoy shopping when they're depressed. And right now we don't feel good about ourselves or our diminished power to affect the world in which we live. We cannot really love the mess we have made of the planet.

We like to think of ourselves as a peaceful nation, but we've been a nation engaged in yet another war. And we've accomplished little or nothing recently in our ongoing wars against crime, drugs, AIDS, homelessness, illiteracy and pollution.

Falling Stars

It's been so long since we've heard good news. Any evening you tune into the news you can be quite certain that none of it will be very good. Of course there are, no doubt, examples of individual happiness here and there. And sometimes the teams we like win football games. And every now and then, somebody does something that rouses our admiration. But one does not reach for the morning paper or turn on the television expecting to be gladdened.

A newscaster solemnly announces that the last great thing America did was to go to the moon. That was more than a generation ago. Our heroes have gone to jail. Even our icons are showing cracks.

This is reality—the new reality. And it's likely to stay this way, even worsen, until we improve our expectations.

A man from Minneapolis called in to me during a television talk show and proclaimed, "You expect too much!" This struck me as the most grotesque assessment of our current situation that I've heard in a recent tour of 21 cities! What can we possibly hope to expect in the future when we no longer expect much from ourselves?

Somehow we must each find the means to rekindle our former belief that it's not too much to expect a better quality of life in the future for ourselves, for our children, and for everything else that's still alive on this tiny planet we all share.

We're misusing words like "recession." This new current reality isn't temporary! This isn't just another down year. We love to believe that it all will be over soon, that this too shall pass, and that soon everything will be all right again—the same as it was before.

Increasingly, it seems we do things wrongly or badly. Now, more and more of us cannot read or write—or dance for joy. Instead, we are frightened and defensive every day we spend in any large city.

We tell ourselves: "Oh, it's not that bad. It could always be worse." There's always something or somebody worse off. This is, after all, America, and how could anything go seriously wrong in a place where so much has always gone right? Things can't be seriously wrong. This must just be indigestion after too much dinner.

Yes, we've been complacent for the last 20 years and no, we can't read as well as we once could. And yes, there isn't a city in the country where you feel secure on the streets after dark and no, we haven't much clean air left to breathe. And no, we don't seem to have much money lately and yes, more people are out of jobs. And no, we don't seem to do anything as well as we used to anymore. But what's any of that compared to, say, Afghanistan where they don't even have a mall to go out to?

Reality Customers

Our customers' minds are distracted as never before, dealing with depression, stress, keeping their jobs, increasing crime, ignorance and indifference. Why should it be surprising to us that all of this just happens to coincide with a domestic crisis in the quality of merchandise and services and prices of goods at which customers laugh or gasp, but, either way, leave the store just the same?

Customers have developed an immunity to the frantic fake sales that retailers have too long used as life support systems for a failing industry. The customer no longer responds adequately to "Sale! Sale!! Sale!!!" The new reality is that the customer is saying, "Goodbye!" And it's time for us to say goodbye to the luxurious frivolities of the aren't-we-clever self-appreciation societies that dreamed up vast exaggerations in order to win advertising awards.

Say goodbye to the silly days of the famous 30-second Apple Computer Super Bowl Commercial that cost $10 million and ran just once—but enough to win a dozen advertising awards. Those days are over.

Say goodbye to the asininities of Infinity automobile advertising. Jay Leno summed it up pretty well for us all when he said, "Sales of rocks and trees are up 300 percent."

Customers are saying hello again to well established and excellent products like Kleenex, Ivory Soap, Scotch Tape, Timex and Keds. Sales of Keds have moved up from $150 million to over $200 million in just one year. Shoe designers are growing pale. They quake as they attempt to bring out cheaper and even more exaggerated running shoes.

The new reality is that customers are being realistic. And those reality customers are seeking good, realistic products for realistic times. We're hunkering down.

Reality customers are the new economic revolutionaries. They're through responding to sales and hype and distraction. They're through getting less quality and no service for their money. Reality customers are determined that they are not going to take it anymore! Many are increasingly willing to stand their ground, speak up and talk back.

Now that business owners are no longer making money, customers are becoming more successful in getting management's attention. And now management is beginning to listen and respond!

The time has arrived for reality marketing. Reality marketing is marketing that deals with reality the way customers perceive it. Reality marketing is giving customers exactly what they want and how they want it and getting paid to do it—just that way.

Stores and all their associated backup systems need to completely abandon their own private versions of reality and come out onto the sales floor to meet their remaining customers on common ground.

Reality to the customer isn't your idea of incredible markdowns or this week's lowest-prices-ever sale. Reality to the customer is walking out of your store one last time and never coming back!

Reality has caused customers to realize that life is possible without shopping, without acquiring needless merchandise, without being insulted by totally uninformed lip service, without ludicrous prices, and without experiencing a meaningless and humiliating human interchange. That's reality to the customer!

Half-price designer racks full of clothing are no longer the distraction that they once were. Life lived as a fantasy is giving way to a more responsible reality, and customers are the first to have gotten the message. Since they also have the money, the combination means that tuning into customers will become a necessity of survival.

Reality customers have changed their priorities about life. They have evolved from creatures born to shop to caring individuals who are concerned about the quality of their lives, their neighborhoods, their country and their planet.

Reality customers want to purchase activities with their money, not just merchandise. They want to do more things like writing poems in a meadow or walking five miles. It doesn't always cost a lot of money to do these things. Growing has always been free. And it doesn't always matter what you wear while doing it. You *do* need courage and curiosity and imagination, but not much in the way of merchandise.

Matters of the heart don't need to be expensive.

Reality Service

In this country where our economy is no longer based on manufacturing but on service, there is appallingly little service and most of that is only lip service. Reality customers are tired of talk.

The only thing that will truly save us is to turn our full attention immediately to real customer service. This subject must surely be confronted—

realistically—starting now. Those few companies that provide genuinely good service to their customers are all currently the new heroes because they are seen to be capable of surviving tough times.

Business owners have always looked at the few good service believers with interest and even amazement. But historically, they haven't acted. They just never seem to get the message that there is a connection between good service and making money. Anyone hoping to stay in business can no longer ignore the fact that the competitive differences in business are all a matter of genuine service.

The only real service the customer wants is the kind of service that's done right in the first place. No screw-ups. No apologies. And customers are beginning to fight to get that service. The use of 800 numbers for complaints has doubled in just the last year as customers discover that their dissatisfaction is finally a concern to the people who want more of their money.

People are increasingly suing for almost any reason at all these days, but particularly for malpractice. One recent cartoon showed a receptionist telling a patient, "I'm sorry, Tuesdays and Thursdays the doctor is in court."

Everybody says they guarantee everything. But when you boil it down, most of the promises are about how nice they're going to be to you after they screw up. Banks, for example, have started giving out apology money when they've made you wait in line too long. We've come to the point of perfecting our apologies rather than our products and service.

The new reality will be that customers will only spend money where they actually get the products or services that are for sale. If not, those customers are going to "walk."

Reality is the new reality. And those of us who work in retailing are going to have to learn reality marketing fast in order to survive. Retailing is about to become much simpler. There will be less of it, and what is left will be better. Superfluous stores will close down soon. The stores that survive will improve. They will enable customers to get their shopping done quickly and get out so they can go on and do the things they care much more about.

There will be successful reality retailers, and you can study them today. They include The Gap, Home Depot, The Limited stores, Wal-Mart, The Body Shop, Nordstrom, Toys "R" Us and a few others. They all share some important similarities. Their stores are all extremely clear about what they do—and they do it precisely, and well. Alarmingly to some, these stores do not do "designer" anything. The only "names" in these stores are brand names the customers still trust. Alarming to even more, they do very little advertising, concentrating their marketing efforts on in-store persuasion. All of these reality retailers are positioned to benefit even further from the mediocre retailers who are soon to be going out of business.

For those who turn and face the tiger squarely, the new reality will be a great and rewarding adventure.

Part II

The new reality will be especially cruel to those in the marketing field, unless they change radically—and soon. In fat times, customers respond to the optional charms of fantasy, fashion, design and sales promotion. The superfluous is readily available, and they'll indulge. Those days are over.

Ask the visual merchandising industry. Ask the advertising industry. Ask suppliers about the new reality. Ask anyone involved in selling goods to customers. Reality is hitting us all.

Perception

The problem, for the most part, is that the customer's reality and the reality of those retailers with whom they have—until recently—spent their money, are two differing sets of realities. And all who participate in this commerce (designers, visual merchandisers, manufacturers, suppliers, advertisers, accountants, et al) need to fundamentally alter their thinking and adapt as fast as possible to the current reality. If they don't, customers are going to take the money that pays all those good folks and stuff it under their mattresses.

New York magazine a few months ago asked prominent New Yorkers to describe what they thought were the city's greatest treasures. The hopes expressed by most of the responsible and visible leaders (John Kennedy Jr., Daniel Moynihan, Ed Koch, Abe Rosenthal, et cetera) dealt realistically with humanity: peace on earth, reductions in poverty, illiteracy, homelessness, drugs, crime, AIDS and a revitalized economy. But the fashion industry, when asked, spoke as it frequently does. Here are some of their thoughts regarding the treasures of New York City:

"There is no other place in the world like Balducci's. It's my favorite place to shop because it has absolutely everything."
— Paulina Porizkova
"The Macy's Thanksgiving Day Parade. I'm totally obsessed by it because it's such a totally New York and American tradition."
— Isaac Mizrahi

"The city's street happenings are uniquely New York, but have a wonderful international flair. I love the flea markets, especially the one on 26th Street, and the antique fairs on the piers."
— Donna Karan

"The New York skyline. Coming back from a glorious vacation over the Triborough Bridge at night, you see this wonderful jewel of a skyline. It's like finding a diamond in the rough. It's very exciting. Like no other city in the world."
— Mario Buatta

"My customer Mica Ertegun. She epitomizes the pure sophistication of classic New York style. Anyone who gets her hair done and wears Bill Blass to a Led Zepplin concert is a genius."
— Marc Jacobs

The fashion industry is not yet as reality minded as either its customers or our politicians. That industry is rapidly becoming a victim of its own making. The executive Director of C.F.D.A. (Council of Fashion Designers of America)—the designers' collaborative that stages massive AIDS benefits and generally raises the standard of image the fashion industry needs—recently said on the way out of the job he had held for nine years: "The earliest casualties will be in the fashion business."

Reality Designers
Designers have gotten as far as offering the public a couple of strained realities such as Donna Karan's DKNY. But that was a half-hearted effort. The public was not fooled by the new "realistic pricing" of a DKNY shirt that did, indeed, cost a couple of hundred dollars less than a Donna Karan couture shirt. But it still cost a couple of hundred dollars too much. The customer said the hell with it and with Anne Klein II and the cheaper Geoffrey Beene stuff as well.

The customer has listened to all the hype, looked at all the extremes, and evaluated all the "you-can-afford-it" nonsense and has sent a message back. The customer has said, "No."

There are, in fact, going to be fewer fantasy people everywhere. One wonders where all those luxurious extracurricular art directors and stylists and location scouts and copy editors and models and agencies and conference calls and lunches and unnecessary rehearsals and revised agendas are going to go when there's no demand for their services. This will be a realistic challenge to many of the marketing and visual types who, heretofore, have been exceedingly self-congratulatory and ever-so-slightly sneery about the tasteless rabble they proposed to educate.

Fantasy people are, by definition, unassociated with reality. But they had better make its acquaintance quickly if they want to keep their jobs. Life nowadays is a realistic matter. And if these marketers and merchandisers of dreams and wishes want to continue to be needed, they'd better do a fast study of reality and learn to like it—or they won't be doing it at all.

It's *"Arrivederci"* to the mindless extravaganzas costing millions but saying little. Who cares that we have 88 rear projection screens, lotsa noise, lotsa hype and lotsa mission statements? It's all suddenly gone. It's over. It's time to realize that the *message* is the message.

Genuine reality marketers—instead of being reviled by their customers for their designs, their manufacturing, their quality and their pricing—find their inspiration and creativity beyond themselves and, while maintaining an attitude of interest and optimism, direct it out toward the reality of their customers—the only reality that matters. Customers will respond and reward those marketers who are perceived to share even a few of the same shreds of reality hitting us all. In the meantime, due to the dearth of genuine reality designers, customers are shifting their allegiance to reality brands.

Reality Brands

USA Today announced: "Consumers of the 90s Value Bargain Brands." This headline was also true in 1949 when Timex invented the first cheap watch that was also a quality product. Timex's 1949 manifesto, "an inexpensive watch that really works," is every bit as clear, believable and valid today. That is exactly what reality customers are looking for—a fresh unhyped truthfulness. And that will resurrect customer faith in brands.

Levi's are the standard for the world of excellence in brand names. They are black marketed in Moscow and Beijing. They are as envied as Ivory Soap and Scotch Tape and Kleenex.

Reality customers trust brands more than designers. But they don't trust all brands like they used to. A headline in *The Wall Street Journal* proclaimed: "Reality of the 90s Hits Yuppie Brands." The sudden demise of yuppies has left a lot of yuppie marketers gasping for breath. We'll see frantic adjustments in the marketing of Filofax, Haagen-Dazs, poor old Perrier and BMW as well as brand resorts like Club Med and even yuppie ridiculosities like arugula.

The newest phenomenon we're seeing in reality brands is that the store itself is becoming a brand. The Gap is a brand of clothing. Victoria's Secret, L.L. Bean and Land's End are brands. Eckerd Drugs and others are making their own names into familiar brands. Customers are learning both to depend on and believe in those brands, and they're making those stores successful.

Reality Retailers

If you ask retailers about current reality, they will tell you that reality is begging banks for credit. Instead of buying lamps in Scandinavia and merchandising them to their remaining customers, retailers are busy merging and acquiring corporations. There is very little hiring going on, almost no training, lots of firing and cost cutting and pairing down, and a host of other realities that all tend to drive customers away.

Ask Macy's about the new realities or Ames or Hills or Sears or Carter Hawley Hale. Or ask Child World or B. Altman or Garfinckel's or Federated or legions of small stores suffering the current realities across the nation. Should this surprise us?

You enter the traditional department store, which is filled with Estee Lauder spritzers and enough ambience to give you hayfever. Yes, the prices are cheap, but they're all fake prices.

Everything has been marked down and down again, and then the customer can take an added 20 percent off the already greatly reduced 20 percent off the original, competitive price. But this time, the customer is sure that the store has gone mad or doesn't know what it's doing. And the customer is just plain tired of helping stores figure out how much things should cost.

I was recently quoted four different prices by four different salespeople for the same turtleneck in a Gantos at Fairlane Mall in Detroit. It was totally unclear just what the price of the item was, resulting in my distrust of the entire experience and my speedy exit from the store.

The new, rejuvenated Lerner's is an outstanding example of a reality retailer. It's a great-looking store targeting value-driven reality customers. Two things immediately have an impact on the customers' perception the moment they enter: the giant signs proclaiming realistic simplicities like "COATS! $10 down, $10 a month" (the precise message the customer is looking for); and a splendid staircase surrounding a nine-foot grand piano where a man is playing Chopin.

Lerner's has achieved all the atmosphere of the good old department stores that used to whisper the word "ambiance" combined with the current reality of recession/depression economics. Studying the reactions of customers as they sweep up the merchandise there is a most gratifying and effective lesson in reality retailing.

Another profitable sector of reality retailing is the warehouse club. Spartan, 100,000-square-foot cinder-block buildings like The Price Club are the retail industry's hottest growth area. Even rich people like Marilyn Quayle, Marlon Brando, Ernest Borgnine and Sharon Gless are among Sol Price's customers.

In October 1990, when overall retailing revenues rose 4.9 percent, most warehouse clubs posted revenue gains of 20 percent or more in stores open for at least one year. As customers do more belt tightening because of the economic downturn, warehouse clubs will benefit greatly. Total warehouse club revenue is expected to hit $22 billion this years versus $1 billion in 1983.

Reality Malls

Everybody loves a bargain whether they need it or not. A multi-millionaire business tycoon I know was recently bragging at a board meeting about the "genuine Pierre Cardin" shirt he picked up somewhere in an outlet store for $4. Factory outlet malls are thriving, as true values generally do in all hard times. In fact, many concessionaires are running bus tours to some of those bus places. Are they running bus tours to your store?

Meanwhile, the mammoth Mall of America—the direct descendant of the Ghermazian brothers' humongous West Edmonton Mall in Canada—is underway in Bloomington, Minnesota. This will present an undesiring public with the unparalleled spectacle of almost 1,000 regular, run-of-the-mall stores under one roof. Although the project is far from complete, it already seems like a hard example of an idea whose time has gone.

Reality Advertising

The current cost of producing a typical 30-second commercial is $178,000. This is becoming too unreal, or so it seems to the Campbell Soup Company. Campbell's has resumed running its excellent old commercials.

Not producing new advertising will seem an alarming and dangerous approach to some, but it does raise the question: How much better is another commercial just because it's new? If your product is a standard brand like Campbell's Soup, it doesn't depend as much on each innovative hysteria of "fashion" to change and change and change again, for better or for worse.

Nowadays people *like* familiarity. It is married to dependability, and that certainly describes Campbell's Soup and Keds and Timex watches and

Levi's. Yes, all three of the latter have new advertising campaigns, and they should. But those companies are undoubtedly asking themselves whether there is enough reality in the new ads for their customers to relate to.

Liz Claiborne's new ad campaign catches current consciousness with certainty—"Reality is the Best Fantasy of All." Done in black and white, the print ads include real people photos of real people doing ordinary things and looking good at the same time. Simple, isn't it? And even believable!

Fortunately, Liz Claiborne products have always had the reputation of being related to reality. This campaign will probably work well to make the vital selling connection between Claiborne and her customers, as will Gap's new ads—big, plain pictures of suede back packs or floral caps.

No fantasy. No designers. No mini-celebs being photographed by other mini-celebs. The merchandise is the message. Watch the new reality develop some very different kinds of advertising from the endless epic of high-budget dream sequences that customers may like when they watch *Twin Peaks*, but which they have learned to distrust when it comes to spending their money on products. And you will surely see some completely inappropriate reality marketing this year from the usual people who hitchhike on any trend, even if what they're selling is ridiculous in that context—like Hermes scarves to save the planet.

Reality advertising will be taking place more and more inside the store. A lot of the money previously devoted to advertising in the papers and on television and radio is now being spent at the point of sale instead. It's more immediate, more convincing, and some feel, more effective. In-store reality advertising isn't exactly "visual merchandising" either. It's usually graphic and informative and persuasive, and it's reaching the proportion of an avalanche as the various extravaganzas try to persuade customers to make their buying decisions right in front of the merchandise.

On the other hand, in-store marketing further clutters the landscape and adds to the confusion. It might include advertiser-sponsored newscasts, commercial loops, electronic and printed signs, signs on shopping carts, sampling and spritzing. Shoppers Video, for example, plans to mount 20 video sets in each of 4,000 supermarkets. And there is more coming, much more.

Advertising has moved into the store where the customer makes buying decisions. Some customers hate it, and some do not. The people who work in traditional print, radio and television are going out of their minds.

Reality Attitude

In spite of everything, everyone ought to be cheerful, if only because pessimism is contagious. Our work, like life itself, dies faster when it is no longer inflamed by hope and energy. And negativity drives us all the wrong way—toward abusing what opportunities there are.

Attitude can make a real difference. A great attitude won't save you if you're being run over by a truck, but a great attitude will head off a lot of other headaches before they ever start.

Too many Americans have a rotten attitude toward customers—a phenomenon not as prevalent in other countries. We don't appear to like customers, and we seldom talk to them unless we have to. We'd rather talk amongst ourselves about ourselves.

We haven't practiced "doing unto others," and those we haven't been doing unto are now deserting us because of our attitude. The importance of attitude will be realized as we come back over to the customer and willingly and honestly provide what we promise to provide. Only then will be rediscover that, in turn, customers are willing to part with their money.

We should all start by being cheerful. Being cheerful is not easy when everyone you know is sending out resumes and scaling back their personal expenditures. And it isn't easy to be cheerful when the customer has told you clearly and unmistakably that your best efforts don't mean much one way or the other because there isn't much money and there isn't much interest either.

People can always find a reason to be cheerful if they want to. You might try being cheerful if only because you still have a job. Perhaps those of us who have jobs should stop complaining about them and focus instead on doing them as best we can. The fact is, the worse things get, the more opportunity there will be for a positive attitude to be of service to everyone. Making the best of a bad situation is much better than making the worst of it.

It's time to go to work with a new disciplined frame of mind. "Heigh-ho, heigh-ho, it's off to work we go!" And add in a little "Whistle while you work," too—a healthier alternative to the usual whining one hears about how much everybody hates their jobs. Reality attitudes begin by starting to re-appreciate those jobs we all love to hate. That will be good for your business, and it will improve your mental health.

More than anything else, our own attitudes primarily determine the reality—and quality—of our lives. Adjusting our attitudes—something only *we* can do—will go a long way toward improving the business of our lives.

THE PAGEANTRY OF HOPE

SEPTEMBER 1991

AT 10 a.m. on May 31, 1991, an unusual crowd was pushing its way into Radio City Music Hall—the graduates of the Fashion Institute of Technology and their families and friends. They nearly filled the biggest theater in the world.

The event was more sincere than I had expected. I had forgotten that at moments of ritual we all become traditional again. That usually means conservative. There were a few barkers in the audience, and some of the students embellished their traditional caps and gowns with a few too many pins or shorts underneath. But nothing disruptive. The students were on their best behavior, and our future was looking bright.

The mighty Wurlitzer rolled out of the wall and thundered "Pomp and Circumstance." Hundreds of flashbulbs popped into the void as friends and families craned and searched and tried to pick out the students they loved— and those they'd probably paid for at this moment of transition.

Graduates, families and friends were cheering. But at the same time, there were nagging questions. What happens now? What good was all this sacrifice, this education, this kindling of hope in the face of reality? This group of 1,445 twenty-one-year-olds had just finished two years of thinking about buying and merchandising, fabric, clothing, styling, accessories and jewelry design, advertising and art history, displays and exhibits, production management—and life. In this instant, they were confronting their future, a future in the midst of a crippled industry and joblessness and a very troubled society.

"Nourish their Spirit," a rabbi spoke. "Guide them to the beauty of the human experience."

The first speaker attempting to provide hope was David Dinkins, mayor of New York City, the home of the decaying fashion industry. Dinkins commenced with a cloud of generalities. He pointed out that the city is a melting pot, a wonderful multi-cultural place for whites, Blacks, Asians, designers, students and the fashion industry. But he said that there were a few little problems right at the moment and then assured us that markets bounce back after recessions. He didn't say much about homelessness or bankruptcy or dysfunctional tunnels, bridges, roads, subways, services, taxes, drugs, crime, illiteracy, racial tension or the 10,000 city employees he was about to fire. He added that New Yorkers are perpetual cheerleaders.

By this time, David Dinkins was levitating. The very building we were sitting in, he said, was built at the height of another depression, in 1932. He didn't mention that it was built by the Rockefellers.

Next, Marvin Feldman, the president of F.I.T., spoke in plain, direct words. "We love you," he said to the graduates. "Graduating at a difficult time like this will make you strong. Remaining hopeful is not simple, but it is a necessity."

Eventually two graduating students took the stage. They were both direct and sentimental, giving freshness to cliches like "hope," and we were captivated. Constance Duerr acknowledged the realities of homelessness and AIDS, the state of the economy, and the decay of the educational system. But she said she knew that hope could be derived from the same realities, and that the solution could be F.I.T. She said she had found—and so could we—that social responsibility and personal fulfillment are, indeed, the same thing.

The power of hope was best captured when Tracie Coleman took the microphone and sang "One Moment in Time," the right song to distill the moment we were experiencing. It was an inspired performance. As the verses continued, one step higher each time, the singer nearly faltered with emotion. But the audience was with her, and she finished in control. When she was through, we all cheered—an affirmation that hope is possible.

We must cheer these students who care so deeply as they embark on rough seas in dangerous times. And we much cheer the education that gives them hope. We must cheer the appearance of great teachers who change lives for the better—teachers who not only know and care, but can communicate until the student actually grows. Outstanding students and teachers together are an electrifying combination that can transform dreams into reality. Education is at one time both the crisis and the hope of the fashion industry. It is the hope of all F.I.T. graduates and the hope of our future.

Education is our best hope.

CREATIVITY

OCTOBER 1991

CREATIVITY IS the continuous improvement of the soul.

Creativity is the evidence of the child still alive in every individual. When you quit playing, you're dead.

Creativity is about you. If you live creatively, you design your life instead of just surviving it. The practice of creativity enables you to live your life in your own way.

Creativity is the courage to express your mind and heart exactly as they are. You must not care about consequences or the opinions of others. Trust your own convictions, knowing that delivering your heart and mind can make things change.

Creativity translates ideas into action. Ideas are not enough, nor are intentions, nor are any of the tribes of might-have-beens.

Creativity does not stop to make excuses. Using what it's got, instead of lamenting what it's not, it continues the adventure.

Creativity does not happen to you. You must begin it, and there is no previous path or certain destination. You must go with no assurance—loving the questions and not expecting answers. Whatever your destination, creativity is the strongest way.

Creativity is the exercise that makes your spirit strong.

Creativity originates while all other actions recreate, coordinate or imitate.

Creativity is the extra ten percent that makes all the difference.

Creativity is a good rehearsal, visualizing the outcome of a project or a feeling or design soon enough and clearly enough to improve the plan before action.

Creativity is control. It changes chaos into order, calms a catalog of fears and brings the future gladly.

Creativity is a grace that has been given to everyone. If you do not use it, you abuse the gift, diminish your hopes of happiness, and cancel your chances to grow.

Creativity can lead you to yourself.

Creativity is your best gift—yourself, unselfish—therefore, a gift of love.

Creativity is the seed of hope and faith and love. These are not easy acts, nor are they automatic. But hope and faith and love can be grown, even from ashes.

Creativity can overcome calamity and arm against the pain of common days.

Creativity can charge an ordinary day with radiance and give wings to your routine.

Creativity can never be defeated. It is your spirit, and therefore, inextinguishable.

Creativity is God in action.

The following quotes are from an assignment called "Creativity is..." as related to Dr. Carole Gilmore on March 19, 1991, by each of the children in the second-grade class of Madison Simis School in Phoenix, Arizona.

Creativity is ...

... art. — Alec Rand, age 7

... something that you make that's beautiful. — Kyle Grone, age 8

... when you make something that no one else can make. — Lauren Stamatis, age 7

... something that you do one time that you can't do the same way ever again. — James Tang-Mills, age 8

... being creative by doing something that looks different. — Stacey Ashton, age 7

... making something. You add stuff to it. — Jacob Howerton, age 8

... something that you do that you think that another person would not do. — Matthew Whitehurst, age 8

... when you do something all by yourself, and you don't copy it. — Alex Gotto, age 8

... something that you make up from new ideas. — Bryan Macrie, age 7

... smart and having good ideas. — Sierra Hannum, age 8

... smart ideas. — Jennifer Oddo, age 7

... you make something up in your mind that doesn't copy someone else. — Brian Petrovich, age 8

... something that you do by imagining it. — Leslie Harris, age 8

... using your imagination and getting something new that you have never done before. — Katie Calahan, age 8

... when you imagine it. Then you build it in your mind. And then you try to build it with tools. If it works, you keep on building them and building them and building them. If you wait a day to build it, what you imagined might change. You take a piece out of your mind, look at it and build it. — Scott Castle, age 7

... you build something. — William Fox, age 8

... thinking what you do first and then doing it. — Toni Puente, age 8

... good work because you think so hard. — Betsy Palaschak, age 8

... that you do an activity. — Wayne Waite, age 8

... having or showing what you can do. — Alena Whitlock, age 8

... fun. You make pictures. — J. Reid, age 8

... drawing something real neat. — Sameer Kanabar, age 8

... when you draw something real good and then add something to on to it.
— Theresa Brindisi, age 7

... unique and different because you have to make it unusual.
— Ben Bonsall, age 8

... being creative by using materials you have never used before.
— Katie Houck, age 8

... a piece of art that is very beautiful. — Carol Globus, age 8

... using your imagination and letting it run far off in a meadow.
— Kimmy Schultz, age 8.

ARE YOU A PESSIMIST?

APRIL 1992

I WOULD LIKE you to ask yourself honestly if you think you're an optimist or a pessimist. You, like everyone you know, are predominantly one or the other. You aren't both, so which are you?

Optimists and pessimists are both very powerful. Consider the power of pessimists. They can destroy any country in the world, any economy, corporation, any store or any anything. Pessimists are often right. They say, "I'm going to fail." And they go right out and fail. And then they win accolades and awards for having been quite correct in their predictions.

The pessimists today are center stage. They're getting a lot of dazzling press and applause from other pessimists, and there are a lot of them around right now. If you're a pessimist, you're at least assured of having plenty of friends. Have you noticed that? Pessimists say, "I'm really depressed. Let's go to lunch." I want to shout at them, "Get over it. Then we'll eat." I'd rather have a snack with an optimist, than a banquet with a pessimist. Wouldn't you?

There's a wonderful woman in Albuquerque—Teresa McBride. She's a computer consultant, and she said, "If your own personal outlook is negative, then that's the outlook for your business."

We have created too much of our rotten news. I saw a headline in *USA Today* that really alarmed me. It didn't say, "Macy's is Closing," and it didn't say, "74,000 People are Fired by General Motors," and it didn't say, "Downsizing. Downsizing. Downsizing." Boy, do we get on these dumb words. Do you know what it said? "Wal-Mart Fires 1,200 People." What they forgot to say—what we forgot to make them say—is that during the same year that Wal-Mart fired 1,200 people, they hired 40,000 people.

Where is that optimistic attitude? What's wrong with being successful? Why do we allow the pessimists to pry into everybody's personal life, everybody's dirty laundry, everybody's personal nightmares and then just use all their communication skills to blast it out through the networks: "Hey, we're failing. We're failing." What kind of dignity is that?

So, don't ignore the bad news. But if you have a choice, just shut up and stick to the good news. That's a wonderful and certainly optimistic possibility.

Ken Macke, the chair of Dayton Hudson Corp., recently said that until consumer confidence rises, retail will not thrive again. That's a very interesting idea. He didn't say until the housing index goes up. He said until consumer confidence rises.

What has happened to our confidence? The consumer doesn't believe in anything. Why? Because of pessimism—an epidemic of rampant pessimism. It has nothing to do with pricing. It doesn't really have to do with unemployment. It doesn't have to do with anything.

The consumer today hates everything. The consumer is bashing Japan. The consumer is bashing stores. The consumer is even bashing the shopping experience itself. And so our stores decline, and consumers decline, and the customers get poor. The customers also get something even worse—frightened, scared! As with any child when trapped, the thing we all do is lash out and hate everything and everybody—including ourselves. But what we really need to do is choose to change our attitudes from pessimistic to optimistic.

Our major job right now is to restore consumer confidence. We need to get our remaining employees up off of their self-pitying, sloppy, pessimistic messes on the floor and suggest they announce to their few remaining customers that they're very pleased to see them. And when any budding merchants have the optimistic presumption to open stores and invite the public to come in and have a look around, they ought to lift their customers' spirits, not depress them.

It's now enormously important that we all do the best we can. That's always been a good principle, but it's not so optional anymore. Everybody has got to fight for their jobs. We all have got to pull together and fight just as we would if we were at war. Only this time, we're fighting for the kind of future that we want to create.

We are certainly a nation of pessimists when we allow a headline to proclaim: "700,000 People Will be Fired in 1992." I think that headline is awful.

What strange times! We have become a country of pessimists just at a time of unparalleled global opportunity. There is no historic precedent. Your research department can no longer tell us what they think will happen. That's why hope and optimism matter so much right now. I think that all of the effective decisions for our future and for the future of the planet and our global community are going to be made not with the brain, but with a new organ—the human heart. Let's follow our hearts into the future.

Optimists can—and must—change the world forever. What are the alternatives? It's important to have a few sort of slightly hopeful options going for you like the power of optimism. That power is certainly a flicker of hope that still burns within every heart, even after we've spent the day being assaulted all over again by the pessimistic headlines and dreadful news reports. Yes, these are rough times, but are there no shreds of hope left after which we can be optimistic? I think there are plenty, even if we don't ever read much about them anymore.

Giorgio Armani has opened a store in New York City—A/X: Armani Exchange—that has so many lines, you can't get in. There are people at the door to handle crowd control. The fact is, every Armani-made item there sells for under $100, and the place is sold out, and they're going to open 200 stores. Very exciting. Are they optimistic?

The thing is, they're there. They're alive. Which would you rather be?

Here's some good news about value, service and merchandise. Gordon Segal, president of Crate & Barrel, said, "Value, service and merchandise— you'd better be damn good in one area and competitive in the other two." What a good idea. Fortunoff's (now remember, the pessimists just reported not too long ago that the jewelry industry went totally out of business) announced plans to open a $194 million mall in the middle of Long Island, right near Macy's. And they'll have one of the their largest stores there. What, are they crazy? Is that ego left over from the Calvin Klein era of retailing? I don't think so. That's a piece of good news.

Inc. magazine carried a story about a gentleman who was opening a restaurant with a small marketing budget in an unfamiliar town. Doesn't that already sound like not a very good idea? But what he did, bless his heart, was to deliver a certificate for a free meal to every beauty salon operator in town. It seems he'd heard that what with all the talking that goes on in beauty salons, beauticians would spread his name faster than any other advertising. He was right, and he showed a profit in his first year.

This is the time for new ideas, and I think that optimism will carry the day. There's a new Sony filmless camera—an innovative and imaginative idea. It's amazing. Has Sony given up? Are they pessimistic? I don't think so.

You'll find new hope and optimistic ideas everywhere, but only if you get out and look for yourself. Yes, there's a lot going on. Maybe the earth is shaking and nations are crumbling and life is uncertain. But does that mean changes are necessarily bad? Fear not. It took powerful eruptions and many upheavals to build our most beautiful mountain ranges. They became the backbone of our continent. Where is our backbone? Is it not, even now, being forged and formed by current events and our reactions to them?

Let's no longer delay our evolution out of fear of change and the unknown, but rather focus ourselves from within our hearts and dare once again to dream a vision of a future with possibilities. In one of his books, Ken Carey said, "Decisions are not made by races, culture or nations, unless they are first made by individuals. The most destructive decision that an individual can make is to give away his or her decision-making authority."

Let's each decide, one individual at a time, that what we do does matter. It does make a difference. There was a time in the recent past when we either didn't know this, or we no longer believed it. Today we are living the results of what happens when we, as individuals, give away our decision-making authority.

One step at a time. We're not going to make a giant leap into wonderful productivity. Winston Churchill faced a lifetime of pessimists, yet he still managed to express a most optimistic thought. He said, "Never, never, never, never give up."

Let me repeat. He said, "Never, never, never, never give up."

BITCHING ABOUT YOUR BOSS

MAY 1992

HOW MUCH TIME do you spend bitching about your boss? It is the favorite pastime of multitudes of American employees. "The boss" is the fiercest and most frequent target of complaining. We devote a huge portion of our working energy to dishing and digging and general negative muttering against the management we work for. Think if all of America's bitching about the boss were suddenly changed into bright, constructive action. Then America might actually turn from contemplating its own mess and pass both Japan and Germany.

Certainly your life is made much easier if you happen to have a genuine optimist for a boss. Then all you need to do is stay and grow and there are those bosses who believe that growing is everything. Their method of management is to leave you lifted. But those bosses are as rare as great teachers. Most bosses are not like that. Your boss is your limitation. You need to know your boss in order to know what your possibilities are. Facing the truth is an expedition that calls for bravery.

Having a bad boss isn't just bad luck—it's *your* bad luck. You aren't trapped by it, though. The oddest thing about people who bitch about their bosses is that they act as if they have to take it. In fact, most complainers love complaining. Some of them wouldn't know what to talk about if they stumbled into an optimistic conversation. They have practiced whining for so long, in so much depth, and with so much energy, that their hopes have rusted. And of course "the boss" is also the most frequent reason ever given for mediocre performance. So that whining lack of action is also perfect shelter for lazy people whose opinions of themselves are low enough to allow them to stay in killing situations. After all, there are plenty of other people there to bitch with, and misery does love company.

Bitching about the boss is—for people without courage—the best excuse in the world for not growing. They would deny this up and down, but they do like it. They act the same way in their relationships. They would rather—in the words of Hamlet—"bear those ills we have than fly to others we know not of." And there are excuses: the economy; I need the job; I can't find another job; I've only got 15 years to go; It's not too bad; It pays the rent; I have no skills; I have no optimism myself; I hate myself; I have no courage.

So they stay, and it's not their fault. Their bosses have put their spirits in jail—not to mention their talent, creativity, hopes and fears, and basic need to be cared for. And still they stay, bitching about the boss, which has really become bitching about themselves. They would tell you a lie and say they have no choices.

Six-Part Action Plan

What can you do if your boss is a pessimist?

• Stop blaming your boss. It's as unproductive as blaming Japan for making the kinds of cars that people want to buy. Giving your boss credit for your own mediocrity is as boring as blaming your unhappy childhood for keeping you miserable 35 years later. It all makes great group therapy. But like most group therapy, it's a cheap feel-good that's based on sympathy and community. There isn't usually much improvement, although it passes the time entertainingly.

• Change your bitching into action. This is not easy, especially if you never practice imagining success. Your imagination is your greatest asset, and you need it to make progress. So, either change or admit that you're a pessimist at heart and you like it.

• Motivate your boss. You probably don't think you ought to have to do this, but if it hasn't happened and you don't take the initiative, you can tell right now what your future will be like. Of course, it is possible that your boss cannot be changed. You'll at least have stopped playing victim long enough to play motivator. Giving up leaves you the loser, and you probably haven't completely tested your resources. If you succeed, it may be the most creative thing you've ever done in your work. You will know the exhilaration of having improved another person and lifted yourself.

• Go beyond your boss. Yes, you could be fired. Or your boss could. This is where the fatal "maybe-I'm-better-off-bitching" paralysis sets in. But if you survive it, you may actually get what you want—although we all know how unprepared most people are for that.

• Stay where you are and propose an idea that changes everything. You may change bosses in the process or even become one, in which case you will run out of things to whine about. And you will breathe the clear, clean air of your own invention. Of course, you then take the risk that the people who now work for you are going to coffee, and suddenly you are the target of the same bitching you used to enjoy.

• If you find there is no hope, quit. Save yourself. Some divorces are the only optimistic idea, as are the ends of the many relationships if they are not continuously growing. You are always your own responsibility, and only you can purge what you do not love about yourself.

THE END OF ARROGANCE

AUGUST 1992

A COUPLE OF NIGHTS before I. Magnin started closing stores, I watched an I. Magnin buyer pushing the limits of arrogance at a fashion industry cocktail reception. She barged out of an elevator, sneered at the sight of other guests waiting in line to check their coats, cut in at the head of the line and said to the hired help behind the window: "Take my coat. I don't wait in lines. I am the I. Magnin buyer."

And lo, the obsequious ocean parted and the buyer's coat—which was, of course, fabulous—was checked in the twinkling of an eye.

I remember, too, the sight of Joseph Brooks, then president of Lord & Taylor, bellowing at a baggage porter who wasn't finding his bags fast enough at Chicago's O'Hare Airport. This may have been caused by the archetypal fear of an arrogant executive caught doing anything as menial as waiting for luggage—and in a lesser town than New York or Paris to boot.

The ogres who ran Macy's used to bark commands at suppliers, expecting instant compliance, no questions, no discussion. A negative remark of mine about Macy's was once quoted in *The Wall Street Journal*, and the man who ran Macy's instantly canceled six people's trips to Chicago (of all places) because I was to speak at a meeting there. Several years before that, the entire staff of Macy's California visual department had been forbidden (from a throne in New York) to attend anything I was involved in.

But nowadays this behavior is rare, since most of the folks who act that way are unemployed. "Reality fades merchant's dream," read *The New York Times* headline, musing about Ed Finkelstein, once CEO and chair of Macy's. You would not wish humiliating demise on any venerable institution—especially on the thousands who work there—but neither will you find anyone who would deny that the great days of Macy's were characterized by spectacular arrogance.

We still live in an age in which the chair of Woolworth's, a man who closed 900 stores in 1991, is the most overpaid retail executive in America, according to a *Forbes* computer model based on performance and productivity. Meanwhile, the most underpaid executive is the president of Wal-Mart, a company which, amongst other miracles, created 40,000 new jobs in the same year.

The arrogance of fashion designers dictating what we will wear is fading fast. These designers are talking almost entirely to themselves, and starving because of it. It no longer works. They still go to Paris where so much food is free, but they are less arrogant on the way back, stuffed into economy airplane seats. The best designers today are those who check their egos and check the streets for fashion facts, then edit and translate them into mass market terms.

Nowadays a new humility and a new humanity must come to replace the tired old marriage of success and arrogance. This new humanity will be more effective at motivating sales and profits and people. There is no doubt that great retailers are powerful people and require enormous measures of self-confidence. But now we can hope that such power will be used to lift employees and customers, instead of flattening them for the greater glory of their bosses.

What will happen after the Age of Arrogance?

We could learn a lesson from doctors, traditionally the most arrogant of all the serving professions. They seem to be changing fast. Read these five notes from grateful customers (sometimes known as patients) to Dr. Spenser P. Thornton of Nashville, who first charges them a lot of money for eyesight-improving cataract operations, and then sends each of them a flowering plant to look at during their recovery.

"Dear Dr. Thornton and Staff, I want to thank you for the lovely plant ... It really is a pleasure to walk in your office and see all of you. Everyone is always smiling and so nice and seem so glad to see you. I just love all of you."

"Dr. Thornton and Staff, Merry Christmas! I want to thank each of you for helping me regain good vision. My better vision has given me a much brighter outlook on life ... Also I'm a better driver!"

"God Bless You, Dr. Thornton ... Thanks to all of you for your patience and kindness during my recent cataract surgery."

"Thanks to each of you for your kindness to me. My dish garden is beautiful."

"I came into the hospital feeling very anxious, but those who prepared me for surgery were so capable and caring. Dr. Thornton, I put myself in your hands, knowing God and you work together. ...The dish garden is beautiful and I have a very special place for it. ...I will remember the givers."

Ed Finkelstein was quoted in the April 20 issue of *Women's Wear Daily* as saying, "Fundamentally, it's the Trinity" that's in charge of running Macy's, referring to himself and two other divinities and reiterating his intentions to stay with Macy's during its bankruptcy reorganization. A week later, on April 27, Finkelstein was forced to resign his throne. I wonder how many heartfelt thank-you notes he ever got from grateful suppliers ... or customers.

HOPE IN ACTION

MARCH 1993

HERE'S what's positive and inspiring me lately: HOPE IN ACTION.

It is both positive and inspiring to witness Bloomingdale's and Bergner's become the first new hopeful heroes bringing their stores out of bankruptcy. Their recovery is the difference between sickness and health, and with health, all things are possible. These stores put hope into action, and saved themselves.

Hope is a quality both positive and inspiring, and we have plenty of it suddenly. Now, instead of feeling sorry for ourselves, we deliver dinner to Somalia. Instead of whimpering with our President, we elect ourselves a new one. That gives us hope. We have enough hope to start rebuilding after the hurricane. We hope that the hate in Los Angeles is close enough to turn us to love instead of killing. The hurricane of AIDS seems permanent, but still we fight, we grasp at hopeful bits of news, we go forward. We have hope.

But hope is not enough.

The best use of hope is to sustain us while we transform sadness into action.

HOPE IN ACTION:

Oliviero Toscani photographs an Ohio AIDS patient five minutes before his death. He publishes it in *Vogue*, right between a hundred ads for dresses and dresses and handbags.

Crazy Shirts in Hawaii prints "I survived Hurricane Iniki" T-shirts all night and sell over 5,000 of them in the first 24 hours—all proceeds for hurricane relief.

The manager of the Home Depot store in Homestead, Florida, ignoring the practice of his competitors to gouge customers while they could, gives hope to his customers in the form of building materials, sold at Home Depot's own cost. He tells his competitors that his customers will remember this forever.

Mother Hale dies. It's been four years since she spoke to us from the stage of Carnegie Hall in "90 Minutes for Life," our industry's AIDS benefit. Mother Hale didn't know much about visual merchandising or profit and loss, but she knew about HOPE because she gave it to over 1,000 babies in her lifetime who otherwise would have surely died, but for the hope she gave them. And now her family—and thousands of those who knew here—continue her positive and inspiring work.

Mother Hale *lived* while she lived. Now she is dead—but we are not. We keep Hale House alive. The man in the Benetton AIDS photo is dead—but we are not. "Seventh on Sale" raises more money to fight AIDS than ever before, and a small store called "Under One Roof" opens in San Francisco—all proceeds to fight AIDS. Most of the babies in the dreadful photographs from Somalia are dead—but we are not. We produce Operation Hope. The Bronx high school principal (shot and killed by one of his 16-year-old students) is dead—but we are not. There are 16-year-olds rebuilding stores in downtown Los Angeles.

Sometimes it seems we have seen so much that we cannot bear so many hurricanes. So many mortal insults make it hard to be positive and inspiring. But this is our material, and we must use it.

What inspires me is the notion of moving from hope to action. Only action can lift us out of sadness. We wake instead of sleeping. We arise, because we can. We begin again. We use our abilities. We create our lives. Hope sustains us, but the action is our own.

Nietzsche wrote, "That which does not kill me makes me strong." I was shocked when I first read that, long ago, but I have changed my mind and now I believe it implicitly. It gives me hope.

SOME DO, SOME DON'T

AUGUST 1993

EARLY THIS YEAR I heard Carol Farmer giving a speech in Chicago. She was describing companies that are struggling or failing or succeeding. In the middle of her talk, she suddenly paused for a second and said something that has stayed with me all year.

"There are two kinds of companies," she said. "There are those that get it, and those that don't."

Carol Farmer was addressing an audience of retailers, and she was using retail examples. But she could just as well have been talking about cars (GM doesn't get it) or computers (IBM doesn't either). She could have been talking about network television. The three blind mice (NBC, ABC and CBS) keep right on programming as if cable had never been invented, and the networks still reigned supreme. The cable companies do get it—all 500 channels. The networks are as sadly mistaken as General Sarnoff of RCA radio was in 1940 when he was presented with TV and said, "Television is a scientific and economic impossibility." He was wrong then; they are wrong now.

Then there's the case of America and Japan. Some whole countries get it, and some don't.

Some people get it and some don't. Some live entirely in the past or in the future (worry, maybe, might-gave-been), and there are those who live in the present. Some don't get it, and some do.

I love what Carol Farmer said. It cuts right through all the explanations. Her list of companies that just don't get it, of course, included some of the biggest, like falling civilizations: IBM, General Motors and, in our own world, Sears, who fired 50,000 people, probably making history as the greatest people-catastrophe in retailing—just as Sears had once been the greatest store.

As for General Motors and IBM, both used to get it. We once said, "As goes General Motors, so goes the country." I certainly hope that isn't true anymore. And IBM was as rock-solid as Gibraltar. Old ladies cherished even three shares as they entered their lavender periods. And those three shares nowadays would be worth approximately as much as three shares of General Motors or Sears.

They just don't get it.

What is the "it" they don't get? "It" is the innovation, growth and change that comes from keeping their connection with their customers. Instead, they fail to listen, understand and respond to the changes customers want. They grow old and arrogant. They cease to use their ears and the result of this sensory deprivation is stagnation, repetition, deafness and decline.

Then there are the companies that do get it. Wal-Mart just announced the biggest warehouse ever built, 1.2 million square feet in a little, nondescript and no-doubt-cheap-real-estate town 30 miles from Phoenix. Everyone else is discussing Mexico as a potential market; but Wal-Mart is opening 100 stores right now. They get it.

Toys "R" Us certainly gets it. President Bush went all the way to Japan (during that famous trip in which he threw up at the dinner table) and one of the things he did was open a Toys "R" Us. We were treated to the memorable snapshot of a company that gets it, entering global marketing with a U.S. President who didn't.

Southwest Airlines appears to get it. They don't promise anything except what customers want most—airplanes that both leave and arrive on time. Other airlines, in various stages of bankruptcy, are trying to sell the public complicated meals, seats that now recline to heretofore unknown lengths and the idea that every individual in the company has but one desire in their hearts—to improve the condition of yours. They just don't get it. But the public does—they choose Southwest Airlines because they want to go on time and arrive on time.

And there are hotels and shopping center developers and advertisers that get and those who don't.

Within your own company, there are employees who get it and those who don't. A manager at Macy's in California used to walk around handing out personal cards to employees. He would walk into your department, hand you a card, walk on and leave you staring down at it. The card said simply, "Some do, some don't." I suppose the ones who got it understood the card, and those who didn't, didn't.

Some of you reading this article get it, and some don't. The biggest number of letters to *VM+SD* recently seem to be from people whining and complaining about the industry. And it is true they *can't* get jobs. But that doesn't mean that if they get it, they can't find a job, make a job, change fields, fix their boss, move around as if they had some semblance of control. The people who don't get it are the people who always think nothing is ever their fault. Except for their bosses, they would have been brilliant. Except for their companies, they would have been creative. Except for market conditions, they would be selling more. Except for the recession, they would be rich. If it weren't for life, they would be living more fully.

But the truth is we each work for ourselves, no matter who we work with. The truth is that traffic picks up at retail when the retailer causes the traffic to come into the store. The truth is there are enormous success stories right now.

Those companies that get it are the companies that create the future instead of waiting for it. Those bosses who get it produce by seeing more in their employees than they see in themselves (instead of waiting for the employees to bow down, thank them and live up to—but not beyond their own standards). Those who get it understand the uses of controlling their own destinies, however limited they may seem to be.

It's very important for every employee to ask themselves whether they work for a company that gets it or doesn't. Your companies, and indeed, your bosses are your ceiling. You cannot rise above them. If you work for a boss or a company that gets it, then your limitations are only your own. But if you work for a boss or company that doesn't get it, then they're putting limitations on your creativity, your ability and your future.

Here's a proposal for each reader: Imagine you are sitting on a mountain top at sunset forging a calm heart after one whole week of uninterrupted companionship with nature. On this last sunset evening, these are your questions: Does the company you work for get it or not? Do you get it or not?

Before the sun goes down, you may want to consider the alternatives. What you can do: You can wait for the economy to pick up, or your boss to die, or your company to crumble. But as long as you work for a company that doesn't get it, you aren't getting it either!

But after a week of introspection, as you sit upon the mountain top and the sun goes down, you know you are committing yourself to those who get it or those who don't. This is a decision you will make as often as the sun comes up. Decide on the subject of your whole life, whether you get it or whether you don't.

If you are one of those people who just doesn't get it, you probably won't admit it. Or even worse, you don't even know it. So it's a good idea, if you want the answer, to ask a room full of 12-year-olds who are free of any political connection to you. Ask them if you get it or not. Armed with the answer, you can decide what to do next. If you work for a company that just doesn't get it, you can stay there until it just doesn't have it, and then nobody will be there. (This can happen soon. This recession may be permanent.)

Last year in Florida, an 11-year-old boy divorced his parents in a blow for his own individual freedom. Divorce is sometimes an excellent thing. It's almost always painful, because you committed to that relationship (or that company and that boss) of your own free will. But people change and grow (or else they don't).

The world is at a crossroads today. Everything is uncertain. The future is unclear. People are tempted to compromise by maintaining bad relationships. They seem to feel that it is safer than no relationship at all. Certainly having a job is better than not having one if you are interested in eating.

But the view from the mountain should give you clear perspective, long-distance panoramas and a glimpse of you own future. It must be a future in which you are using your time instead of wasting it or passing it or killing it or spending it. And it is worth at least a week of introspection in a beautiful place and a long climb up at sunset to strengthen your courage, your resolve, your sense of your own possibilities. It's time for all of us to get it.

WHO KILLED SANTA CLAUS?

SEPTEMBER 1993

IN A REMARKABLE FEAT of prestidigitation, *The Wall Street Journal* announced on July 20, 1993—150 days before Christmas—that the Christmas selling season was going to be a failure.

This is the text of the large headline over the first-page main story of the business section: "As Shoppers' Debts and Pessimism Mount, Stores Start to Lose the Christmas Spirit." It's not quite as bad as the tabloid headline "Woman Gives Birth to Chimpanzee in Tragic Sperm Bank Mix-up."

And not so funny, either. Christmas is the most important event of the year to any retailer. No other business risks so much on the last eight weeks of the year. No other business gets 40 percent of its annual sales and at least 50 percent of its profit between the day after Thanksgiving and December 24.

So retailers are fully alert when the word "Christmas" comes up. And when *The Wall Street Journal* screams the words "Christmas" and "Stores Start to Lose"—in July headlines—it will get readership.

The Wall Street Journal has power, and therefore, a responsibility to its readers. Its readers read the newspaper and react, because they trust it. In this way, *The Wall Street Journal* can influence the plans (and therefore the prospects) of its audience, including retailers. Of course, the paper could be saving a lot of retailers a lot of money by warning them now, that there's time to change plans in some areas.

Because of its influence, this newspaper is now causing even optimistic readers to think twice, especially if they are guilty of optimism. They must avoid the ultimate sin of stocking up on merchandise and planning to make the season a success. Thanks to *The Wall Street Journal*, U.S. retailers today will have plenty of time to revise their prospects downward, planning for failure in an orderly, businesslike manner. And because of years of erosion, stores are more vulnerable to pre-Christmas panic.

I hope *The Wall Street Journal* isn't going tabloid and using scare tactics to boost circulation. They must have some idea of the incredible profits of sensationalism. It is hard to imaging that someone at the newspaper doesn't know that Oprah Winfrey makes $80 million a year entertaining people's fears. Surely, some vaguely creative soul somewhere at *The Wall Street Journal* watches "Street Stories," "Hard Copy," "Inside Edition," "A Current Affair" and "Cops"—in secret—and may be trying to persuade the newspaper that misery sells.

Just think! But for the press, we would be in danger of making Christmas successful. We would be designing Christmas as if it were going to be magic.

But for the influence of pessimistic journalists, we would even now be hiring and training the right people to do the right job for customers; we'd be stocking the shelves with hearts' desires. We'd be planning the advertising, boosting morale, even hoping somehow to conquer the molasses of the last few years.

But no! Now, instead we are canceling those expansion plans. No new store openings, refurbishings, get rid of the research, and if the buyers still have to travel, make sure they fly coach to Taiwan and back. They ought to double up in rooms in Milano; Milano is an expensive city. Now we can get an early start on cutting costs and slicing into attitudes. Cancel the Christmas parade, shorten store hours, slash the staff, speed up the early retirement program and unscrew half the light bulbs. Energy is expensive. And the community-helping-the-homeless program we wanted to connect with Christmas will have to wait until *The Wall Street Journal* tells us we have money to spare for the needy. Right now we are needy ourselves, and we remind ourselves that charity begins at home.

Why not, finally, put a sign up over the front door, borrowed from Dante: "Abandon all hope, ye who enter here." Let's take *The Wall Street Journal* 's bad attitude and pass it right on to our customers.

Pessimistic journalism is dangerous. Yes, I am one of those cranks who connects the endless violence on television with the endless violence in my front yard. And I resent the golden fortunes piled up by Sally Jesse and Joan and Geraldo and Phil and Jane and Montel and Oprah as they celebrate the agony of everyday life. They all makes money by catering to the lowest common denominator: trouble, misery and failure. And I can't help noticing that even *The Wall Street Journal* in its lust for readership has its editors killing Christmas eight weeks before Labor Day.

This Christmas will be as good as the optimists can make it, and as bad as the pessimists can imagine. Both sides will be right; the failures will say "I told you so," and so will the successes. More than anything, it is the attitude they carried with them from the beginning about their jobs, their lives and all their prospects. They will each approach the big event of the year with all their characteristics intact. The failures will fail and the successes will succeed.

Last Christmas I was reading the *San Juan Star* when I noticed the slogan under its masthead: "Give light and the people will find their own way." It hit me. I liked it. It seemed right to me. The most we can do to motivate other people is to enlighten them to a better sense of their own possibilities. I believe that enlightened companies are managed in that way. The managers give "light," and then the employees and customers get to be themselves while enriching the company.

I don't know whether *The Wall Street Journal* has a slogan, or whether it matters. But they could rewrite it in the best tabloid tradition, and there would still be truth in it: "Give darkness and the people will follow."

Most journalists manage to convey the facts, presenting the news as it is, truthfully. But the genius of communication of any kind is point of view. Why didn't *The Wall Street Journal* present this Christmas forecast story with a different tone? It could have ministered to Santa Claus instead of killing him. It could have moved toward greatness, using its power to guide its readers to rise above the trash of common expectation.

P.S. Eight days later, July 18, 1993: *The New York Times* runs this headline story—"Strong Holiday Retail Sales Predicted."

USA Today's lead business story was headlined, "Retail Analyst Sees Cheery Christmas."

So much for journalism! Yes, indeedy, it's definite: Christmas will be either (a) a total disaster; or (b) a complete success.

CONTROL YOUR OWN DESTINY

MARCH 1994

THAT'S NOT MY TITLE, but it's a great one and it applies to you and me and to the future of our work. *Control Your Own Destiny* is a book subtitled, "How Jack Welch is making General Electric the world's most competitive company," by Noel M. Tichy and Stratford Sherman.

I was reading this book while vacationing at Little Dix Bay, and I realized I was the unwilling customer-victim of a business that had completely lost control of its destiny. This resort could as easily have been any store or manufacturer I work for, so I was struck by the illuminating coincidence.

The moment I finished reading (and writing this article), this remarkable ad appeared in all our national newspapers: "Presenting a new chapter in a Caribbean classic. Little Dix Bay has been recognized for over 35 years as one of the most unspoiled tropical resorts in the world.... Rosewood Hotels & Resorts announces the reopening of this Caribbean classic following a meticulous renovation."

Little did I know that "someone else" was waiting in the wings to take over and control the destiny of Little Dix Bay. Imagine your company, your job, or else.

Read the story and meditate. Controlling your own destiny is not an optional exercise. You have to do it, or else ... or else ... or else ....

There is nothing sadder than leaders who used to lead, aren't leaders any more, but still keep the job. As changes come faster and faster, tired leaders keep the pace back at their earlier success rate. Witness the woes of IBM, Kodak, Sears, Delta, United and American. All were leaders. So were NBC and CBS and ABC. The Harvard Business School used to lead, but now people laugh and call it medieval.

This story is not about a worldwide corporation, or a state or a country or the fate of the planet. It's really about my vacation. But don't quit reading yet — it does have a couple of Rockefellers in it.

Once upon a time, the Rockefellers created Rockresorts, a marriage of luxury and nature conservation, to be the standard for the world. The government of Virgin Gorda agreed to let them purchase more land than they needed, on condition that they conserve it. So the Rockefellers saved great wilderness land and gave the Little Dix Bay resort access to 22 unspoiled beaches.

The island had no water. From the beginning, it was all shipped in. Nothing was too good for Rockresorts. The buildings' peaked pavilions rose along the main beach, reflecting the mountains behind them. They were preparing to charge more—and deliver more luxury and service—than any other resort. They studied every detail, every knife and fork and trash can; the floats were the best floats available and so were the towels; and there were gardens and space and staff in wealthy quantities. Virgin Gorda locals were hired, trained and aimed at Rockefeller performance.

But the service wasn't good enough.

After opening, the management did a daring thing. They closed the resort, fired everyone and started over. This time Rockresorts brought in staff just as they had brought in water, and Little Dix Bay reopened to world-wide rave reviews. It was rumored to be impossible to get in. This lasted for years.

If the Rockefellers could experience their prize resort now, they would understand exactly how emperors lose touch with the hearts and wallets of their citizens.

Why did Little Dix Bay decline?

It is important to keep in touch with your customers. Sam Walton knew that; he flew himself unannounced to as many as 19 stores a week, so he could see for himself what the Wal-Mart experience was like from the point of view that matters most: the customer's.

Sears didn't. On the day the *Chicago Tribune* announced the mass layoff of 50,000 in early 1993, a reporter remembered an appointment with Edward Brennan. As John McCarron reported:

"Two years ago, I had the opportunity to visit with Sears' Chairman Ed Brennan at the company's executive offices in the Sears Tower.

"To get to his office, my colleague and I first had to check in with a Sears press officer, who, in turn, presented us for screening to a senior vice president for corporate affairs, who authorized our final ascent to the executive suite, where we were greeted by Brennan's departmental secretary, who, in turn, introduced us to his personal secretary.

"By the time we were conducted into the sanctum sanctorum on the 68th floor, where we awaited our audience with the man himself, I had a pretty good idea what Sears' problem might be ... or at least one of its problems."

Mr. Brennan had forgotten where the store was.

Today Little Dix Bay goes halfway. They leave an ordinary guest comment card in your room, but they don't want to read it, and they don't like answering. I wrote to Michael Glennie, president of Rockresorts. I gave him details.

THINGS: Food plates and cutlery uncollected at our door for two days and nights; overflowing trash cans in the bar; broken overhead bed lights; beach umbrellas that rusted shut (discovered only after being dropped for a three-hour stay in full sun on a beach with no shade); limes delivered daily as requested, but never with a knife; a lawn mower—only three years old but the loudest machine on Virgin Gorda—in your garden daily.

PEOPLE: Taxi ordered never arrives; staff doesn't care; only the general manager can call another one. Noisy beach staff gather every afternoon to laugh outside the louvered door of the massage room.

A long-anticipated trip to solitary Spring Bay includes the shock appearance of over 100 tourists dumped there by a cruise boat—information readily available to management.

The porter drops guests' luggage six feet down into a boat instead of carrying it.

Our snorkel trip is canceled in mid-ocean when the motor fails (which is fine), and the boatman pours all the overflowing oil right into the ocean (which is not).

And the music blasts at night whether you like it or not, and there is more, much more mediocrity ... you are not happy, and they do not care.

After returning home, while waiting for Mr. Glennie to answer, I saw an ad for Little Dix Bay in *The New Yorker*: "Sentence yourself to a week of solitary refinement." Surely, this could not be a joke? On guests? Again?

"There are no television sets because nothing is as entertaining as what's outside your window"—the infernal lawn mower man.

"And there are no clocks because the sun still rises and sets very nicely without them"—yes, and the taxis don't arrive and the umbrellas don't work and you must cut your lime with your teeth.

"Resting calmly on a secluded beach in the still unspoiled ..." Stop! You have spoiled the ocean with boat oil and spoiled our retreat with 120 vibrating snorkelers.

And finally: "Not just a resort ... a rockresort."

Think about the promise. Not just a machine ... an IBM. Not just a car ... a Plymouth. Not just film ... Kodak. Not just a business school ... Harvard. The emperors have forgotten to talk to the people.

I did not hear from Mr. Glennie, so I called him. He, of course, was not in. His secretary, Cheryl Scriven, told me that my letter had gone to Mr. Brewer at Little Dix Bay. I did not hear from Mr. Brewer. Eventually I got a form letter from Mr. Glennie, which contained not one reference to a single detail covered by me. "This is the way the world ends: not with a bang, but a whimper."

FLASH! Eighteen thousand miles away—at Amanpuri, Phuket, Thailand—a resort with an identical aim: to be the best on the planet. Same goal, same price, same class, same customers.

I went to Amanpuri because I saw a photograph of their great staircase in a travel magazine and I wanted to stand on it myself. And you can stand there at the head of 120 steps by the pool in the palm plantation, down to the beach and Andaman Sea, with nothing between you and this enhancement of nature.

The Amandari never gets between you and your vacation. You could tell from any one detail that everything was right. The outdoor brass fruit bowl was polished every day, but you never saw them do it. The flowering orchid plants in the bathroom were rotated daily, unless the bloom was past its peak; then it was taken to the nursery and replaced.

In this state of bliss I was standing at the head of the staircase next to the manager, Anthony Lark. He and I were admiring the sight.

He suddenly said, "Excuse me," and spoke to an instant waiter. A moment after the waiter disappeared, an electrician appeared, carrying a light bulb. Mr. Lark spoke to him briefly. The electrician then ran down 120 steps, kicked off his shoes and went fully dressed into the water. He waded out to a rock which broke the surface and screwed the new light bulb into an underwater light.

Standing at the top of the staircase, we could see one more small light now. A slight improvement, a thing done right, a little more light from the manager.

Little Dix Bay needs an Anthony Lark. Anthony Lark is evidence that perfection is possible, even in a complicated enterprise. He is a manager who stands with his customers and cares and acts on his observations. He makes everybody happy, and he makes money. He is a leader.

Sears needs Anthony Lark, and maybe he should also visit IBM and Kodak and Procter & Gamble and Harvard. Yes, Amanpuri and Little Dix Bay are smaller. But Sears started out with a single store, and so did Wal-Mart. And IBM and Kodak and Delta and United and American and ABC and NBC and CBS—ancient icons, all of them, nodding off on their thrones, with no one but their customers to tell them they have no clothes on.

PART SEVEN
FASHION

MODACIDE

NOVEMBER 1988

THE MULTI-BILLION DOLLAR fashion industry has only been around for 80 years. In all the time before that, we poor human beings got along without it. And now it looks like we may get along without it again.

The fashion industry is dying, and it has no one to blame but itself. Call it "modacide" (moda is Italian for fashion)—a form of suicide in which fashion kills itself.

In the whole previous history of civilization, we struggled along without *Vogue* or designers or Seventh Avenue or pret-a-porter or *WWD* or swatches or knitwear or colorists or double-truck fashion ads. How did we survive?

Now, we want to get dressed and get going, but the fashion industry hopes that we'll get dressed and then get dressed some more and then get dressed all over again. They've invented seasons and openings, and they introduce designers ad infinitum. (Quick, name two important clothing designers from the Renaissance.) They thought up "fashion shows." (Name a fashion show from the Greek theater or Elizabethan England.) They set themselves up as oracles telling people what to wear. (Erasmus and Plato were teachers, but what they had to say about hemlines is not recorded.)

Only in this century have we seasonally rushed to any country except our own to see what people in other places were wearing and brought the sophisticated word back to the mal-dressed heathens at home. (Did the Spanish conquistadors wear Japanese designer garments when they shot the Incas in Peru? Not known.) Somehow, those 20 centuries of barbarians managed to get along without a fashion director. (Did Columbus' crew include a fashion forecaster so the troops would look cute when they discovered America?)

All this incestuous party-going is very fine as long as the public pays for it. But the public is showing ugly signs of having had enough and they're not going to take it anymore. Consider the customer's point of view—and by customer I do not mean the professional who borrows samples to go to clubs and parties, then returns the dress to the designer in the morning with a pair of pantyhose still in the pocket. (This actually happened.) I mean real customers—the folks who are supposed to read all this drivel, follow trends, put up with lousy stores and their nonexistent service, and then pay money in the hopes of living up to some fashion editor's expectations.

They've gone along with this for years. So why make them angry now? Why are they taking the money they used to spend on endlessly renewing their wardrobes and spending it on activities instead? It's the fashion industry's own fault. Just to be sure it really works, the industry is committing modacide two different ways: insane pricing and lack of direction.

Insane Pricing

These are the prices of some garments shown in Paris in July 1988:
- $11,000 for an Yves St. Laurent evening jacket (not couture)
- $7,000 for a red leather day suit
- $1,900 for a white evening shirt

Christian Lacroix, last year's hottest designer who had the fashionettes in downright orgies of praise, posed a $4.2 million loss in the first year in business for himself, according to *Women's Wear Daily*. The first Lacroix dress in America was unveiled at Bloomingdale's in September '87. It finally sold in September '88 to an unnamed customer for $6,000 (Lacroix's dresses begin at about $14,000).

In the September issue of *Details*, the brilliant and courageous writer Bill Cunningham reports the fashion news from Paris, Milan, London and New York City. It is a 99-page report. He says, "The most important trend, at all levels of design, was the excessively inflated prices, which may be telling us that the death of highly innovative fashion is imminent, as modern design turns to investment clothes to justify pricing."

Lack of Direction

Pretend you live in Denver and you subscribe to *Details* and you read Bill Cunningham's entire fashion report. Here is an abbreviated list of some of the trends he sees coming up for spring. Try reading this aloud to someone.
- 1920s jazz age
- Renaissance brocades
- un-extravagant style
- Spandex and Lycra bodyclothes
- jumpsuits
- Botticelli
- stretch dresses
- colossal evening wraps
- great quantities of jewels
- monastic simplicity
- mid-60s copies of *Vogue*
- French Ye-Ye

- swinging London
- Ungaro's 1967-68 icons
- masterpieces from the late 50s
- empire dresses cut from authentic 1800s patterns
- simple cashmere clothes
- sculpted coats
- a new sobriety
- new realism
- the traditional Sicilian peasant woman
- the grace of impoverished nobility
- no-nonsense tailoring
- familiar sharp silhouette with less-blazing sensuality
- escapist Oscar Wilde fops
- soft medieval armor
- 30s matinee idols
- jackets cut like sweaters
- another fabricated hemline, like last year's hysterical rising
- minimalist 1954 high-waisted sheath
- multiple appliqued swirls of cloth, texture, color and fur
- winter coats without backs or fronts
- strange evening dresses with trains that resemble caterpillars
- hats the size of enormous balloons
- 25 models carried by bodybuilders to *Aida*
- vampires in black dinner jackets worn backwards, with devil's tails
    hanging down front
- the magical Land of Oz
- the revival of the portrait collar
- prophetic knife-pleated suit skirts
- surface texture through crunching fabric
- yard-wide palazzo pants
- gossamer silk net for evening
- evening wraps designed with intense thought.

There is more, much more. Clear, isn't it? Doesn't it make you just want to rush right out and buy a whole load of gossamer, crunched, frontless, yard-wide, evening palazzo pajamas for spring?

I sent this list of highlights to a stockbroker and his wife in Phoenix, asking what they thought of it. They sent back a simple customer-type message: "Don't ever do that again."

So, with this in mind, how do you think business will be next spring? You'll be able to see it all at your nearby mall. Or, you may not need to wait that long.

Modacide has already hit the stores. For the last two seasons, fashion sales have been a disaster. Stores don't tell their customers what to buy, and they charge them astronomical prices. A friend of mine picked up a white cotton shirt with a price tag of $385 made by Comme des Garcons. She said, "This ought to be called Comedy Garcons."

Meanwhile, we read that Anna Piaggi of *Vogue*, famous for her outfits and advice, was wearing live grass on her head at fashion shows, and journalists noted that it continued to grow during the collections. Don't you think this gets fashion a lot of respect in Grand Rapids, Michigan?

I think most people think that fashion people are a bunch of fools. And, alas, meanwhile the stores are announcing a "Return to the Classics." Stores always make this announcement when they have nothing to announce. "Menswear sales weren't great last year, so makers decided not to experiment too much," says *The Wall Street Journal*.

I think most people think that retailers are wimps. People in Atlanta, Billings, Cincinnati, Dallas, Edmonton and Fairfield County are not going to wait forever for sanity to invade the fashion world. We got along without it for 4,000 or 5,000 years. We may get along without it again.

BYE BYE BLACK

APRIL 1990

I'M SICK of the color black. Except for businesses that long to be "in the black," and lately aren't, I can't think of a single use of the color black that lifts the spirits. That ol' black magic just isn't magic anymore.

Black is the color of cats who bring bad news. Motorcyclists and executioners have always worn black. So have witches. And if you think that witches don't exist, go to any party south of 14th Street. Black may have always been "the color of my true love's hair," according to the folk song, but black is *now* the color of one's true love's clothes, accessories, home furnishings and attitude. One shops for black clothes and objects in hard, concrete surroundings. Most of those shops look like parking decks attached to malls. It makes me want to wear all white, but there would be a lot of screaming about cleaning bills and stains. In fact, all white would be unimaginative, too. All anything is unimaginative.

We invented black, and the problem is that black is too much with us. The people who wear black are very good at defending it. "So simple," they whisper. "So right. So classic." Too many designers protest too much about the purity of form as seen in black. They love to show the subtleties of cloth and cut and fit and shape and material—in black. True, that's design anatomy the way its taught in the classroom. It should be left there, and the students should take a course in color.

It must have been insecurity that caused those quasi-religious Japanese fashion designers to start cutting illogical holes in useless places in their black clothes and adding extra sleeves to their black sweaters. They must have suspected that black on black on black was a little bit boring.

Suddenly, though, those same detached Japanese designers have slipped into something slightly yellowish. I recently asked one of those tied-and-twisted, black-clad Comme des Garcons salespersonages why they suddenly were showing a garment that was not black. "That's our holiday collection," she breathed.

So now, thank goodness, there are some signs black will not be back. That will be good for business—and good for the soul. The people who always wear black haven't bought any new clothes in years. They don't need to. But maybe the revolution will be caused by customers leaving the designers with a black plague of markdowns hung on stark concrete walls.

Black is still the color of fashion people, though. The last refuge of the unimaginative. For a group that claims so loudly to be individuals, such conformity. You can see them in the front rows at fashion shows, ranks of ravens muffled up in black making notes about color. They privately intimate that for them, black is fashion salvation. Black is, in one of their own memorable phrases, "to die for." Black implies that these dictators are so extraordinarily busy telling us what we will all be wearing in the future that they don't have the time to get dressed for it. They wear black importantly, priestly, beyond mere trends. They teach individuality, but dress in uniforms. They preach change, but they always look the same. The very sight of them is a contradiction of everything they ought to represent.

When God the Designer colored the world, he left out black. Nothing in nature is entirely black—even a crow's wing has color. I sit writing this in a garden almost drowned in riotous hibiscus, surrounded by hovering hummingbirds, next to a sea which blossoms into turquoise every morning when it is hit by the sun. I will eat papayas and mangoes and watch the sunset system of colors glow again this evening—color all day long.

I will never go into the garden to gather black flowers or swim in ebony waves at noon, and I will not wear black for these excursions into nature. I will see that back in the city, where color is drained away into ashes. And I hope that even there I will remember enough about what is beautiful to put some of it onto myself and shed every face of black.

Black is the color of death. Let's bury it now, and move toward morning.

THE NEW YORK RODENT SHOW

SEPTEMBER 1990

THE EDITOR PREDATOR rodents all know how to get tickets for every fashion show. The ground hogs gather, the moles poke their noses into the air, and the ferrets catch taxis to the Pierre.

Geoffrey Beene, the master, is giving a fashion show. All the editor rodents show up at the door wearing marvelous coats. A thousand noses twitch, exchanging kisses—kiss-kiss at everyone they see, including those they may actually know, kiss-kiss as frantic as the day the males are released onto the females back at the mink ranch.

The rodents are getting ready to gnaw their way into the ballroom. They all show up as avid as a pack of starving beavers facing a forest. The minor rodents have to wait outside the ballroom—standees, the hamsters, gerbils and me. As we wait we get to watch the main parade of muskrats, minks, the rare white mice and the chinchillas all move majestically past us, ushered right inside. They all have seats. The lucky woodchucks, ground hogs, hairy marmots, nutrias and porcupines all make it in. The crush and bustle make us all look like lemmings.

"I am from Saks," a belligerent nutria announces. "I sit on the left side, always." An angry rat shouts at a security guard, "I'm a licensee. I have a reserved seat." A prairie dog comes up and barks, "I am a prairie dog. I don't stand in line." Miss Muskrat from *USA Today* is turned away by a frantic Beene weasel with a sweatshirt tied around his waist. A standee gasps, "That was Francesca Ferret, of *The New York Times*," as though the Pope has just strolled by unnoticed. A gopher speaks to a hamster: "I think plaid is really in this year." And a very superior ground squirrel snaps, "I expect this bullshit in Europe, but not in New York."

Every time a raving rodent makes it in through the ballroom doors, the roar of rehearsal slips out. We are 40 minutes late. We look divine. We wear our scarves identically tied. We shove, we keep our places in this mean, pushy lineup. We are just like mice driven mad by too many lab experiments.

Finally, the big doors swing open and a major weasel calls to the assembled crowd, "Let the standees in." We rush the door. This is the New York Rodent Show, the professional fashion industry at work. Inside, behold the panorama of the rodent show in action. See the hysterical host/assistant/helper weasels dart in every direction checking pedigrees and seating charts, tugging at latecomers, pushing standees.

All the front-row moles, writers, editors and celebrity customer rodents wear sunglasses—everyone knows rodents see better at night. They sit there lifting their sensitive noses up toward the runway, blinking and sniffing out stories and twitching for trends. They are the trusted conveyors of mystery and beauty to the world.

Get out of the way of the fashion photogs and the videotapers, the to-hell-with-fashion grubby types entrusted with immortalizing the mystery. Those types wear anything, as long as it has dozens of pockets to hold lens caps. They are not rodents at all—they are marsupials.

Look for the buyers, the frazzled department store porcupines who all need haircuts, including women. They keep themselves in disrepair to let you know how very, very busy they are. They translate "moda" to the masses, making lots and lots of money. Nonetheless, they sometimes feel insecure as they sit close and watch the insolent nipples of the models bouncing around in front of them.

The downtown fashion students are also in the crowd, an anxious pack of gerbils dressed in black—all poverty-concealing reverential-and-ready-to-worship black. Some wear metal confections and safety pins in unsafe places.

Make way for the Japanese, a family of happy waving badgers, the national symbol of good luck. Wave back or they'll make waves for you. They could easily buy the building if they wanted to.

Read your program. The blazing title is "Geoffrey Beene, Wings of Desire, Winter Nineteen Ninety" (rodents love to spell numbers out completely). On the cover a distorted fashion model squats, showing off her triangles. The writer explains: "For Fall 1990, Geoffrey Beene reveals an almost pagan appreciation of the elemental power of clothing ... This season Beene breaks down the notion of silhouette by carefully manipulating abstract shapes to enhance the body's sensual appeal. After defining the shoulder blade of a black suit with a triangle of red satin, Beene discovered that this fundamental configuration highlighted the mobile allure of the upper back ... Instead of evoking the eternal, restful pyramids of Egypt, they (the triangles) suggest the gliding grace of an albatross' wing.

" ... From the front, the whole dress seems to hang precariously from the triangle's fragilely attenuated tip. This same gravity-defying, tenuous construction is repeated in an austere black dress where the lines of force, here traced in gold, become even more suspensefully galvanized." And there is more, much more. This is rodent ranting at its best.

The show begins. And a humorless, joyless show it is, too. This is "art" and don't you ever forget it. Prepare to be deafened by mean-spirited music, blinded by inaccurate lighting and stupified by the spectacle of fashion. The show is slow and sad and badly synchronized. The models start every scene upstage in worn-out Martha Graham Greek tragedy poses. Then they move out, slinking down the runway like very expensive otters. Nobody smiles—ever. It could be "art," or it could be too much choking by neck accessories.

The first eight outfits are black. The second eight outfits are also black. Fear in the fashion industry always gives birth to black again. In unified despair, the entire rodent pack prepares to declare that black is back again. Suddenly, a model appears in all black, but daringly accessorized with green gloves. This gets applause. Then more black—black lace, black sequins, black for evening (strobe lights, wow), one purple dress (applause). There are flowers on black, gold on black, embroidery on black, and giant paisley on black. Each scene ends with a model reposed in Clytemnestra agony under the dimming lights.

The flash bulbs flash and the pencils scribble. And thus it is over. At the end, the whole acclaim of rodents—overcome—all rise to their feet as one, as if they had just attended the world premiere of *Parsifal*. They have been present at history. There's a curtain call. The Master scurries out to take a little bow, a nervous blinking curtain call, and a quick retreat. The rodents stand amazed, applauding, bringing their little paws together, some in tears.

About one hour later, Beene's secrets of the universe will have shot around the world by way of fashion columns, photographs, video, fax, magazines, cable and knock-off entrepreneurs taking triangles to speedy tailors in Taiwan—on and on, until the unsuspecting world of ordinary people is expected to acknowledge the "attenuated" and "tenuous" nuances of the deeply meaningful triangles of Geoffrey Beene.

The New York Times is generous in its coverage of the New York Rodent Show and almost never critical. The major designers and the bulk of the U.S. fashion industry, many of the *Times*' best advertisers, are located in New York City. In fact, on the morning of his fashion show, Geoffrey Beene ran a full-page ad in the *Times*, using the same photography of the triangulated model that was featured on the cover of the program for the show.

The next day the *Times* published a review under the headline "Beene, as Usual, Forges Fashion Path." Here are some excerpts: "The Beene show was most powerful. His attenuated (there's that word again) sculptural line had a simplicity that reminded some viewers of Brancusi's birds in space. To those who share his adventurous spirit, the clothes will be a revelation ... So the cries of 'Bravo' and the sustained applause at the end of his show yesterday seemed thoroughly warranted. The audience was also applauding itself."

What we have really seen is fashion archaeology, a weakening nostalgia for the days of the old dictatorial emperors of fashion—the same kind of emperor who had, of all things, no clothes on the day when the public gasped and then lied when they saw that the emperor was naked. That is still the situation today when Geoff and the other fashion decliners strut their stuff and show us what they imagine they still have up their sleeves—no clothes at all.

There is more fashion in an instant in line at an Almodovor movie or scouring the racks at Canal Jeans or in what folks wear to tear down the Berlin wall or to stop tanks in Tianamen Square than there is in all the sub-textual pseudo-religious "attenuations" of Geoff and the other triangulators. No wonder they all wear glasses jammed up on their heads. If they used them, they would see that they are looking at nothing and then they would be jobless in fashion land.

A black thought crosses the intersection. Herbicide, pesticide, insecti-cide—rodenticide. Maybe we'd better kills the rodents before the rodents kill the fashion business forever.

DEATH BY PLAID

NOVEMBER 1991

THE NEWSPAPERS have bulged again with fashion promises for fall. The magazines have swelled with ads and editorials. (Calvin Klein ran the biggest ad ever in *Vanity Fair*'s October issue: 116 pages separately printed and bound into the publication—the world's first "outsert"). And what is the message? Plaid!

So, out of some ancient atavistic reflex, I went out shopping to see what was new for fall. I saw plaid in 100 percent of the stores I visited and in all of the ads for the stores I didn't.

In Bergdorf Goodman Men, I was not approached during 40 minutes, although the staff was certainly talking a lot to one another (some pondering plaid, but mostly talking about Madonna). Across the street, Charivari was completely deserted at noon. There were, however, several employees with severe haircuts doing paperwork, no doubt about plaid. The *plat du jour* at Bendel's restaurant was fresh fish, and you could smell it from the front door all the way up to the couture department where they were serving up plaid fashions. Saks was stripped of all decor except for some flowers in the cosmetics department and no longer looked like a world-wide destination. The person at the information desk knew a lot about plaid but had absolutely no idea where I could find the Joe DaHun shirt editorialized in that morning's *New York Times*.

At Bloomingdale's, I saw plaid as security types followed close behind. But I was never approached or greeted by a salesperson. Inside Macy's main entrance, the information person sent me to seven in search of Evan Picone's plaids. But later I found plaid Evan on three. When I came back down to the main floor to inform her, she'd gone to lunch.

Once again it seems that "fashion" forgot to wake up and smell the coffee. Stores are still talking to customers the way they did ten years ago. Reality has passed retailers by, and chances are customers will sit this season out if retailers start dictating fashion again.

Herewith, some amazing excerpts from the new fall fashion advertising campaigns:

• "Isn't it rich? Casual luxe from Calvin Klein"—Don't you think homeless people will appreciate that sentiment as they line their cardboard box homes with this ad from *The New York Times*?

• "When America goes plaid, keep your eye on Lord & Taylor. [Thanks, I'll try to remember that.] Albert Nipon just rustled up [cute] the latest dance craze—Black Watch silk taffeta. [I didn't know taffeta could dance.] Bare shouldered and pouf skirted, it is, quite simply, one of the most romantic dresses we've seen." [Ahh, isn't life wonderful?]

Tell this one to your toddler at bedtime:

• "Has America gone plaid? Yes, happened overnight. [That's quite a sentence.] Plaid dresses so enchanting we positively cannot face fall without them. [Yeah, just face fall wearing plaid, and there will be no crime, no drugs, no hatred, violence, illiteracy. Yeah, just rush to Lord & Taylor to solve the problems of the universe.] Plaid suits. Coats. Even plaid shoes. [You can't face anything without plaid shoes.] Buttoned up plaid. [My favorite.] Pared down plaid. [You gotta take the good with the bad plaid] Plaid with pleats. With zip. [What the hell is plaid with zip? Or without it? Don't you just hate a zipless plaid?] Everything fresh-faced plaid. [Fresh-faced what? Fresh-faced plaid?] Vibrant. And so beautiful you'll be mad, mad, mad for these fabulous new plaids." Maybe that's why the wards at Bellevue are waiting-list-only. Too many New Yorkers went mad, mad, mad at Lord & Taylor.

Other manifestations of plaidness:

• One *Wall Street Journal* front page story led off with: "It's a plaid, plaid, plaid, plaid, world." Now you don't suppose the reporter writes for Lord & Taylor too?

• Ralph Lauren is showing a $9,286 mahogany highboy with tartan drawers. Evidently conspicuous consumption is not over.

• Houston socialite Lynn Wyatt bought an original Ungaro tartan ball gown. "Tartan," she said, "makes it less formal. Considering the troubled times we're in, anything that is overdone is inappropriate." The dress cost her $20,000. Wyatt's sense of current events exemplifies exactly what people think is wrong about Texas.

• Saks devoted 13 pages of its latest catalog to plaids, and *Vogue's* October issue had a plaid cover and 24 pages of Linda Evangelista romping in plaids.

Bad plaids are ugly. Good plaids are expensive. Plaids make fat people wider and thin people cartoony. And you get sick of plaid right after you wear it the first time. It's very, very visible and usually visibly unattractive. Its only advantage seems to be summed up by Loni McKown fashion editor of *The Indianapolis News:* "This is one trend that even people out here will get." Yes, they'll "get it." But will they buy it? *The Wall Street Journal* reports that even Bloomingdale's is having trouble pandering plaid. An article talked about one saleswoman who tried to sell red plaid stretch pants to heavy-set women: "Wear them with a LONG black top!"

Let's face it, the consumer isn't consuming. Fall sales have been worse than even the pessimists expected. Plaid may be a trend invented by the fashion industry that turns out to be disposable before the consumer buys it. This plaid fad madness: Is it lack of innovation? Archaic marketing techniques? Lack of interest? No, it's simply fashion gone bad. It's death by plaid. And that's sad.

PIT BULLS WITH ATTITUDE

SEPTEMBER 1992

THE NEW YORK fashion community has never been noted for good manners, but it recently set new standards of rudeness.

On March 3, 1992, about 250 people—editors, photographers, buyers, marketing people—had been invited to a new showroom to see a new clothing line and to hear an unusual message in an era when all of us should hope for any possible good news. It was the launch of the new Susie Tompkins line and it was the scene of the most disgraceful behavior I have ever seen.

The fashion industry relishes its own disgusting reputation. We hear constantly of the piggish way Americans beat their way into French fashion shows. We see ourselves screaming in Italian airports, abusing limo drivers who are three minutes late. We've all been bruised by the bitter pushing of small, strong men and women who want better seats and to whom the whole superficial extravaganza actually matters. Then we publicize our own erratic antics. No wonder the whole world wonders what is wonderful about the fashion industry.

We have no manners at all.

I posted myself at the foot of a major romantic staircase to watch the mobs get out of the elevators. They were a mostly angry group, tired, ready for cocktails, depressed about business, infuriated by having to wait even a moment for elevators, enraged by having to stand in line to check their coats, and itching to get at the free drinks and food.

There were a lot of lip-smacking air-kissers watching over the shoulders of the kissee in case there was someone they should have been kissing more. Most people avoided direct eye contact because it might have meant looking directly at someone not worth looking at. It was a mean-spirited group.

The new clothes were displayed in the showroom, while upstairs past the bar, chairs were set out for a unique program that did not include a fashion show. It wasn't easy getting the guests to sit down so far from the bar and all the overheated networking. One sensed that 80 percent of the people there had their resumes out circulating, and now they too were circulating.

They did sit down, but nobody heard a word Susie said in her welcoming speech because they were too busy continuing their own conversations. Most were therefore surprised by the sight and sound of a gospel choir shouting "hallelujah." Some listened politely, trying to hear over the din of cocktail chit-chat, but most didn't like what they were hearing.

Then came a man whose ministry feeds 300 people a day in San Francisco, who writes editorials for *The New York Times* and who is a beacon of hope to thousands of people whose lives have "slipped through the cracks." Rev. Cecil Williams is an eloquent, exciting speaker who came from San Francisco to speak to us for 15 minutes.

As soon as he began, the crowd got louder. Five minutes after he started, people started leaving their seats and the bar was jammed. There was so much noise that Rev. Williams could not be heard, even with a microphone. One woman trapped in heavy metal (Chanel) said loudly, "I didn't come to hear this kind of shit. I want to see product."

Liquor always turns up the volume, and by now even free food didn't seem to slow the rudeness of the crowd. The reverend was announcing optimism, caring and the responsibility of making a difference, but the fashionettes weren't listening.

Bad fashion behavior is bad enough on ordinary days, but here religion had intruded, and the New York City audience justified every nasty thing ever said about it. We are an insensitive, loutish lot dressed up in hard-edged black conformity, as frantic as rats in a failing experiment, as insensitive to our friends as we are to our customers.

I wonder what the out-of-town buyers thought of all this.

It is Susie Tompkins' right and privilege to introduce social responsibility into business. It's precisely what has made Anita Roddick the International Businesswoman of the Year. It's what makes Rhino Records and Ben & Jerry's not only successful, but urgent study for all of us.

The reverend was talking about our collective responsibility and the privilege of caring. It is the audience's privilege to disagree and even to express that disagreement.

But occasionally we are guests. If any of these mean, rude fashion casualties had acted this way at home, any decent mother would have spanked them. The spectacle of greedy people choking down free food and drink and walking out on a 15-minute religious speaker is not an inspiring sight.

By the time Rev. Williams had finished speaking and the gospel choir was into its finale, the ultimate hallelujahs sounded through a space that was half-empty, soon to be a showroom, soon to show clothes that the hosts of this event hope to sell, all in the hands of an audience that just walked out.

Even the current increasing unemployment of these people evidently wasn't enough to shock them into decent behavior. Our manners have vanished with our success. Our pride has been punctured, and we are taking it out on everyone. We grow ruder as we fail, and this is dangerous, because it stops us from being able to see a good thing when it comes.

This behavior reflects the same insecurity that is causing hate groups to spring up all over America. In 1992, the country is full of homophobes and neo-Nazis. David Duke has 44 percent of the vote in South Carolina. College students stage raids on Jews. Los Angeles is Los Angeles.

Hard times are bringing out the violence in people, and the fashion industry is turning into a pack of pit bulls with bad attitude.

Shame on them all.

They could use a little salvation.

FEEDING ON GRUNGE

JUNE 1993

Q. What is "grunge"?
  A. Ugly clothing.

Q. What's the look?
  A. Depressed. Dirty. Poor. Anti.

Q. Anti-what?
  A. Not sure.

Grunge is what is worn by slackers for slacking around expressing anti-attitudes. You do not find these customers browsing the racks at Saks or Nordstrom. They are happier recycling old clothes than spending money on new ones.

Fashion is so inventive. There is no "grunge" in the dictionary, so they made it up. On my way to not finding this word in two dictionaries, I strolled the "grunge" neighborhood in these good books, and I found some defining companions. Here are those old-fashion favorites: grim, grime, gross and gruesome. "Gross," for example, sounds a lot like "grunge." It means "dirty, slovenly, base, contemptible." Here is "grubby," which is much more vivid for me now—it means "infested with fly maggots." And "grunt," which I knew," but not this precisely: "the deep, short sound characteristic of a hog."

Partridge's Concise Dictionary of Slang is more helpful. It acknowledges "grungy" as "dirty, unwashed and smelly; squalid."

As the fashionettes would say (as they do when English fails them), "C'est la grunge!"

In its second season, the trade magazines are struggling to make grunge palatable; one editor in Milan faxed back a fashion flash about this trash—"haute hobo." Other desperate names include "ragamuffin" and "vagabond"—and it is still ugly. The real question about grunge is not "What is it?" but "Why would anyone want to wear it?"

Grunge has always been the costume worn by people who protest. I found grunge 23 years ago on the first Earth Day, when I saw a protester in Central Park carrying an empty poster. It had nothing written on it at all. I asked him what he was protesting and he said, "I haven't decided yet." He was anti without a cause. He was wearing the regulation anti-outfit: grunge. He was

23 years ahead of Seventh Avenue.

Yves St. Laurent had a brief brush with grunge 12 years ago. He decided to dress his customers as Ukrainian peasants, at roughly $12,000 an outfit. Of course, this was not called grunge, but there was something ineffably grunge-like in the sight of very rich women dressing as peasants.

This idea once entertained Marie Antoinette before she lost her head. *("Apres moi, pas de grunge...?" "Le grunge, c'est moi...?")* But the antis in the 20th century didn't like it, nor did St. Laurent's customers. They protested by not buying it, and St. Laurent went speeding back to opulence.

The latest incarnation of grunge is credited to the Seattle music scene. Seattle is an attractive city, famous for its Starbuck's coffee bars, incessant rain, a billion boats and annual productions of Wagner's four-night opera-thon "The Ring Cycle." And right now Seattle is the source and soul of the new post-techno, sub hip-hop-rave anti-music known as grunge.

Tina Brown's hot new *New Yorker* contains an item titled "Apres Seattle" (evidently the English language is as inadequate for Tina Brown and pop music as it is for fashion).

The cultural juggernaut known as grunge has spawned several new idioms, one of the more fearsome of which is "the next Seattle." At the moment, several cities—San Diego, Columbus, Providence, Chapel Hill and Halifax among them—are vying for that particular honor, but the front runner seems to be Portland, Oregon.

For those in Seattle who overdose on too much Wagner or too much basement rock and roll, there is also Spam-O-Rama. This is a speed carving competition which raises money for a food bank and expands the creative boundaries of ground ham, pork shoulder, salt, sugar, water and sodium nitrate.

The revival of grunge coincided with the decline of George Bush. We had become a nation of losers, and we dressed for the occasion. The movie *Slacker* appeared as George Bush disappeared, and the grunge band in the film is called "The Ultimate Losers." Wearing grunge expressed our depression with ourselves perfectly.

These antis are more articulate today. You don't need to ask them what they are against—they will tell you endlessly. They are protesting the government, big business, the education system, ecological destruction, lack of corporate responsibility, animal experiments, racial injustice, sexual harassment, their parents, chemicals and fur coats. In fact, they are against fashion.

This is very bad news for Seventh Avenue. Customers who had always worn grunge had always found it without any help from fashion designers. They already knew the best advantage of grunge: you don't need to pay big money for it. You just go to used clothing stores and pile it on.

So what was Seventh Avenue to do? After several failing seasons, and faced with another season or two without an idea, they decided to upgrade grunge. The accountants told the designers to get busy.

And so the fashionettes pierced one ear and took their limos to the Salvation Army for inspiration. They stayed out all night in damp Seattle basements going deaf and doing research. Then they went to work poking holes in perfectly good garments, shredding seams, viciously mismatching patterns and charging big money for the workmanship.

This cuteness became comedy the day the jokers at Chanel presented the world with their version of Doc Marten boots at $1,600 a pair.

But the cutest of the cute was Marc Jacobs, the latest in a long parade of Stephen Sprouse-ish darlings who go in and out of business often because their cuteness does not sell. They are fashion industry inventions, propped up against reality by their own fashion show and each other, talking to themselves but telling all America about it, as if America cared. Marc Jacobs had four years after the death of Perry Ellis to earn his living by shocking people with the cleverest of all clever inconsistent combinations. But after four years of losing money every time and a final grunge fashion show that cost $300,000, he was fired. C'est la grunge.

Grunge is backfiring where it matters most: with customers.

Now there are two groups of customers, and both are anti-grunge. The first group is the original rock-band-student-thrift-shop antis, who have always worn grunge, and bought it cheap and always will.

The second anti-grunge group are the faithful fans of fashion who appreciate good clothes, because they look good when they wear them. These people got over grunge a long time ago, and they aren't going to spend a lot of money going back to it now.

That leaves a third group, the fashionettes, who, bereft of ideas, consumed with cuteness, are busy going bankrupt and dwindling away. This gang of happy cannibals is finally answering the old question for all of us —

Q. What are you "anti"?
A. *Ourselves!*

PART EIGHT
SERVICE

MR. SWIG, MR. THORN, AND MR. EHRENBURG

JANUARY 1987

CUSTOMERS forever say they only meet employees who seem to hate merchandise, stores, bosses, customers, their company, and probably their country. I think I have finally found out why employees don't give a damn. It's because management doesn't give a damn. Dig under the skin of any dead employee, and you will find a dead manager in charge.

The difference between one store and another is presentation. So is the difference in hotels. Here's the story of two experiences in two of the country's top hotels, both in San Francisco. It's really a story about management. One deserves to be booked up full forever. And the other, even though it is utterly famous because it is the setting for the silly series *Hotel* deserves to lose its license. At that hotel, the employee who dazzled me with his caring and ingenuity was refused even the slightest recognition by the owner of the hotel, a man so obviously taken with himself that he can't even answer a letter or compliment a clerk.

The good news first, though. The Campton Place is the best city hotel I know—anywhere. (The Bel Air in Los Angeles is even better, but only because it has swans and acres of gardens, which would be truly tricky on downtown O'Farrell Street.) This tiny hotel welcomes you back with the same room, a handwritten note from Richard Thorn (the manager), a thousand microscopic services and the uncanny ability to respond to disaster in an instant. When you rip your blue linen jacket pocket wide open on a taxi door handle in front of the hotel, the housekeeper will be standing in the lobby with a needle and thread by the time you slam the cab door shut and walk back in to change clothes. Nobody knows how this is done, except by caring coupled with instantaneous communication.

Every hotel has soap from I. Magnin, terry bathrobes and remote-control T.V. All you have to do to get these frivolities is to pay a lot of money. But you can't buy happiness, and the Campton Place doesn't charge for it. Name three stores who react to customers that way, and I will buy their stock before lunch today. I dare you. But go back to the Campton Place Hotel after a nine month's absence and they will remember that you want *The New York Times* in the morning, valet pressing in the evening, and someone to run over to Gumps to collect the Baccarat after it's gift wrapped.

Now go up the hill and pay the same kind of prices at the Fairmont. You'll get groupies screaming for Hall and Oates in every lobby and tourists lurking behind the garish red wallpaper in case the stars of *Hotel* pass by (don't count on it; I doubt they stay there). And just hope with all your heart the zombies behind the desk don't put you in an old, unredecorated room. For the same $200 that the right people get big views from, you get crammed into a dark pit with a single ceiling light that looks like the London Underground at dawn. If you go back out and raise absolute hell, they will move you, but only to keep your mouth shut so the other guests can't hear.

For one week I endured this incivility, encountering the kind of condescending service that only comes from staff who secretly know the place is ripping you off. Elizabeth Taylor may get caviar in her baked potato; you get dismal swamp coffee with every late, cold breakfast. But—and this is important—an assistant manager, who for reasons undetected works at this tourist trap, did a deed so good, so daring and so entirely out of sync with the rest of the experience that I wrote a letter to the owner praising him. I suggested the owner do the same, and requested an answer as I cared about the consequences. Here's the letter:

Dear Mr. Swig,

"This is an opportunity for you to recognize a remarkable employee. I left a $1,200 plane ticket and valuable documents on a table in room 662 on October 1, 1986. They were thrown away. Assistant Manager Peggy traced but could not find them, then reported to your accounting department. The end. My loss. The Fairmont's regrets.

"*Not* the end. Chris Ehrenberg (more a "guest advocate" than an assistant manager) went through your garbage with your sanitary engineers and found everything. This was reported to me by "Haydee," yet another assistant manager. You are vastly fortunate to employ Chris Ehrenberg. You must do something extraordinary for such an extraordinary employee. As an interested guest, I will hope to hear what you decide to do for Chris Ehrenberg. If you are successful, it is because you encourage and reward employees who exceed the requirements.

"People are more important than things. The greatness of the Fairmont is not in its physical existence. It is in the initiative of its employees' efforts on the behalf of its guests.

"Please respond!'"

Nothing. Zero. Null. Void. Zilch. Nada word. Not even a Leona Helmsley form letter. (Isn't it sad that she's been accused by *The Village Voice* of escaping payment of $36,000 in sales tax at fabulous New York jewelry stores by sending empty boxes to Florida and taking the contents home to her hotels and telling us all how much she cares about details?)

Mr. Swig does exist. Tributes to him in the form of photographs of himself with "celebrities" cram every page of your in-room reading. But he obviously is too busy hosting Imelda and Ferdinand Marcos in complimentary suites to bother about the lowly clerks who actually deal with the sad and ordinary human beings who pay for their rooms.

I am not giving up. I am sending him a reminder today. After all, he may not have a secretary, or he may just wish to answer the letter himself after deep thought.

I want to say to him, "Dear Mr. Swig, GO PRAISE YOUR EMPLOYEES if you want them to go down into the garbage to dig out a customer's valuables. If you don't, Mr. Swig, they may take your valuables one of these days and put them into the incinerator. Or they may go work at Campton Place. Why haven't you answered my letter?

CUSTOMER SERVICE IS LIP SERVICE

APRIL 1988

ISN'T IT IRONIC that "service stores" or "service departments" are the ones where you have to stand in line to get waited on? Just try getting served at the shoe repair or credit department without waiting in line. In some of those places you even have to take a number and wait until the number is shouted out before you get the service you came in for.

H. Michael Hecht, chair of The Broadway, is quoted as saying, "There is no perceived lack of service; there is no service." An honest man. Everyone today is talking about customer service—in every department, in every store. And that's exactly the problem. We're all talking about it, and nobody is doing it.

Customer service is this year's favorite personnel ballet. There are training manuals, mission statements, motivation rallies and even ads to tell their customers about their service. According to every CEO in America, their company's greatest single priority is—yep, you guessed it—customer service. They bang on podiums during speeches to emphasize how much they believe in customer service. They've seen it coming for years. They've been muttering all the trendy catchwords, like "getting close to the customer," "seeing the customer's point of view," "management by walking around," and that all-time department store favorite, "He's on the floor."

These speeches are always greeted by really hearty applause from the audience, signifying that every person present has just undergone the customer service conversion, and the first thing they're going to do when they get back to their business is emphasize customer service. But then when it's time to figure out the budget cuts that need to be made, they just haul off and give it to "customer service."

Customers are also talking about customer service. They say it's "lip service." They're angry and determined to do something about it. They keep right on ordering more and more from dependable catalogs because catalogs don't lie as much about customer service.

These customers—and there are lots of them—hate not only stores, but also airlines, hotels, the U.S. mail, the entire bureaucracy of the U.S. government. They are just ripe for customer service. What an opportunity!

When will somebody see that a customer's need for genuine service is the most important thing a store has to sell? The time is right—right now—for some visionary merchants to realize this. These dreamers would see that they're selling trust instead of toasters. They would make the obligatory speeches at meetings and even participate in every rally. They'd have the campaign and the ads ready to go. They'd come in with serious funded, disciplined plans in place and every word they said would be believable. They'd be greeted at first with astonished employees who've heard them mouth off about customer service for years. But this time, their employees would realize they mean it, they believe in it, they'll pay for it, they're ready to recognize and reward it.

For a long time, the customers may not react. They'll either ignore it because they don't believe it or they won't be able to experience it because they've shopped for years without it and have become deaf, dumb and blind to it. Or they'll wait for the store to get over this temporary spasm of decency and go back to normal. But if it keeps on going, finally customers will stop, look and listen to the message they have longed for so long to heart.

Friendliness. Honesty. Sincerity. Courtesy. Entertainment. Information. Genuine interest in customer needs. Concerned. Caring. Thinking more about customers than about themselves. They never say, "It's not my department." They never say they're going on break. There are plenty of them everywhere. They love their jobs. They love their store. They love their

merchandise. They love their customers. They even love themselves.
It's like a dream. But dreams are what profits are made of.

WHAT'S THE DIFFERENCE BETWEEN ONE STORE AND ANOTHER?

JULY 1989

BRIGHT AND EARLY on an April morning, I was in a linen store asking about some merchandise displayed in the window. The woman in the 1,000-square-foot shop didn't know what linens I was talking about.

"Can you describe them to me?" she asked, standing about halfway back in her small shop. Instead of just going to the window, she made me help her paw through samples while we looked to see whether there were any linens like the ones displayed there.

I decided to leave. She said, "Why don't you pick up one of our catalogs by the door? If you find it in there, you can always mail order it."

The salesman took my charge card when I told him I wanted two medium black silk pants and two medium black silk T-shirts from the display rack next to his cash desk. He wrote up the sale, got my signature and telephoned to verify my card. But then he found that he'd have to tear up the charge slip and cancel the sale because he had just looked at the merchandise and there were no mediums left.

The front of one menswear store stopped me cold: A Pirelli carpet was rolled right out the store's front door, across the sidewalk and down to the street. It was imprinted, "Tenere, Tenere, Tenere!" A huge sculpture stood in front of the store, and banners shouted, "Tenere!" What may be the biggest single department store window in America continued the blast with more black and red and sculptures and banners and "Tenere!" and five male mannequins dressed in identical pairs of terrific black pants with many, many pleats and tight ankle-clutching bottoms. There was a big, fat-frogged belt at every waistline. Terrific show, terrific pants. But what's "Tenere?"

It's a new Paco Rabanne cologne for men, but I had to ask three people to find that out. I must have shown up too early.

The staff was standing there spraying and wiping the counters and combing their own hair. The first one had never heard of "Tenere!" I told him about the windows. "Oh," he said, "the staff comes in from the back way. Only customers come in off the street."

Was he rude? Was I insulted?

Another saleperson allowed as how "Tenere!" was "some kind of new cologne they're pushing." And the third salesperson stopped adding eye shadow to her eye shadow and come over to join us. "Yeah," she said, "and it's g.w.p." Because I'm a retail consultant, I happen to know that means "gift with purchase."

That was easy. Now the pants.

This conversational encounter group and I were standing at the very first counter in the store, approximately 15 feet from the big, big window. And there were six more mannequins wearing six more pairs of exactly the same pants on six display ledges right above our heads. But nobody knew where the pants were. One suggested I try downstairs. One suggested I try upstairs, on the second floor. The g.w.p. lady said I might find them in "Designer Collections."

I persevered. I went downstairs and was met with, "I don't know." I went upstairs only to hear, "I don't know." I asked in "Lifestyles." They didn't know.

I toured through Armani, Yohji, Gaultier, Ferre, I toured through private-label land. I tortured the salespeople in every department asking them about the pants in the window.

Nobody knew nothin'.

After a while, a perky department manager appeared and said to me, "Persistent, aren't you? Let me see if I can help you find those pants!"

Alarms went off. A person who cared! This event should be declared a national retail holiday.

She called the one department I hadn't yet visited. No pants. A stockperson said he was just a stockman and didn't know anything at all.

She called the buyer. The buyer had no idea what pants she was talking about.

Then the perky person had an inspiration. She beeped the display department. Two minutes later she hung up the telephone flushed with answers, victory and customer service. She had found the display department and the explanation. She was as pleased as Miss Marple at the end of every story. "Those pants don't look like that at all," she said. "The effect was created by the display department. They pinned them in at the ankles and bunched up extra pleats. The belt is from women's accessories and wouldn't fit you at all. Those are Union Bay pants and they're down in the basement. Come on down with me, and I'll show you right where they are."

We went back down to the basement to find the pants. They were out of them. The display department had taken them all for display. She started apologizing again, but I didn't stay to listen. For all I know, she may be standing there to this day outside the store on the "Tenere!" carpet right in front of the sculpture next to the window with all those pants.

Here's another story—a Nordstrom story. A man called the store because his wife had died, and he wanted to settle the account. She owed the store $1,000. The store canceled her outstanding bill, explaining that she had been an excellent customer for many years. And then the store sent flowers to the funeral.

The difference between one store and another is customer service.

THE AGE OF APOLOGY

AUGUST 1990

THROUGHOUT HISTORY, there have always been ages named for dominant characteristics of the times. There are golden ages and Middle Ages as well as the Age of Enlightenment, the Age of Reason and the Machine Age. But what will we call the present age?

We could call this the Age of Apology because being in business in the United States today means you have to say you're sorry all the time. Doing it right isn't much of a concept in the Age of Apology. There is no particular need to do things right since you can always apologize later and fully expect to be forgiven. In fact, as a customer nowadays, your most important quality might be forgiveness. "This is my first day on the job," the cheerful whiner explains, preparing you to expect exactly nothing from the interaction.

You have to forgive TWA which begins its menu with "We apologize in advance if your luncheon entree selection is not available due to the requests of other passengers." Shut up and eat what's left. The choices on the menu are just there to keep you entertained with what you might have had if TWA had done its job right in the first place.

"I'm sorry," the fragrance bar lady at Bloomingdale's told me, airing her whole week's batch of dirty laundry. "We don't have Francesco Smalto except in this one size. They're not shipping us things nowadays." Bang. The end. They're sorry.

Perrier takes costly nationwide ads explaining how sorry they are that nasty old benzene slipped into your drinking glass. AT&T took full-page ads everywhere offering reduced rates on Valentine's Day calls because they screwed up one afternoon and blacked out phone service across the entire country.

Exxon keeps leaking all over the map, infecting whole coastlines. Then they apologize and leave to leak somewhere else. Even L.L. Bean, for many years a near-religious experience in customer service, is having apoplectic seizures of apology. In 1988, dissatisfied customers returned $82 million worth of goods. That cost the company $2 million in return freight charges, or 14 percent of sales. They are hastily retraining 3,200 employees in techniques that may help them do less apologizing and more selling.

I ordered a reading table featured on the cover of the Levenger catalog, and three days later a chipper little voice called me up to say: "Mr. Glen, I have good news and some not-so-good news!" Isn't that cute? Cuteness often precedes apologies. "The good news is," she chirped into my ear, "that the table you ordered is now available in three finishes—not just one. The bad news, however, is" (and I could have lip-synced this next part right along with her) "that our deliveries are running a little bit late. This item is so popular that we're temporarily out of it." (I had received the catalog exactly three days earlier.)

What was I supposed to do? Rejoice along with her at the company's successful sales rate? Praise the buyer for buying such a hot item? Be glad for this latest opportunity to practice the art of forgiveness?

I tried to buy five inflatable penguins from The Nature Company, although I know that they are often out of whatever you want. Sure enough, they called almost as soon as they received my order to say that deliveries were running a little bit late. The penguins would not be ready in February, as the catalog promised, but by April 15th. Would I like to keep the order in? I said yes.

On March 4, they called again. It seems that the penguins were arriving at The Nature Company, but there was still a problem. I was told that if you picked them up by the wings, they came apart. So, The Nature Company was going to make new and improved penguins and fully expected good ones to be available for shipping by the end of May. They very, very sincerely told me how very, very sorry they were about all this. But I was assured that the penguins were really, really cute and that I would enjoy having them—eventually.

Who cares? Why Advertise? Why lead me on while I stand around like an idiot waving money at them? I spoke to a supervisor who promised she would have (at my request) the president of The Nature Company call me. He never did. I suppose he was too busy apologizing to someone else to get on the phone and apologize to me.

About a week later, I got a message on my answering machine telling me that someone in customer service would be happy to help me if there was anything, anything at all they could do. They left a telephone number in the 415 area code, which would have cost me $4 if I had returned the call.

I did not invest in the telephone call. At this time, I have no idea whether or not I will ever see those penguins. But if I do, I know that they will make a cool display during the dog days of August or September when the smog is yellow and the deliveries get straightened out.

The dictionary is so great, so precise in its definition of "apology." And it is obvious that the message is not lost in—although it may not appear in—the mission statements of L.L. Bean, Exxon, TWA, Levenger, The Nature Company, Perrier, all the automobile companies and others too numerous to forgive. The dictionary says: "an admission of error or discourtesy accompanied by an expression of regret." What can I say dear, after I've said "I'm sorry?"

If all businesses did things right in the first place, they would never have to apologize. Loving your customers means never having to say you're sorry.

MY SUMMER VACATION

OCTOBER 1992

I TOOK A NAP this summer. I needed a break from trying to keep track of the L.A. riots, California earthquakes, Yugoslavian wars, horny naval aviators, raging rap groups and our pitiful performance at the Earth Summit in Rio, where we stood by and did nothing while our planet hemorhages in the emergency room. I needed a vacation without any news about Alexander's retail bankruptcies and Sears' cheating its customers.

And then I woke up and prepared to revisit the world. I knew I could find out what had happened fastest by talking to customers. What changes customers changes us all—and customers are changing a lot lately. I expected to see some good, constructive changes in stores and in service, because I know that hard times bring out the best in good people, and I believe that through suffering we get smarter.

I went to the mall, because any mall at all is where America lives. (Even a mall with 950 stores—and 58 bathrooms—in Minneapolis is still a mall.) I wanted to see new stores, and old stores doing new things. I expected to see more businesses exploring their social responsibility. I even expected service. I was optimistically primed to discover that service is finally being taken seriously, that people care about their jobs, their work, themselves and even others. I expected joy after darkness, and profits being made.

I was wrong.

The mall I visited has six big anchor stores. The four department stores are Wanamaker's, Bloomingdale's, Macy's and Strawbridge & Clothier.

Each of these four department stores has an atrium. The other two anchors, Sears and Penney's, do not have atria. (Sears doesn't even have trusting customers.)

In each department store I was told that the atrium was an innovative architectural feature. All four of these stores had been playing "My atrium is bigger than your atrium." But customers tend to mistake one atrium for another, so the song really should go, "My atrium is exactly the same as your atrium and so is my business." (The customers might respond if the stores recognized their existence instead of leaning so hard on their atria.)

Actually, the atrium at Strawbridge & Clothier was different: It had a pig in it. Or rather, a boar, the famous wild boar of Florence, in cunning reproduction. You could rub its nose and deposit money for luck, just as if you were in Florence.

Passing through each of the atria, I found myself floundering in Father's Day promotions. I saw big piles of Madras shirts, brought back in the hopes of selling last year's markdowns this year. But the merchandise was not the message. Signs said:

Macy's: 20% off, 35%, 40%, 50% ...
Bloomingdale's: 15% off, 25%, 30% ...
Wanamaker's: 10% off, 15%, 30% ...
Strawbridge & Clothier: 20% off, 25%, 30% ...
Sears: I didn't go in.
Penny's: I didn't want to walk through 24 cartons being unpacked in the front doorway.

Not much had changed. We cling to sameness. It covers the earth.

I did find evidence of people using social responsibility as a way of doing business profitably. Estee Lauder introduced "Origins." Store shelves now have CDs in short boxes and deodorant in no boxes at all. Wal-Mart recently announced that it intends to actually Do Something about education by partnering with vendors (and when Wal-Mart calls, you answer the phone) in raising funds to educate people who need it (an almost unimaginable task).

Outside the anchors, I found less of everything: stores, merchandise, success, customers. I had known this was happening, but the actual sight of so much vacancy made me believe it.

I am still—as always—searching for service, like some pilgrim trusting only to faith. I clocked the following times spent inside each store, handling merchandise, carrying pieces from place to place, draping garments on my self in front of mirrors ... fading ... aging ... without once being approached by a saleperson:

Macy's: 11 minutes
Bloomingdale's: 9 minutes
Wanamaker's: 6 minutes
Sear's: 4 minutes

Not much had changed.

But I still needed hope, so I went to one more store. I walked the mall until I came to The Disney Store. Same mall, same time, same day, same customers, same country. I walked through the front door of The Disney Store (no atrium) wearing two cameras and half a dozen clanking accessories.

Instantly a young woman wearing mouse ears came toward me and I knew she was going to say, "I'm sorry, you're not allowed to take pictures here." All six anchors stores would have done this. (And the Gap tries to take away your film.)

But I was wrong again, just as I had been wrong in hoping for progress until now. The mouse ears were joined by a cute, cute youth with 40 bright white teeth, who said, "Give me your camera. I'll take your picture!"

I surrendered my camera, stunned. I smiled. He took my picture. He handed me back my camera.

"Why did you do that?" I asked.

And they both replied together: "Because we love you!"

And then I realized, not much had changed here either. They're always like that at Disney.

On my way back out of Macy's, a woman carrying nine garments stopped me near the atrium.

"Do you work here?" she said to me. I had to say, "No, I don't."

"Well, neither does anybody else," she said. "I've been here at least 20 minutes (I knew what she meant), and I want to buy all of this merchandise and I cannot find a living human being to take my money. What more do they want than that I should be standing here rattling hangers and hoping to give them money?"

I couldn't have said it better myself.

And that was the way it was. I came back to the world by going to the mall hoping for improvement. It had seemed such a good opportunity—but not much had changed. No service, no fun, no news, no innovation. I felt like taking another nap.

What does it take, I wondered as I wandered through one final atrium. What does it take to wake us up?

BATTERED BY BARNEYS

JANUARY 1993

ON SEPTEMBER 16, 1992, *The New York Times* men's fashion issue ran two full-color pictures of a white winter coat by Dries Van Noten—available at Barneys—in its "Fashion Forecast" section.

What more could a store in a recession want? Gorgeous full-color, free photos addressed to millions of customers pre-selling a $655 coat. I, and perhaps others who loved the coat, called the store to find it.

Hah. The switchboard operator knew nothing and admitted it. Then began a telephone-tag extravaganza that has yet to end at this writing.

The switchboard connected me to Designer who knew nothing and switched me to Advertising, who, after many trips through hold finally told me (as though I were young and slow to understand) those photos were not advertisements, they were publicity, so why was I talking to them?

Advertising switched me to Public Relations, who hadn't seen *The New York Times* yet. (This info after three phone calls—I had stupidly inquired at lunch time when the P.R. personables were all at Le Madri experiencing the autumn wild mushroom festival and making deals for more free designer garment publicity.)

I was switched back to Designer, then to Designer Sportswear, then to Outerwear, and back to Public Relations. Nobody had ever heard of Dries Van Noten, or his coat or *The New York Times* advertorial.

Then I called the President of Barneys. An Executive Assistant answered and informed me everyone named Pressman was unavailable, whether President, Chair or Other, and what was this in reference to? (I should have known they were probably in Japan getting mo' money to open mo' stores.)

I explained I was a Customer reacting with enthusiasm to their merchandise, but that no one could find the merchandise; they'd never heard of the editorial, hadn't read the paper. And I announced I thought 50 minutes was enough of a customer investment to get their attention, but I was failing and thought—whimsically—the folks running Barneys at some Executive level might still be interested in selling coats.

I don't think she liked my attitude, but she promised to get back to me and I hung up for the fifth time and waited for her to ring me.

She did. She was switching me, immediately, to the waiting Buyer, who, if anyone, should have known where the elusive Dries Van Noten coat was.

The buyer was a hoot. He delivered a monologue that showed he would have been better doing impersonations of fashion fatigue at a Madonna-thon than buying at Barneys.

"Oh God!" said Vince. *"The New York Times* just makes me crazy. They picked that coat even though we didn't order it, and now I've got to try to get the damn coat into the store. Only it comes from Dries in Belgium and you know what Dries is like. He's a great designer, just fabulous, but getting any merchandise from him is an incredible experience. Why don't you call back in a few weeks and see if we've go the coat—only I've got to tell you his sizes run large, so if you're small, forget it because the medium is huge and even the small is large. Plus, Dries has been having trouble with the Italian fabric people—you know what they're like—so it might not be in the same fabric as the sample anyway...."

That was only the beginning. My telephone log reads like this:

• Next call to the buyer: "Dries is shipping next week. I'll call you."

• Next week; my call: "Dries didn't ship, but he's shipping this week, and it should be in Customs next week. I'll call you."

• Next week; my call: "I don't know if the coat is in Customs yet but I must tell you we're only getting one piece and I don't know what size it's going to be. I'll call you."

• Next week; my call: "The coat's not in Customs yet, but I expect to clear it this week and it should arrive at the Distribution Center by Wednesday. I'll call you."

• Wednesday; my call: "We don't have the coat yet. You know what Belgians are like. I'll call you."

• Next week; my call: "This is Nicole. Vince is on vacation. What coat? Could you describe it? I'll try to trace it and call you...."

Surprise! No call. No coat. No follow-up. No sale.

How's Barneys' business? Terrible. But Barneys has great windows. And great ads. And great publicity. But no coat. And no sale.

As of November 4, it is exactly 49 days since the coat appeared in the Fall Fashion Forecast of *The New York Times*. It is cold, as winter came early this year due to global warming. Vince is on vacation, and I am cold. I know there are other coats in other stores, and I could, like most decent Americans, go on wearing whatever I have been wearing in recent winters.

But I was persistently looking for signs of life in the retail industry, brandishing my $655 at Barneys and hoping to meet a Salesperson.

PART NINE
AIDS

A MATTER OF LIFE AND DEATH

MARCH 1987

"Since 1981 some 16,000 people have died in this country because of AIDS, and well over a million may be infected with the virus that causes the disease. The official projections for the next five years have become familiar—a tenfold increase in cases, more than 179,000 in the U.S. by 1991."—*Vanity Fair*

WHY DOESN'T THE RETAIL INDUSTRY *do* something about the catastrophic health crisis facing friends, customers, members and, indeed, the entire nation?

Why does Elizabeth Taylor, who has spent most of her life just being a world-famous movie star, suddenly rise to greatness, raising $4 million to fight AIDS, saying, "I promise you, I have committed my life to fight for the cure." While we stand by.

Why does the interior design industry, crushed by the death of Angelo Donghia, rally, advertise, publicize and evangelize in the cause of AIDS? While we stand by.

Why does the fashion industry, galvanized by the death of Perry Ellis, unite to support AIDS research with star-studded benefits and celebrity-filled magazine ads? While we stand by.

The New York Times in 1986: "Designers finally came out in force to take concerted action against the killing disease AIDS. There was no greater moment in fashion this year than the night its leaders gathered at the Javits Convention Center to raise money for AIDS research. Way Bandy, the make-up artist, asked friends to announce his death as AIDS-related ... several companies involved with fashion gave contributions to AIDS researchers in lieu of holiday gifts ... among others, Mark Goldstaub Public Relations, which represents entertainment/business clients, and Mitchel-Manning-Batter Associates, which represents clients such as Murjani International (Gloria Vanderbilt, Coca-Cola, Tommy Hilfiger).

"In the spirit of the holidays, Ralph Lauren's 1986 gift card read, 'We have made a contribution in your name to Dr. Wm. Haseltine, Harvard School of Public Health, for the purpose of AIDS research. Season's Greetings.'

"Fashion made no more significant statement than that in 1986."

The January 12, 1987, *New York* magazine cover story is "Fighting AIDS."

There will be lots more, which makes it even more embarrassing that we are standing by.

What is the reason for our delay? Maybe it's because we haven't had a martyr yet. Martyrs always ignite causes. Maybe that's what it takes to motivate us—the death of a hero. Then, and only then, our of grief, action begins.

No. We must not wait until a hero dies, and we are finally forced into action. We must not wait while thousands of less well-known people die. There's plenty of company on the sidelines, where we stand by. But that's no excuse.

The truth is that the only real action of any consequence is taking place in the fashion design, interior design and movie industries, and a few related magazines. These professions are logical: AIDS hit them first. But AIDS is not confined to them any longer. It wanders everywhere amongst us.

Rock and country musicians, who are very good at causes, don't yet have conspicuous AIDS organizers. They've been very busy with food and farming.

The classical music world, led by its own constant evangelist Isaac Stern, staged a big night at Carnegie Hall, with disappointing results. And it remains an isolated event.

In sports, the drug-related deaths of Len Bias and Don Rogers shook the world, but when the Washington Redskins' Jerry Smith announced he had AIDS, there was very little publicity. Shortly thereafter, he died.

What has big business done? General Foods? General Motors? General Electric? Or any other *Fortune* 500 company?

And where are the renegades? Ross Perot? Lee Iaccoca? Malcom Forbes? Peter Ueberroth? Donald Trump? Jane Fonda? Ronald Reagan?

Many have done a lot. Many have raised funds, produced concerts, marathons and sports events. Many have given their time, their money and their hearts in tireless ways. Blessings to every one of them. But private action is not enough. There has always been power in numbers. The whole has always been much, much greater than the sum of its parts.

What has our industry done? As far back as 1981, when AIDS was being called "the gay plague," Levi Strauss took action. Top management members of the Haas family educated staff about AIDS. They sat at desks in the lobby of their international headquarters pioneering in the early fight against AIDS. But name one other major American corporation that has done this. Where's Esprit? Georges Marciano? Nike? Liz Claiborne? Are we leaving it all up to Ralph Lauren and Murjani?

What has the visual merchandising industry done? At the recent NADI

(National Association of Display Industries) show, someone thought up some very small, cheap stars which were sold out in four hours. They cost $2, although some gave more, and everyone obligingly wore them for a few days, as if to clear their consciences by making this minute gesture.

There was a raffle before that, in June 1986. Lots of people gave merchandise to be sold. Proceeds went to AmFAR, The American Foundation for AIDS Research. The results were dismal; this ill-fated raffle raised about $25,000. *Crain's New York Business* ran a story headlined, "AIDS benefit sputters, starts." Referring to industry members, it said, "The trade group realized what AIDS victims already know: Despite all the publicity, people still prefer to keep their distance from the disease."

So what will the visual merchandising industry do next? Well, NADI is irritated and exasperated, and much more is planned for June, 1987. There will be a really big auction, with details to come.

WAVM (Western Association of Visual Merchandising) is devoting its industry party this March to raising money for AIDS research. And, believe it or not, except for vital individual contributions, that is about all the visual merchandising industry has done about AIDS. Where are the trade organizations connected with retailing? These associations are the single central gathering places for everyone concerned. But they mostly just stand by.

What have visual merchandising manufacturers done? One company ran a full-page memorial ad in *VM+SD* magazine after a key employee died. We need more action, though, and fewer memorials.

Where are all the usual industry leaders? What have retailers done? Here's a multi-billion-dollar industry that welcomes every citizen in America, but they're scared. You can't name one single store or chain or one shopping center developer that has done anything to fight AIDS. Oh, maybe Kenneth Cole, who ran ads reading, "This season, buy one less pair of our shoes and contribute the difference to AIDS research." Or Patricia Fields and a few other shops selling Bruce Weber's new Rio book for $60 per copy, with all proceeds going to AIDS research.

Good for Kenneth Cole and Patricia Fields. Dare one ask where Macy's, Melville, The May Company, Marshall's, Mervyn's Neiman-Marcus, Nordstrom, Kmart and Sears are? The Rouse Company? Les Wexner? Milton Petrie?

Many visual merchandisers say things like, "We can't bring this subject to our corporate board." Too bad. All they have to do is wait, and the subject will be brought up for them. *U.S. News and World Report*, January 5, 1987: "AIDS will begin to figure in the nightmares of mainstream America in

1987. In 1987, the federal government will spend $79 million on education and $317 million on AIDS research. More will be spent in 1988."

What have our trade publications done? *VM+SD*, on a few occasions, has donated free ad space for the NADI's AIDS raffle events and publishes this column that will reach many.

I realize, too, that I am as delinquent as so many others in this emergency. I'm going to work. This matter of speaking out, of shouting opinions, is a privilege we all have. I'm a columnist and speaker. You're also a person in the public view. You belong to a community. You can express opinions; opinions have power. They can create revolutions. They can cause good things to happen.

The spirit of courage is beginning to creep in, but the spirit is slow—far too slow. The tragedy grows. It will not diminish; we need our courage now.

We go to memorial services and run memorial ads. Our grief is sincere, but we do not look ahead. Nothing we can do is going to cure AIDS immediately. But we cannot let that be our reason for quietly standing by. Just imagine what could be done if we were doing it together. The accumulated power of all our associations, publications, manufacturers and stores all using our collective imagination (that's what we're famous for) would be extremely strong. We need to be a unified community all fighting together.

This has not yet happened. Why don't NADI, WAVM and WORLDSTORE sit down together and plan? This would be a true summit meeting of all the powers in the visual merchandising field. They could invite some retailers, too. Just one afternoon with all these determined people in one room would make a mighty start. What are we waiting for?

I wonder what it takes to motivate people. Isn't it enough that everyone you know has lost friends to AIDS? Do we still need a martyr to inspire us?

Rock Hudson, Angelo Donghia and Perry Ellis made action unavoidable. Don't you think those industries wish they had initiated action before those tragedies?

Are we afraid? If so, so what? There is no room for fear in matters of life and death.

In our industry, we have the cause, we have the power, and we have the influence to fight against AIDS. And we're not doing it enough. We must stop the waiting, the gossip and the fear. We will be fighting for our lives, not waiting them out. We can turn this crisis into this industry's finest achievement.

We have always been colleagues in work. Now, we are colleagues in fear. It is now, *right now*, that we can use the privilege of life to fight fiercely for life.

HALF WAY TO CARNEGIE HALL

AUGUST 1987

"This hall will intertwine itself with the history of the country. All good causes will find here a platform. From this platform men may be spurred to aims that end not with the miserable self, but here an idea may be promulgated which will affect the world, or here a good cause may be promoted."
—Andrew Carnegie, May 13, 1890.

A LOT HAS HAPPENED concerning AIDS since my last article in *VM+SD* (March, 1987). Many industries, reluctantly or otherwise, have begun to help themselves by joining forces, pooling their talents and all their hopes and fears, and acting against AIDS. The display and retail industries have continued to act individually ...

• Bloomingdale's had memorial ads and windows for Antonio and Willi Smith.

• Marshall Field announced Fall Benefit events that are expected to raise $1 million.

• Levi Strauss made an "AIDS in the Workplace" film that is being shown to all its employees.

• The National Association of Display Industries (NADI) staged a big auction in New York City on June 15 to raise money as well as display community consciousness.

• *VM+SD* magazine donated 5,000 reprints of my March column, "A Matter of Life and Death," for distribution around the country.

• Kenneth Cole continues to use advertising space to focus attention on AIDS issues.

• Retailers, including Crazy Eddie, Aca Joe, Madderlake, New York Man and Tower Records, sponsored an AIDS Walk in New York on May 17.

• The North Face held a $3-million sale in San Francisco, donating proceeds of $32,500 to the AIDS Foundation.

• Katherine Hamnet is designing clothes with special (labeled) pockets for condoms. And Filo Fax, the manufacturer of quality appointment books, now offers a special insert pocket for carrying condoms.

• Seven Continents, Toronto, is celebrating the opening of new facilities with its fourth (almost annual) summer event, and 2,000 people are expected. Each person will be charged $25 admission, all of which goes to the AIDS Committee of Toronto towards the fund for Persons With AIDS.

- Bruce Hoover, a major Broadway theater stage manager, donated services as general stage manager for the recent NADI auction.
- John Fariello, a sales representative for several display companies, donated ten percent of his commission on opening day of the California Visual Merchandising Market this past March.
- Roth Display, Garden Grove, California, donated funds in lieu of its annual party during the California Visual Merchandising Market.

So there is a continuing and growing patchwork of diverse individual efforts—but nothing yet as a community. However, one good deed can be obliterated by one cruel piece of ignorance: A chain of stores in Washington, D.C., posted a notice on all employee bulletin boards, in a disastrous attempt to be amusing. The notice said, "Due to the AIDS epidemic, it is no longer mandatory to kiss the boss's ass." This cartoon was sent to me by one of the store's employees who's been diagnosed with AIDS.

Other industries have banded together to achieve tremendous influence. Here are three important stories:

- "The Art World Goes All Out Against AIDS"—what a headline in *The New York Times*! Over 70 New York galleries and 600 artists joined "Art Against AIDS," a week of art sales raising millions and worldwide awareness of AIDS in one great week.
- The dance world is going all out—13 New York-based companies will perform together in "Dancing for Life" on October 25 to raise money and unity. Their goal is $1.4 million. How did it happen? Lar Lubovitch called a bunch of managers and choreographers to his studio to talk about the response of the dance community to AIDS. The organizer said, "To my knowledge, this is the first time anything like this has happened."
- Malcolm Forbes became a true hero on May 28 by facing the entire business community of America with the subject of AIDS. On the 70th birthday of his magazine in the presence of the titans of American business and politics, he presented Elizabeth Taylor with a check for $1 million for AmFAR. In this single gesture he probably did more to open and illuminate the subject of AIDS than any "celebrity" so far. This took even more guts than money, and its influence will reach far beyond the $1 million.

His example either irritated or gained the admiration of his guests, but got the attention of them all with a generous, compelling example.

If any retailers attended, they were not mentioned in the *Times*. And here's a very odd thing—*USA Today* wrote up the party, but didn't mention the $1 million for AIDS.

Now, finally, the retail world is going to get together to act as a community against AIDS. We, the retailers, can participate in a great beginning—"90 Minutes For Life," December 8 at Carnegie Hall, where 2,800 retailers will gather for the first retail industry event to raise money and to make plans for fighting AIDS.

The producers of this event are NADI and the Western Association of Visual Merchandising (WAVM). Their determined cooperation makes the entire industry proud. Here's some information from the first press release for this event:

"NADI and WAVM will present Peter Glen and Friends in an enlightening benefit and celebration of an action plan against AIDS. Peter's program will present ideas and actions undertaken so far by retailers and manufacturers in three fields related to AIDS—research, education and care. Peter's 'friends' will be eminent industry leaders testifying to the audience in one-minute presentations about what they feel and do in their companies, and what they feel this influential audience can do in their companies.

The morning has two objectives: 1. To raise money and 2. To teach the audience how to spread the word. We will endeavor to have a national television network underwrite and produce the program, making the tape available for distribution throughout the retail industry. It can also be syndicated as a public service through national television. The videotape will greatly expand the Carnegie Hall event to millions of employees in the retail industry.

Many people and companies are contributing talents and time to ensure the success of this project. To make it great, we need you. Your influence is mighty, and we need it now."

Already people are contributing ...

• NADI and WAVM have appointed committees and committed resources to produce and stage the event. This is the first time the two major display organizations have combined to produce a project. Their commitment is making this possible.

• Tom Holliday and the Newspaper Advertising Bureau have located suppliers for stationery and envelopes for the entire project; Tom has personally contributed one-third of the cost.

• Douglas Raymond of the Retail Advertising Conference will act as consulting producer for December 8.

• Craig and Diane Carl of Craig Carl Inc. have designed and donated the logo and artwork.

• Jo An Pagenetti was first to announce the project in *Retail Ad Week*.

- Robert Moss will act as general stage manager.
- John Ryan & Company, Minneapolis, will design and donate posters for the audience.
  - Susie Tompkins, co-owner of Esprit, will be among the vocal guest stars.
  - All Esprit employees can turn trash into cash at the Many Happy Returns Recycling Center. Proceeds go directly to the San Francisco AIDS Foundation and the Shanti hospice project.
  - Esprit News, the company's paper, has constant updates on AIDS. And next season's advertising campaign will include statements on AIDS to increase awareness and understanding.
  - Dr. Mathilde Krim, co-chair of AmFAR with Elizabeth Taylor, is supporting the project.
  - Marshall Field is the first corporate sponsor, as, indeed, Marshall Field is the first major American department store to host an AIDS benefit anywhere. Other corporate sponsors will shortly be announced. (Are you among them? You might volunteer.)
  - The Chicago chapter of the Institute of Store Planners has made my July 9 presentation an AIDS benefit. A portion of every admission goes to AIDS research.
  - "Fashion Cares" is a Toronto design event that sold T-shirts and threw a June 10 fashion show and party. All proceeds went to The AIDS Committee of Toronto.

Many more committed people are on the way. As you read this, we are just half-way to Carnegie Hall. Think what you can do to join in this great cause. It is time for courage, and courageous people will gather to speak out and plan. Think what you and your company can do to contribute, participate and act. We all need to act to fight AIDS. We are late, but this is our opportunity to make a great beginning. We are on the way to Carnegie Hall.

A DAY IN THE LIFE

DECEMBER 1987

I WAS OUT in San Francisco recently, meeting with people to discuss "90 Minutes For Life." Tom Wrubel, president of The Nature Company, picked me up at the St. Francis Hotel. Tom had already agreed to become a sponsor for the program, but he wanted me to meet Ruth Brinker.

We drove to St. Gregory's Episcopal Church, where Ruth cooks 300 meals in the church basement every morning. She's recruited some of the best chefs in San Francisco and organized a regular schedule for them.

At 4:30 every afternoon, ten volunteer drivers appear and deliver the meals to AIDS patients. Because they're so sick, some of the patients give the volunteers their house keys so evening meals and bag lunches can be delivered to their bedsides.

Ruth started doing this instead of retiring because she knows one of the biggest problems for many AIDS patients is getting food. Said Ruth, "We give practical support, and food programs are practical." Ruth's organization is called "Open Hand." They use no processed food. Volunteer vegetable choppers start early in the morning. A hot dinner entree and a bag lunch, delivered, cost $4.25 per person per day.

Ruth Brinker is one of the six individuals to be honored in Washington by The National AIDS Network. (Others include Whoopi Goldberg and Robin Williams.) I asked Ruth what she would say to 3,000 retailers if she were talking to them at Carnegie Hall. "I would say that AIDS is affecting all of us, and we need to help. Most of the public is aware of this. Stores are saying 'It might hurt sales.' People only know the statistics. They don't know face-to-face what this disease is actually like.

"AIDS patients are often so weak they can't get up out of a chair. They can't walk to the kitchen. In very hot weather, a patient might have to make one of two decisions: to open the window or get to the refrigerator. He can't do both. Nobody terminally ill should go through this. They need to feel that people care about them.

"I see people thoroughly involved in their own personal lives. I see them at opera openings, so concerned about their appearance. We need to shake them. If they send in a check for $100, they feel they do their bit. I don't want them to get off the hook that easily. I want them to commit regularly."

Ruth is working to establish a foundation across the country. Her tribute in Washington will probably help.

As soon as Tom and I left the church, he turned to me and said, "We'll still be sponsors for '90 Minutes,' but here's what else I'd like to do. Three friends and I want to bring Ruth Brinker to New York, buy her tickets and hotel and have her appear on stage at Carnegie Hall."

Ruth Brinker will be at Carnegie Hall.

One hour later, I was telling Gerry Greenwood, executive director of the Western Association of Visual Merchandising, about Ruth. He said, "Let's have a seminar next year on March 29. You can do '90 Days After 90 Minutes For Life' to tell everyone what's happened since December—another uplifting event. Proceeds of all tickets will go to 'Open Hand.' "

How quickly good things can happen when people act because they care. On the same day in San Francisco, I ...

• visited Wilmer Weiss, Jay Licht and Barbara Bass at I. Magnin. I collected material about "Raise the Roof," an AIDS benefit performed under a tent on their roof as long ago as last year. In November, the grand opening of their new men's store was an AIDS benefit. I will show these great events at Carnegie Hall.

• photographed Peggy Mendelson, Chris McKenna and Tim Keller at Neiman-Marcus. They and their "store family" are responsible for putting panels from the "Names Project Quilt"—a two-block-long patchwork, each three-by-six-foot patch memorializing someone who has died of AIDS—into their Union Square windows in August. This courageous event galvanized the store family and the city itself. Afterwards, the entire quilt was taken to Washington, D.C., where the 3,000 victims' names were read in a ceremonial reading on October 11. I will present this retail event in Carnegie Hall.

• visited Wilkes Bashford to explain "90 Minutes." He put me in touch with Angie Thieriot, not a retailer, but an extraordinary fighter who has built The Planetree Model Unit at Pacific Presbyterian Hospital—the most humane hospital unit anywhere in the country. A mere eight lovely rooms are gathered in a circle around a kitchen, living room and nursing station, staffed by avid humanitarians who encourage patients to fight. I wonder why rich people on this earth do not build dozens of these facilities to make the epidemic slightly more tolerable in human terms. A million heartening details include the delivery—free—of both menus and lunches each day from the neighboring Alta Plaza to patients with AIDS.

• met the composer of "Deep Breakfast," Ray Lynch, along with Allan Kaplan, head of Music West. Ray said, "Death is a terrible prospect. But death is not an ending. Death does not end consciousness." Ray Lynch's new music can lift the soul and give hope. We planned an inspiring finale at

Carnegie Hall.

• met with Kristin Joyce of Esprit. That company's guts and caring radiate like the sun through ads, stores and community relations. Together with Doug Murphy of AIDS Awareness Week, Esprit is gathering a band of warriors and celebrants throughout the city. Susie Tompkins will fly from Hong Kong to New York to appear at Carnegie Hall.

It was quite a day. I wouldn't have found so many great people in many other cities, but soon there will be people everywhere acting for other people. San Franciscans are motivated sooner because they have experienced more. Experience is what finally goads us into action.

The day was not yet over, though. I met for just five minutes with a man who has long been visual director for another very famous San Francisco store. Two weeks before, a friend of his was diagnosed with AIDS. I asked whether his store would become a "90 Minutes For Life" sponsor. He took the material and said he would ask. But he said not to count on it. He said he doubted very much they would be participants.

T.S. Eliot wrote, "This is the way the world ends. Not with a bang, but a whimper." So, to lift my own spirits I went back to St. Gregory's in the late afternoon. The kitchen was electric. Macaroni and cheese, chocolate cake and sandwiches were all being bagged and boxed, and the drivers were arriving. There was joy in the kitchen, and soon there would be food for many.

I remembered what Jay Licht had told me at Magnin's. He said he had an old videotape of mine and that he treasured the last sentence. I was startled by the long connection through time and asked him what it was. He said I'd quoted Dr. Samuel Johnson, "May you live every day of your life."

Here's another quote: "It is always morning somewhere."

A MESSAGE FOR DISCOURAGING TIMES

DECEMBER 1989

IT HAS BEEN TWO YEARS since our industry produced "90 Minutes for Life" at New York City's Carnegie Hall. I finally got the courage to sit down and watch the videotape of "90 Minutes" again. Two of the speakers for that evening now have died: James Terrell, founding partner and former president of the interior design and architectural firm Hambrecht Terrell International; and Sam Dunn, designer and founder of Sam Dunn Visuals.

AIDS is still with us. We still have hope, though. And finally, we have some encouraging news. People who test positive for the HIV virus can now proceed with immediate treatment that works in many cases. They can take AZT to delay the onset of ARC and AIDS without the intense side effects that come when the illness has progressed. It has also been proven to prevent pneumocystis pneumonia. And another drug, DDI, is going to be available shortly.

This all means that people at risk must be tested. Of course it's not pleasant to be tested for the HIV virus. Nothing about AIDS is pleasant. And up until now, there has been nothing for an HIV positive person to do but wait for symptoms to begin. But that's changed. People at risk who are not tested are acting irresponsibly—both toward themselves and others.

Talk to a doctor you trust as soon as you can. If you want to live longer, get tested now. Start the new year with courage. In a world of grim realities and such pervasive sadness, there is hope for everyone alive.

Every person reading this essay knows people who have died this year. Those who can bear the facts now know that by 1995, there will be ten times the number of AIDS cases that we have today. It's very hard to imagine what that will be like.

We cannot dwell too long with sadness. We long to feel the clouds disperse and to revive. We reach an almost infinite tiredness; we scrape at life to find more courage, humor, wit—anything just to keep fighting until we win. "One day at a time" makes more sense now than ever. We cannot allow our energy to be infected, our optimism to wilt. There's work to do.

We must not wait, but act. Let's start with our talents. We create, we dramatize, we make things beautiful. Our powers of persuasion are our greatest pride, our highest individuality. It's what we do for a living.

We must use our talents to live as strongly as possible. We can cause others to live more strongly. That's why we must seize each day we have and love it. While we live, we have that privilege. We know all this, but it is hard each time it happens all over again.

Watch the videotape again—crushing evidence of how time goes by. It is not a happy spectacle. But you will also see that hope sustains us. You will see how you can gather up your tools and go to work.

Laurence Olivier died this year. He was asked how he felt as the greatest actor in the English-speaking world. He said, "You do the very best you can. You can't do more, and you mustn't do less."

This December, remember to keep fighting as the gift-giving time comes back again. The best gift you can ever give is the gift of yourself at your best. Our greatest strength is ourselves, and we have a mighty cause to fight for—life.

Love and hope to all!

IT'S NOT OVER UNTIL IT'S OVER

DECEMBER 1990

HERE COMES another Christmas in the Age of AIDS. And here's the recent news on how the battle's being waged in New York City:

From the Fashion Industry...

The New York Fashion community staged its strongest AIDS effort yet. The Council of Fashion Designers of America (CFDA) and *Vogue* magazine (published by Conde Nast) produced a major event at the 69th Street Armory on November 29. Guests shopped a "dream store" of designer samples, with all the proceeds going to the New York City AIDS Fund. Tickets started at $1,000. Apparently the fashion industry has finally realized that by pulling together it can use its considerable accumulated power to motivate itself and others.

WNBC's "Live at Five," New York City's NBC affiliate, ran a three-part syndicated series on AIDS and the fashion industry that forcefully presented the facts about the talent lost because of AIDS and the current prejudices that stop manufacturers from hiring men as designers. It was a hard-hitting series. Footage from the videotape of WAVM (the Western Association of Visual Merchandisers) and NADI's (the National Association of Display Industries) "90 Minutes for Life" Carnegie Hall benefit held back in December of '87 was included in the presentation.

The Fashion Institute of Technology Student Association presented an AIDS benefit fashion show on October 11, with tickets selling for $100. Proceeds were given to Northern Lights Alternatives, an organization that trains volunteers to care for AIDS patients, and DIFFA (the Design Industry Foundation for AIDS).

Designers Rifat Ozbek and Jean Paul Gaultier have created special clothing lines, the profits of which will be donated to AIDS causes. It's all part of "Red Hot and Blue," a benefit that included a record album and video of musicians signing Cole Porter tunes. Musicians include Sinead O'Connor singing "You Do Something to Me," U2 rendering "Night and Day," and David Byrne crooning "Don't Fence Me In." (The clothing line of sweatsuit styles in psychedelic and harlequin prints will be available in February.)

From the Retailing Industry...

NADI has donated its December Market entertainment budget to DIFFA and Broadway Cares, a non-profit corporation made up of more than 30 leagues, guilds and associations for the New York Theater community.

Arthur Court, a San Francisco-based display manufacturer, has donated booth space to DIFFA during the NADI's December market. The company also donated space at NADI's last market.

May Department Stores contributed $200,000 to organizations that assist people with AIDS. The National Community AIDS partnership and DIFFA were each the recipients of $100,000 from the retailer. May's Chair and CEO David Farrell said, "With AIDS affecting increasing numbers of people, we want to offer direct support to help meet basic needs for food, shelter and other assistance."

This is a stupendous piece of news because it is a sizable and aggressive public gesture put forward by a major department store chain. I don't know of another company that has made such an effort.

Conran's was a major sponsor behind "Heartstrings," the traveling musical about AIDS that had sold out performances in New York City. The retailer gave a grand party after the opening performance.

From the Entertainment Industry...

Longtime Companion is an excellent movie that probably brought more understanding about the nature of living with AIDS to more people than any other "entertainment" so far.

The off-Broadway musical *Falsettoland*, a follow-up to the phenomenally successful *March of the Falsettos* ten years ago, updates the story to the Age of AIDS. *Time* magazine calls this the central musical event of the 90s. I would do anything possible to see this show during NADI's December market in New York. It will lift your spirits and renew your determination about AIDS—and life in general.

AIDS activist and performance artist Diamanda Gallas was banned in Italy after she performed there this summer. She recently performed "There Are No More Tickets to the Funeral," a piece "for the damned of our day," at the Cathedral of St. John the Divine. A cathedral spokesperson said, "Let's face it; she wouldn't be able to do this at St. Patrick's."

The first "Music for Life" concert was held at Carnegie Hall four years ago, and on October 28, 1990, the second one that had been planned by James Levine and the late Leonard Bernstein took place, assembling every classical superstar in concert. This needs to be done again and again.

And Yet...

There is still more bad news than good news, and we must renew our efforts as quickly and as strongly as possible. A major story in *The New York Times* declared that "AIDS Advocates Find Private Funds Declining: Advocates for people with AIDS are expressing concern that the public is growing weary of hearing about the disease and that a sense of alarm has given way to a resigned acceptance, making it harder to raise badly-needed private funds."

There is a general perception that AIDS is not as urgent as it used to be. And this is not only true in New York City. The California legislature announced that it was cutting its funds for AIDS by 12 percent. Equivalent reports are in from Dallas, San Francisco, Washington and New Orleans. And, of course, many such events go unrecorded.

Trend forecasters tell us that the national mood and its attention has shifted. And who is to say that help is not needed for children, literacy, homelessness, drugs, crime, the entire national health care crisis, the worldwide crises of the environment, starvation and possible war. Those are all gigantic issues and the role of the individual may not seem to matter on such a scale.

It is understandable that we are tired, worn out, exhausted by AIDS, and that fighting for so long with such small progress is dispiriting. And yet, it's not over until it's over. That's why it's important—as yet another season of love and joy and renewal comes to us shadowed, as every Christmas seems to be, by the constant undercurrent of unabated AIDS—to use our powers this and every season to do the best we can as individuals, as companies, as countries, as the world.

We are the world; we must continue to be the world and to fight until our tiredness gives way to action, until we live—oh, how we need to live again—in an age where AIDS is banished from the earth.

PART TEN
FACING FORWARD

PALLADIUM: THE END OF AN ERA

SEPTEMBER 1985

THE PALLADIUM is New York City's newest, hottest disco. And it's a great example of an idea whose time has gone.

You've seen it all before. In fact, you seen it for 25 years. Twenty-five years ago, The Peppermint Lounge and the Whisky-a-go-go killed live entertainment. Go-go boys and girls were the last of it. Record albums appeared. The music was dead, and so was the audience. It was all just right for those new years of "me-me-me" and "me and my mirror."

The Palladium is new and big and arty and flashy, but a disco is still a disco. And its ideas are stolen: the theater is from Studio 54; the inside structure from The Saint; the art from Area; the music from every dance joint in town; the videos from Private Eyes; the limos from Limelight; and the truly desperate public from wherever they were last week.

When an idea is new, it gives designers plenty to do. They invent new architecture, decor, graphics, sounds, lights—everything. But when the idea has been around, one of a kind decor is just a substitute for the last and the more things change, the more they stay the same. How many ways can you flash a light?

What's needed is a new way to spend the evening.

The Palladium pretends to be new. God knows, it's frantic. The major part of the mob is made up of too many people-per-limo and too much makeup-per-person and too much economy during the week to be able to make it to Saturday. It's old like *Saturday Night Fever.*

The astonishing thing about all this "individuality" is how "groupie" it is. The sole major motivation is to get in, fit in and to join. There have always been more joiners than leaders in the world, but this is a very extreme form of the Moose Club, Elks Club and Rotary; it's just a big frat house with all the despair that precedes being accepted.

The doorman at Palladium has become the local version of Saint Peter at the Gates of Heaven. The limos swarm up. The Day of Judgement is at hand. The sinner approaches the Throne.

Unfortunately, the current version of Heaven looks quite a bit like Hell: People dress Mean and Sinful; Rich and Aggressive; and they walk through anybody's face to get to the Head of the Line to pay their $18.

The music seems to matter, but all you ever hear is that it's never been heard before. Thank God we're first. But why doesn't anybody ever say they *like* it?

You can retire from the dance floor to the same old niches, the snotty waiters who used to be naked (but now they're dressed), and the superstar private rooms with overflowing ashtrays and the same old tortured flower arrangements. Lord, how those flowers must feel to have lived in the eye of God only to be cut and jammed into rented vases at the Palladium.

THE EARTH IS NOT A TREND

JANUARY 1990

THE OVERWHELMING ISSUE facing humanity today and from now on is the fate of our planet. Every other issue—including business—depends on it. Businesses must recognize this opportunity and act on it.

The fate of the earth is more important than crime, hunger, drugs, over-population, literacy, AIDS and the economy. There are many smart people who not only think it is by now too late to save the planet, but that idea is not even worth considering. If we do not decide to fight for the planet, we need to consider the alternative, and the alternative is ugly.

People in China and Japan wear surgical masks because they cannot breathe. People in Western Australia wear sunscreen all day, every day, because the thinning ozone layer is burning their skin.

The British do nothing at all to stop acid rain, although they create it constantly. All the chemicals they toss into the air are carried immediately northeast—away from Britain—by strong prevailing winds to Sweden and Norway, where it falls back to earth killing every lake and tree.

Russia won't tell anybody just how bad Chernobyl was. Already we are forgetting that Exxon infected Alaska and then departed. People are not reading the book *The End of Nature* because they find its thesis unbearable.

Our biggest fight still lies ahead. The earth is ill. We have always made the earth serve us, but we do not serve the earth. The planet has always provided for us, unconditionally, asking nothing back. And we have exhausted the earth without exchange. The earth has a fever; the temperature climbs. The climate has changed. The immune system of the planet has begun to fail.

The sun goes down, and we admire the sunsets caused by acid rain. Our winters are worse, and our summers hotter. Things don't grow, and cattle and people die. The air is foul. Ice is melting, and the oceans rise. Our trees are gone, and the earth has trouble breathing.

We must provide. Now we must turn and serve the earth. We will need courage, faith, imagination and fervent optimism. We are suddenly like some absurd nurse who confronts a patient with 20 minutes to live and says, in an old cliche, "Can I help you?"

The earth is our department, and everything we do depends on it. We must all do the best we can.

Retailers are already engaged in battle—from big stores to chain stores to independent stores to catalog operations. And they find it good for the soul. In many cases, customers are ahead of the stores, demanding that stores cooperate in order to deserve their patronage. There is plenty of choice in stores. The choice is now a matter of personal conscience, as much as it is price, location and selection.

It has never been as clear as it is today what stores must do—what all of us must do—to survive and thrive. If you are not involved in the life of the earth right now, it won't stick around while you wait to change your priorities.

You can be involved both in your official company role and as an individual. Eighty million Americans did volunteer work last year. This year, the participation is growing.

So, right now "the earth" is "hot," and everybody is doing something very trendy about it. How soon will they all have something new to be hot about? Do all these businesses realize that the fate of the earth is not just a magical moment in merchandising, but a fundamental change in our way of doing business and living that must become permanent?

Here is a warning: The earth is not a trend. The environmental issues are in danger of becoming a trend. This means it might not be taken seriously enough. The environment is not a fad. It is a permanent emergency.

Trends die fast. Something new replaces them. This is the essence of the merchandising business. Any moment now we will see a manager turn to someone who has just presented another planet-saving idea and say, "Why don't you just shut up? We've done our share."

Our biggest job is to convince our companies and ourselves that the fate of the earth is not a project or a trend. It is the right way to live.

It is the only fight that can give us back our future.

MARKETING THE MILLENNIUM

MARCH 1990

"IT WAS the best of times, it was the worst of times." Thanks, Charles Dickens. Good quote.

Here beginneth the nineties, the new decade, the countdown to the millennium, the most critical years of this century and therefore, of our lives. The Chinese say, "May you live in interesting times." These are.

A lot of things are forecast, ranging from world peace to the end of the planet. But one collective concept stands out as the most urgent and immediate merchandising activity—the home. Home is where the heart has always been reputed to be. And now, it's where you'll find the office, the garden, the health club, the communications center, the bank, the theater and the store. So since everything is taking place at home, then that's what retailers must go after.

Home—there's no place like it, all the comforts of it, let's keep its fires burning, be it ever so humble, and I'll be there for Christmas. We will possibly rediscover love and family life at home.

Many millions will discover they don't have to commute to work. We will work at home. A lot of money will disappear from dressing and transporting ourselves; closets and garages will get smaller, soon. Saving time and travel will add a cumulative total of several years to every working life. Those years can be used for pleasure or productivity instead of low-grade anger trapped on a freeway, even with a fancy cellular phone.

This escape from the office will require buying high-tech tools for a work-at-home revolt. Computers, telephones fax machines, all the forms of electronic mail, office furnishings, supplies, decor, et cetera, are already a $5.7 billion market.

Home will be a private piece of the environment that we can control. We will invest in seeds, bulbs, gardens, greenhouses, land, space and privacy. We will experience the joy (and health) of our own vegetables, planting, growing, nourishing, pruning, ripening, cutting, pickling, admiring and eating. We will need to buy things to get all this done.

We will be entertained at home. We need Nintendo, dozens of cable channels, videos, pay-per-view programming and multiple VCRs. The home itself will change to accommodate extended families and activities. The home will be our major investment. The kitchen and the family rooms will become the heart of the home. Bigger, fancier baths will be places where people can sit and talk and read and light the fireplace. There will be porches, places to sit and enjoy the evenings. Better computers will be inside the house taking care of the temperature, the appliances, lights and security.

We will do our banking at home. Banks are returning to the scene of one of their biggest flops—home banking. With better software and delivery systems, some banks are trying it again, knowing full well that if 250 million customers could be spared the trauma of actually going to a bank in person, they would give those banks *all* their money.

We will prepare and cook and eat at home while restaurant business declines. This is happening now. Safe, healthy food, exciting food, food within the price of reason will all taste better at home than at the end of high-priced travel. Gourmet food, international food and healthy food will become the property of everybody, and it will be consumed at home.

We will shop at home instead of haunting the malls. We will read catalogs, watch video and order merchandise without false promises of good service. In fact, we'll find that the selection, the honesty and the guarantees of good catalogs—and even home video shopping—are more sincere and less disappointing than shopping in a store.

Electronic shopping will take place at home, as soon as it gets straightened out and progresses beyond cubic zirconium. Meanwhile, there will be fewer, but better, catalogs. Nobody is going to bet on the decline of Smith & Hawken, Spiegel, Lands' End, L.L. Bean or Tweeds.

We will protect our homes. Already there are specialty stores that sell equipment, devices, gimmicks and paraphernalia ensuring the safety of our homes. The last ten years of the century are not likely to become less dangerous; crime and drugs continue to be our biggest national defeat. So we invest in razor wire, guard dogs, private police, sophisticated survelliance systems and alarms.

How sad it is that we will miss the irreplaceable charge of the Super Bowl in person, the jolt of sleeping in Yosemite National Park. But nowadays the Super Bowl is completely sold out, Yosemite is unnaturally jammed. Home had better be an attractive alternative.

The home improvement field will come to be connected in the customer's mind with life improvement, and former optional hobbies of "do it yourself" and decorating will become exploding passions for potential purchases. Being at home will change the spending emphasis of America from what we look like (there goes "fashion") to where we are and how we feel about it. We will invest and improve and furnish and rejoice in our controllable surroundings, cocooned and couch-potatoed, spending money on the nest.

But this will not be laziness. All his concentration will produce new gifts of time and opportunity to merge our hobbies with our happiness, to exercise our bodies and our minds right in the heart of home with and the people we love.

It would be nice if during this decade we could eliminate oil spills and acid rain and AIDS and homelessness and starvation and dwindling species and apartheid and war and crime and drugs and toxic waste and nuclear warheads, et cetera, et cetera. We will continue to fight for the sudden amazing possibility of a unified world, a global community, peace and the salvation of the planet.

Meanwhile, we will turn to what we can control—our homes. There, we can witness and participate in the rebirth of the family and family life. We will feather and furnish ourselves during the countdown that has already started on to the millennium, that time of reckoning when all our hopes and fears will coincide—and we will know the future.

LIFE AFTER EARTH DAY

JANUARY 1991

NOW THAT Earth Day has come and gone, what happened? Did people act or just talk? Has anything changed? Was it a dream or a dud?

Like most events that require effort and participation and a genuine point of view, some did and some didn't, some still do, and some don't. Yes and no. A hundred million people celebrated Earth Day in the usual three groups: followers, leaders and joiners. The followers contributed a little cheap cosmetic hype by calling themselves "green," which, in practical terms, accomplished nothing at all—except to ease the consciences of those marketing spectators who hoped that Earth Day would leave them alone.

The majority of people went along with Earth Day. They are joiners, as the majority always are. They saw a large parade moving down the avenues of the world, so they went over and sniffed at it and marched along for a few blocks until the became tired of the effort. But there were leaders, too—the only people who matter. And some of them were big businesses making big decisions that saw Earth Day as the right event to galvanize their own parades. The tuna industry, for example, no longer fishes with nets, causing tuna prices to rise and 100 million dolphins a year to go on living. McDonald's assigned $100 million to building future stores of better materials, and they're now using packaging made from recycled paper (as are the pages of this book).

Most of the leaders are individuals, as leaders always are, with a few multi-national intercontinental big boys with car phone networks making gestures at the earth. But we must believe that individuals care enough to see the sense—and even the necessity—of demanding paper bags in supermarkets and sorting the family trash into recyclable piles for intelligent collecting.

Manufacturers didn't do much. Some added scribbles of philosophy to hangtags on their garments; others hastily screen printed piles of sloganeering T-shirts. And none of them wanted any hassles from leftists and leftover hippies celebrating Earth Day.

Manufacturers certainly can and should make differences as well as products. General Motors, for instance, can make and market an electric car. And they should do it. If they don't, Japan probably will. That means Japan will take over the market one more time and help save the Earth as well.

The most responsive retailers attacked Earth Day two ways. First, they educated themselves and their employees to respect the earth while using it up, and they still made money. If the tuna fishermen can do it, retailers can do it, too. Second, retailers used their privilege as public businesses to wear their hearts on their sleeves for all their customers to see—an audience of 250 million folks who can save the planet. Some retailers did this well, some did it badly.

The informationists did a great job on Earth Day. There was certainly no lack of stickers, posters, pamphlets, newspaper supplements, rallies, parades, radio blitzes, heartfelt advertising and dire, artistic television specials. Earth Day itself probably generated enough new trash, biodegradable and otherwise, to completely bury the home of our "environmental President," the White House.

A lot of this thrashing turned out to be more motion than action. As usual, the North American public didn't lack ideas or information. We lacked action. The question after Earth Day isn't "What shall we do?" The question is one of motivation—"Why don't we do it?" But most people don't get motivated until life hits them right in the face. They keep smoking until the surgeon says, "You've got three months to live." Or they suddenly start indulging in safe sex when some partner is found to be HIV positive. Or they finally apply for a gun permit after someone they love is murdered on the way home to dinner. There's nothing quite like catastrophe to get people to do what they should have been doing all along.

The plain truth is that the plight of the planet hasn't exactly motivated everybody. There still is, and always will be, an overload of other, smaller issues. There's making a profit and greed and indifference and apathy and ego gratification and more, much more, to get in the way of saving the earth. Our best hope for life after Earth Day is that the situation is serious enough, persistent and personal enough, to affect us all until we live as individuals and citizens of a single planet.

So, Earth Day is over again, another superannuated dateline. Maybe again—in another 20 years, if there is such a thing—the whole celebrity shenanigans will happen all over.

Now what? We need to get moving again immediately, with no intention of stopping. We need to get moving differently. We need to move all over the earth. Most effective Earth Day events were individual and local. The problem, however, is collective and universal. We must stop thinking of global warming as some kiddie classroom issue, such as whether or not the distant Seychelles Islands will be buried, vanished, gone, by the time we think of where to put the next Club Med. We must stop thinking that the reason the population of the planet cannot breathe is because of some irritating Brazilians with bulldozers.

No individual has ever been an island, and now we are locked in one single breathing space together, sharing every respiration. The earth is everyone's department. Every day needs to be Earth Day!

THE SIMPLE LIFE

UP IN Burlington, Vermont, tie-dyed garments are not "fashion"—they are clothing. People carry babies around in slings and meditate on incredible new recipes with vastly organic ingredients. A couple of months or years ago, these people worked next to you. But they didn't like it, so the left. They wanted to live in the present, but enjoy it more. They clarified their lives by asking themselves what they wanted and then set out to find out how to get it. Now they enjoy themselves and are fulfilled in their agreement to keep their state in a state of nature before it's too late.

Vermont is gorgeous. Lots of places are gorgeous, but there it re-enters your life. Even the architecture plays background to nature. The inevitable downtown Burlington Mall is discreet, and the Gaps are tucked away inside old downtown buildings that look like they were not designed, but just plunked right where they are. Four miles from town there is wilderness. Not even developers have gotten to the Green Mountain National Forest.

I'm sure there is trouble in paradise, though. The trouble is the current human condition. So if you're looking for drugs and crime and economic woes and mediocrity, I suppose you can find them even in Vermont. Or in the remotest islands of the South Seas—if that's what you look for. But you'll find a few things in Vermont that are in short supply in other places. People are nice. They are decent. They may even be honest. They are cheerful, animated, energetic. The make money, if that's what they're trying to do. They lead a simpler life, if that's what they want to do. They go fishing—a lot—if that's what they want to do.

The folks at Empire Video in Burlington are slick, full of good ideas and discipline and passion, and so is their store. They are nice. When I visited my local Blockbuster Video in New York City, the kid was cheerful, and I was surprised. So I asked him why he was so cheerful. "Drop acid every day on my way to work," he said. That's the New York way of getting to be nice.

Good people make good places. These Vermont folks are not dull dropouts. Madeline Kunin is the only female Jewish governor ever in any state. She was elected three times in Vermont. This is the home of Ben & Jerry's ice cream, a state where billboards were banned 15 years ago, and authentic hippies are directly descended from Thoreau. There are radical publishing companies in Vermont. There's great food. Green Mountain Gringo Salsa and Stowe Corn chips are exported to Zabar's and Balducci in

New York. The Brattleboro Food Co-op is better than food stores in New York. The Common Good co-op restaurant has been packed for 20 years. Even the average pizza slice is excellent. You'll probably find that the chef quit a vice presidency at Batten, Barton, Durstine & Osborne two years ago.

This is the simple life of *Time* magazine's cover story not too long ago and of 15 people you know who recently vanished from "fabulous" jobs and who now make far less money but are happier. Are you one of those people? Have you been thinking about it? Talking about it? Trying to find out what other people think about it? Are you doing it?

The Northeast is often thought of as the old, decayed foundation of our country. Is the paradigm of the terrible deterioration of America, our failed economic system, our endless social woes, our crime, our physical decrepitude, our disability.

You can look at it that way. And the view is dreadful. Or you can look at it another way: I'm not talking about the Northeast or even any particular "country" location. People are going out of town—they are out in search of themselves. They are armed with the disappointment of the life they have been leading lately, and they're looking for a change of values in another system—different economics, better schools and medicine. They're looking for fearlessness on ordinary days. They want to live with less razor wire supplementing their burglar alarms.

People care about everything they do, not just about how much money they make. This is a change in the consumer condition that borders on betrayal. It often means not getting and spending money. Suddenly we need less and we want less, and it's this brand-new "wantlessness" that is destroying a large section of business. We never wanted less before; we always wanted more. We still want more—more clarity, simplicity, more joy.

The simple life can take place anywhere. It's a lot harder in the depths of New York City than it is in Burlington. It's probably exceedingly simple living in a tent on a glacier near Banff, but the simple life can take place wherever the spirit has been simplified. This requires some introspection, a quality for which Americans are not noted. Some questions must be asked, like: What do I want? What is the purpose of this? What's going on here? Am I doing the best thing for me? Do I live in the present? What do I enjoy? How could I worry less?

There are several places that aspire to a living present. Ithaca, New York, is another surprise for those who don't know it. Many of the "Vermont" principles apply. The place is all nature, mostly preserved, with an aggressive intellectual life maintained by 60,000 students and their teachers at Cornell.

The standards of restaurants, theaters and daily life are high. Everyone is involved in expressing themselves—like "talk-back" from the audience to actors at the Hangar Theatre after the show or the intense examination given by customers to ears of fresh corn in the farmer's market. The restaurants are hard to get into without reservations, and worth it. Baker's Acres is a garden shop as good as any in the land. Cornell itself inspires everything. People smile, they are polite, they seem contented. The lady that served me pie with pride said that most people she knew had never been to New York City, and she made it clear that they had no desire to do so. Yes, many people are overweight, and, no, stores and fashion are not much of an issue, dealt with strongly.

There is contentment today in certain American places like Ithaca and Burlington—and even money to be made. This version of the simple life results from questioning, exploration and well-though-out choices. Many people thriving creatively like this have mastered the task of living in the present and liking it.

P.S. *The New York Times* beat me again—and just as I finished writing this column—with an immense headline: "Made in Vermont. Marketing the Myth You Can Eat." Here are two excellent sentences from the story: "That's the Vermont of purity, wholesomeness, rural values, tradition, self-reliance, trustworthiness, simplicity, honesty, hard work, environmental awareness and closeness to nature, which residents and visitors alike described in interviews with the State Agency of Development and Community Affairs for a 1986 survey on the image of Vermont. For many, the report concluded, 'experiencing Vermont becomes a religious experience: oneness with nature, oneness with self, oneness with the universal life force.' "

And then there was a comment from the special projects manager for the much-admired Ben & Jerry's Homemade Inc. Alan Parker said, "There is an ache for our rural past that goes beyond nostalgia. I think that people feel there's something missing in general in the path their lives are taking, and images are part of the way we try to reclaim what is lost."

PARADISE AND PROFIT

JULY 1992

TWO YEARS AGO when I was going around screaming about the environment, I was greeted with every attitude from skepticism to indifference. But suddenly this year people have started asking for a progress report. The bad news is so bad that the planet has finally gotten the attention of business as well as customers. But there has been progress.

The first good thing I wish to report is that few things will thrill and rejuvenate your heart and spirit more than running out to the nearest Body Shop—or local bookstore—and grabbing a copy of Founder Anita Roddick's book *Body and Soul*.

The first paragraph begins: "I hate the beauty business. It is a monster industry selling unattainable dreams. It lies. It cheats. It exploits women. Its major product lines are packaging and garbage. It's no wonder that Elizabeth Arden once said that the cosmetics business was the 'nastiest in the world.' " And it goes on from there.

I dare you not to read *Body and Soul* standing up. I danced all over the place—it was so damn good. Anita Roddick is not just some aging sixties hippie trying to stop people from cutting down trees in Brazil. She's actively trading with downtrodden, dispirited people from her soap works in Edinburgh to hyacinth paper makers in Nepal to rain forest people everywhere. She believes in "Trade Not Aid," and she'll make you believe in it too. She's grown her business entirely on her own values and in her own way by listening to and caring about the environment and native peoples everywhere. But most of all, in the process of caring for the environment, she's become a vastly rich lady.

In *Body and Soul* Anita declares, "Environmentalism will be the most important issue for business in the 90s." Do you believe that yet? Many are still waiting for their research departments to discover it.

What's headline news today is that if you do business with environmental awareness, and if you do it with your heart—from your heart—customers will respond, appreciate it, and do lots of business with you.

People are going to the Body Shop because they know there's very little difference between one face cream and another, but they just love the idea of doing business with the woman who has taken such a stand against testing products on animals and the burning of our rain forests. The Body Shop has developed terrific and imaginative products tied directly to the environment. The best gift my next door neighbor, ten-year-old Alexander Milligan, got for Christmas was a box of five soaps in the shapes of endangered species. It cost just $8.25. He took them to school for show and tell. About half his class went off to the Body Shop that very afternoon to get theirs too.

Almost as powerful as that kind of word-of-mouth advertising are Target's ads. They tell kids, "You and your friends can start a club to save the Earth." There is a most interesting linkage here, that children will do more about the environment than adults. I think they're right. Target has devoted most of its environmental public awareness toward getting children involved. So has the Gap with its "Earth League." Do you think we're talking about two very successful stores that just happen to be playing around with the planet, or do they really mean it? I think they do.

Robert Redford has turned the environment into a business. His Sundance catalog is full of turquoise button covers and other nonessentials. But if you happen to love the outdoors—or if you just love Robert Redford—you're giving him your money. I'm sure it's profitable and it's all dedicated to the environment by association.

Are you getting packages like I am with notices that say: "Due to environmental concerns we will now be packaging with popcorn instead of polystyrene void fill. Please be aware this popcorn is not fit for human consumption."

Why on earth not? I fired off a note to Stew Leonard Jr., and I said, "Hey Stew, you sell a lot of great popcorn. How much more popcorn do you think you might sell if you sampled it to your customers by using it as packaging in your mail order shipments? You could enclose a message like this: 'Unlike most not-fit-for-human-consumption popcorn that shippers are using for packaging these days, the popcorn we use to pack your order is the same delicious, premium grade quality popcorn we proudly provide to our customers and associates at Stew Leonard's everyday. All Stew Leonard popcorn is popped fresh the day your order is shipped to you. As long as your package arrives intact and undamaged, our popcorn should be perfectly safe for you and your family to enjoy.' "

Although I prefer popcorn, in many of my presentations this year I have been demonstrating a water-soluble packaging material called "Eco-foam." I got it from Berkley Publishing Co. They've started packing all of their book cartons with it. It costs two cents more per carton—God they must have had *board* meetings about that! The stuff is made of cornstarch, dissolves in water and is gone—forever—in about ten seconds. It's great. And it's a thrilling magic act for audiences to be able to see it all disappear before their eyes—just like that.

Does this seem like a minor thing? It isn't. We're talking about hundreds of thousands of cartons of books shipped out every year by a single company. Is it improving their bottom line? Without question, it *would* be if businesses were made to be responsible for the disposal costs of the materials they use.

At Wal-Mart because of Sam Walton—arguably the planet's single most effective advocate right to the very end—you can, today, buy Sure deodorant that's not in a box. It's now sold without a box. How did this happen from a huge company like Proctor & Gamble? Sam must have rattled their cages something awful down in Cincinnati.

I don't think sales of Sure deodorant will drop even one unit because it no longer comes in a box. Do you? I think people will buy it simply because they don't have to scatter trash on their way out to the parking lot before they even get deodorized. That's important progress.

Rubbermaid, an innovative and inventive company, was recently featured on the cover of *Fortune* magazine—right along with Wal-Mart—as one of the nation's most admired companies. Rubbermaid reinvented the lunch box which has now become one of their hottest selling items.

When you and I grew up, it was thrilling to have lots of trash. If my trash was bigger than your trash, it meant I was probably richer than you. Now Rubbermaid's new lunch boxes are the most popular lunch boxes in America, and they never get thrown away.

The CD long box is gone. The indestructible jewel boxes for CDs are not gone and will still outlive you. But the pointless, wasteful, long box is gone. Every record store in America will have to refixture its CD bins. This will cost many millions of dollars. But it's less than the billions of dollars we've been paying for needless packaging.

An even faster way for us to fix the packaging disaster would be to make it absolutely mandatory that all packaging and product disposal costs are included in the price of every manufactured item. Customers would instantly communicate to manufacturers their willingness to live with less packaging and avoid these new costs.

Esprit's new $10 million advertising campaign is based entirely on customer responses. They ran ads asking, "If you could do anything, what would you do?" 40,000 people responded. And still some of you continue to believe your customers are apathetic. It turns out half of the responses received by Esprit expressed concern for the planet. Does that suggest anything to you? Esprit's customers are very interested in all sorts of issues like giving back the land stolen from Native Americans, and they speak out on abortion, and they speak out on Mr. Clinton. They speak out on everything, but you wouldn't believe how much of it had to do with cleaning up the messes we've made. Esprit had a great idea.

The first photograph the astronauts took of the Earth floating in space evokes an almost universal emotional response. When you look at it today, you still think the thoughts you had when you first saw it, that our planet is an unquestionably precious and beautiful place God created—and it was good. But now and forever, when you look at this picture a question forces itself into your consciousness: how long will it last? Isn't it beautiful, and how long will it last? That's a sadness that's now turning into action.

The Body Shop put out an environmental broadsheet for its customers about the violence being done to the planet. Go to the Body Shop and see if you can get one. It will give you lots of ideas.

Patagonia is a great company that for years and years has given ten percent of pretax profits to saving the places that their customers like to climb to and survive in. They continue to make their catalogs more and more beautiful and more recyclable and devote even more space to the environment. Patagonia is a profitable company.

Elements is a handsome new magazine published by Timberland. I think you'll want to get on their mailing list for your own personal delight. It's a great magazine, well written with beautiful photographs. It's about 80 pages, but only has two pages of advertising. The rest is all articles about how to climb Mount Everest and how to save the rain forests and so forth and so on. What you won't read much about is shoes. It seems that Timberland had discovered its customers love reading scholarly articles about saving the planet and has focused on giving them exactly what they want and how they want it. It won't take you long to realize Timberland is putting its heart into caring for the environment.

Buying a Christmas tree is perhaps the single most unifying purchase a family makes together all year. But IKEA won't sell dying Christmas trees. For a $10 deposit and $10 rent, they'll provide you a living tree—in a pot. You can bring it home and put it anywhere in your house. After Christmas, you bring it back. In 1990 IKEA rented 18,000 trees. They could have been quite pleased with that and helping to save the planet and the press coverage and all the rest. But for 1991, IKEA went on to order 30,000 trees and rented every one of them along with a gift coupon entitling the renter to come back this spring for a free seedling. It's important to constantly improve what works.

Sure, it was a hook to bring you back to IKEA. I liked it. I imagine a considerable number of those 30,000 people—quite likely at the urging of their children—came back to IKEA this spring to get their living seedlings, take them home and plant them in their yards. A great idea and a wonderful family activity.

The most surprising Christmas card I got this year came from Irvine Development Co., an Orange County, California-based shopping center developer. Irvine has Fashion Island and a whole bunch of other places trying to sell books and soap and all the rest of it. It said:

"As 1991 draws to a close, we look forward to a New Year filled with hope and prosperity. 1992 promises to be a year of ... [opening the card, it contiues] ... positive change, renewed growth, environmental awareness. Shifting our lifestyles back into balance with the earth is no longer an overwhelming task. The ability to make things happen begins with you. We're entering a decade of environmental awareness with people joining together to protect the most important asset we have—our environment. Resolve to make a difference throughout this year."

They didn't stop there. These people are great. They went on to make it individual and personal. They ask you to write down your pledge. They enclose an attractively lined card that stares right back at you on which you're supposed to write down your commitment to save the planet—even if it's only turning the water off while you brush your teeth. On the top of the card is printed, "My personal resolutions for 1992." And on the bottom is printed, "Saving our earth starts with each of us. Influence others with your actions. Make 1992 count."

Brian Shauhnessy is store manager of CVS drugstore in Keene, New Hampshire. He's become CVS's version of Johnny Appleseed. He organized the planting of 350 trees in New Hampshire's Pisgah State Park. It always boils down to one person getting going and starting some thing. You can't make a huge chain of drugstores do very much. It's people like Brian Shauhnessy working in them that make things happen. What a motivation. What a person to work for. Is it related to CVS's business? I couldn't prove that, but I will argue that Brian's heart is certainly in the right place for planting trees for us all.

Individual Amway representatives are recognized by their management for their work on the environment with a check for $2,500. That's a lot of money to hand out to your representatives. Amway represents a very powerful environmental force both in its products and its representatives. I think they're putting their money where their soap powder is.

Here's a memo starring Kenneth Banks, vice president of Eckerd Drugs—who threw a small fit one day against TBS and *Time* magazine's "Man of the Year," Ted Turner. (I agree, by the way, that Turner might be the most influential person of the year. God knows, you go out to Timbuktu and turn on a television set and there are his people telling you everything that's going on.) Kenneth Banks wrote:

To: Ed Stanley, Turner Broadcasting Service
  Dear Ed,
  I was particularly interested in the news about TBS Network Earth. I was amazed at the amount of paper your every other Wednesday memo takes. I suggest you duplex it (copy on both sides) and save a few trees every other week. Another suggestion is to cut your highlights from nine or ten to four or five. Not only would that save a couple more trees but increase readership by more than double.

TEN's immediate response:

Turner Entertainment Networks
  To: Ken
  From: Ed Stanley
  A big thanks to Ken Banks, VP marketing communications of Eckard Drug Company, for his stellar format suggestion. Copies on both sides (save those trees) and a shorter format for higher readership (save more trees).

Fast action from the vast empire of TBS and TEN and CNN and all the rest of the subsidiaries. Was it worth a few trees every other week to write a memo to them? It worked. It helped.

People have started to listen up, stand up, speak up, write memos and beat each other up and, in the process, discover that doing the right thing is exhilarating. It benefits us all. How many of these kinds of letters and memos have you written this year? How many recycling traumas did you nip in the bud?

White Rose is a chain of stores in Canada which will replace any plant they send you that dies, or any plant they send you that you kill, or any dead plant from anywhere —if you just bring its poor dead body in to them—they will give you a live one free. Smart.

Some people didn't believe this so to prove it—the only way reality seems able to be proved these days—they made the following television commercial;

"Thanks to white flowers, my granddaughter thinks I'm a pretty good gardener. But wouldn't you know it, the one plant she brought me for my birthday didn't make it. That's when my wife reminded me of the incredible White Rose guarantee. White Rose would replace my granddaughter's plant free even though she hadn't bought it there. Sure enough, they did. And what a beauty.

"You know, my little pumpkin still thinks I'm a big-shot gardener!"

What a warm, nurturing, alive and heartfelt ad that is. Are your ads for real these days? It's what customers are responding to. As I go all over reporting what good news I can, all the companies I mention are making a profit. I no longer want to hear or talk about people who are doing the right thing but not making money. I hope you can see, if only by these few examples, that the environment is now directly related to your customers. It's in their hearts and in their homes and in their gardens and backyards. Whatever it is about caring for the planet, it's working, it's powerful and it's profitable.

If we are to preserve that beautiful picture of our planet floating in space, we must restore our belief in the power of the individual. It's the power of individuals that will save the planet that allows us to live together in a place that could be Paradise Found—again.

58 TOILETS AND A CEO

NOVEMBER 1992

I WENT to the Midwest today to find out how we are, and it is alarming. If you live in reality-exempt places like New York or San Francisco you only get virtual reality, by reading about it or watching it on television. For the true zoom-lens view you must get on a plane and go to Ohio.

So I sat midair picking at a sad little Danish snack on bankrupt Continental Airlines. The morning papers weren't serving up fake confidence this morning. CONSUMER CONFIDENCE WILTS, they said. Other headlines read—IBM: 10% OF WORKERS WILL RETIRE EARLY; STRIKE LEAVES PITTSBURGH IN THE DARK; ADVERTISERS LAMENT LACK OF BUSINESS; WORRIES SEND BOND YIELDS PLUMMETING—et cetera, et cetera. Just another day in paradise. Then I arrived in Cleveland.

How Ohio is, is how we all are. This is not the view of economists, futurists, publicists or politicians. It's reality through the eyes of two very different people I met: a maintenance woman who cleans 58 employee toilets a day and the chairman of the board of her company. Two months ago he fired 100 people from the central office of this retail giant, and even now he cannot be absolutely sure the immune system of the entire company isn't getting ready to quit. The woman who cleans 58 of his toilets has not been fired yet, but her husband (she told me as she drove me to the airport after my meeting) will not get up in the mornings depressed now, because he has been fired from two jobs already this year, and her two children (21 and 23) cannot find work.

Both this woman and the chairman of the board are unprepared for the reality hitting them now. Both find too much collapsing too fast. They don't know what to do with a husband who won't get out of bed, or 1,000 stores across the country that aren't producing sales. Neither knows what to think when the government woo-woos tell them everything is on the upswing, and why don't they just run right out to their local mall and spend a lot of money, honey, and everything's going to be just fine.

This company has been cutting expenses and consolidating and right-sizing itself on a modest basis for some time now, but the mass dispersal of 100 people at once was something of a novelty. And the sight of all those people walking out of their corporate headquarters was the first concrete sign of the possibility that their company might not, in fact, survive.

All of this is as plain—or even plainer—to the woman who cleans toilets as it is to the board chairman. That is the way it is today in the real world of America.

And so is this: Across the monstrous parking lot at this headquarter campus for a company operating over 1,000 stores is a building two years old that never would have been built if the idea came up today.

It's the company's employee day-care center, and it is an aspect of Ohio reality that can give us hope.

This is no ordinary child depository. Ninety infants and toddlers gather in eight suites, according to their age groups, playing, sleeping, eating—and learning. It is art class and reading school and gym and creativity of every kind. Because this is America, this inadvertent miracle might be the only introduction to the arts that these children will ever see. Art is no longer taught in most American schools, nor is reading or writing or music. We just don't have it in the budget. But we have it here, in Ohio, in a serene and energetic site of hope for our future, just across the parking lot from the national headquarters of a grim American company.

Maybe one of these days the employees who run the day-care center will be fired, but it hasn't happened yet.

Who knows what's to come? The chairman, wondering (appropriately or not) if he has let these thousands of people down, suffers. So does the woman still cleaning toilets, grateful to have a job, wondering whether they will need so many toilets cleaned if they have fewer people to use them.

Meanwhile, the little kids are painting faces on each other, learning to tell each other stories, spelling with computer keyboards. I noticed a vast profusion of hearts in this building: kids painting hearts, heart-shaped note paper, and arrangement of dried flowers hung in the entrances in a heart-shaped basket, a huge red heart mural covering an entire wall. Two of the bathrooms had red heart wallpaper, and believe it or not, one two-year-old was fast asleep on her cot wearing only a diaper and cover dotted with hearts. These kids are learning a heartfelt lesson. One hopes they will be able to use their education.

As I zoomed out, back to New York, I looked down and saw thousands of neat Ohio houses, many containing people not getting up in the morning, having nothing to do, not knowing where to turn and watching their children pick up their attitudes. All these homes and families got smaller and smaller as we flew away, but they are there, and that's how they are. And so are we. It's alarming.

P.S. I was wrong. Even California-the-reality-exempt is failing. The next morning's paper (no airplane, no danish, no Cleveland) tells me: CALIFORNIA, LAND OF CRISES, MINGLES DESPAIR AND HOPE. "Disastrous earthquakes, drought, fires, freeze and floods have now been joined by recession, cutbacks in military spending, deadly racial disorders, and the biggest budget shortage that any state has ever faced."

P.P.S. Just run right out to your local mall and spend money, honey, everything's going to be just fine....

HURRYING TO THE MILLENNIUM

DECEMBER 1992

I DREAMED I went to Minneapolis, on my way to the Millennium, to see the Mother of them all, the Mega-Mall, the Mall of America.

The Mall of America! MOA! Moa. Say those initials over and over and hear the projected 40 million shoppers chanting the message: Moa, Moa, Moa. It's an idea we used to believe.

Sometimes I seemed to have dreamed this dream before, like the time of Biosphere II, that vacuum capsule of virtual reality, the laboratory for our future after the destruction of the planet. All was well in Biosphere II until the people committed to living entirely inside for two years were caught sneaking out for sandwiches.

One time I dreamed I was in Las Vegas, in the Forum Shops, the *Mallus Romanus*, a lollapalooza showbiz shopping ritz-and-glitzerama shopping experience, where gigantic statues of Roman emperors come to life every hour to tell the theme-world dreamers what time it is.

But in the Mall of America my dreams took wing until I approached the meaning of the new Millennium. I dreamed of living in MOA, in virtual reality, forever. In my dream I knew that living in a future in which the real biosphere is destroyed.

Time magazine knows it too: "As overpopulation makes the real world less congenial, artificial realities will become more attractive." (Fall 1992 special issue.)

MOA is perfect already: airtight, clean and safe, sealed off from the problems of the universe, filtered, waste-and-climate controlled, and entertaining enough to stop you from ever doing anything yourself. One could live here with one's needs fulfilled, one's aspirations quenched, one's popularity assured. Everything functioning, everything perfect, everything dead.

I witnessed a world of people standing mesmerized, like pilgrims, before a 45-foot inflatable Snoopy. Were they waiting for it to explode like the Hindenberg? Or to rise into the heavens in some gaseous resurrection? Could anything so big be cute?

MOA is the apocalypse of bigness, another idea we used to believe.

I did not have my ears pierced, but I could have. I could have been tattooed, temporarily or forever. I strolled a dozen streets that weren't streets in a town like no town anywhere—perfect. I ate food labelled "seafood parts" and mixed fruit jellies, a lot of things that taste like things they aren't, to fool you so you think you're eating something you aren't. But it's fast and cheap and you do get full, so you can turn your attention to something else like shopping or getting your face peeled free, as a gift with purchase, in a department store.

You can go into an amusing amusement park or see movies, most of which star Eddie Murphy and Kevin Costner, in 36 theaters (so you can sit withdrawn in the Cineplex watching reality once more removed) Or you go deeper, stand in the virtual reality machines that used to be video games, and you're in an even smaller box within a box within a box. Chances are, the very air within this ZIP code is a manufactured substance better for you than the air outside. You're in a biosphere selling T-shirts. No hurricanes here, just what America needs: Moa merchandise, Moa fun. Lullaby, America, sleep tight, we're open all night.

In my dream I caught up with two customers when, having seen only 165 stores, they stopped to refresh themselves in a food court offering 132,465 choices, all of them fast and most of them awful, before they continued through 135 more stores, passing 35,000 plants (all spathiphyllums), accompanied eternally by "Stranger in the Night" on 14,000 invisible speakers. Suddenly, dazed in a department store, in a moderate-better-transitional-bridge dress department, they seized up, rigid, no longer able to tell where they were, or how, or what for.

They turned, and so did I, as customers do turn when they have seen too much. We dreamed as hard as we could, imagining our departure, passing back through the amusement park, the Hormel cookout area, the pool, the nightclubs, the movie-plex; through European, Broadway, high-tech, and art deco decors; under the promise of five acres of skylights, to somewhere outside. We ran out through one of 58 exits, into the world's largest parking lot. Hurrying to—or from—the Millennium.

BLUE SKIES AND BULLETS

JUNE 1994

BLUE SKIES AND BULLETS—that's the way we live today. It's not the happiest theme you've ever heard in your life, but turn on the television for 15 minutes and you want to kill yourself. What can we do about it? This is a tough one, but reality is our business, and making something of it and lifting people is using our business powerfully.

A couple of years ago we were talking about optimism versus pessimism, and then we were talking about hope versus action and how action is more important than hope. And now we have a word that has never really hit the whole nation quite as clearly before. We're dealing with fear—what a cheerful beginning! But the fact is that if you were in New Orleans last week, they told you not to go out of the hotel without a companion. If you're in Florida, which nobody ever is anymore because you're going to be shot as you rent a car, *that's* not funny.

We live on a smoking mountain of violence. My thought is that maybe each of us could stop just one bullet. Does that have anything to do with business? Yes, I think so. I don't know what your experience has been, but your tolerance for this subject will depend directly on how strongly *you* feel about the necessity of creating blue skies because there aren't any.

That's all there is to it! And there are some amazing examples of blue skies. In my endless quest for the improvement of dismal, disgusting, rotten, violent customer service, I walked into a store this year that had an enormous sign saying, "Bless all ye who enter."

I went into a coma—I mean, that is not what you get in the average store, is it? I feel that this applies to you, because you have a job that could bring us all a blessed year instead of a horror show. Keep in mind that there is at least one store in the world that blesses its customers on the way in. That's a very strong word.

On the other hand there's another kind of sound that has become one of the most familiar sounds in all of American life. It's like this—

[LOUD GUNSHOT]

I want to tell you that there is a violent crime committed in America every ten seconds. During the 90 minutes in which I talk to you, that translates into 540 major violent crimes—and a lot of them are taking place in your parking lot and your shopping center and your home.

Forty percent of the people would like to do something about the fact that they don't want to lock up their children every morning or take them to school in a guarded van. What does this have to do with you?

[LOUD GUNSHOT]

I'm sick every time I hear that noise. It interrupts every song, blots out the sky, and clouds your customer's mind! Imagine a picture of a little girl with a gun in her mouth. This is "virtual reality." This is the kind of popular art that is now selling in card stores. Last year I talked to you about a hurricane, and this year everybody out in the lobby is saying, "How's your flood? How's your robbery? How's your earthquake?" We don't say, "How are your children or family?" anymore.

And yet. And yet. It's funny because the worse things get, the better the good stuff gets. Look at what Banana Republic did. They ran ads featuring people in their 70s. Those people are extremely beautiful—with the kind of beauty that *no* 21-year-old could ever have!

There's a store in Los Angeles called Fred Segal that has a blue sign in the parking lot. It says, "We the people of the earth, pledge allegiance to the creation of harmonious and sustainable planet for the future generations..." *that's* an ad. Well, what does it say in the parking lot of your store? Because that's a first impression.

I wonder what happened to the environmental movement? What happened to AIDS? We have *so many* things to deal with now, and yet you've got to do it just one sign at a time. Right in Los Angeles—picture a peace garden in the back of the store. What do you call the back of *your* store—the smoking area? The parking lot? YOU can have a peace garden.

Now here is the future—a store run by eight-, nine- and ten-year-olds. It's "Biz Kidz" at Orlando Fashion Square. This is different from inner-city living. These kids are brought in by bus as a class every day. The store is open from ten to two. They learn how to run the register, how to do the buying, how to do the inventory. They learn how to get dressed. They learn discipline and creativity. Man, if school isn't doing it, isn't it great that a shopping center is doing it? Why isn't the shopping center a school?

I was in on a story of resurrection this year that was very exciting. What happened at Carson Pirie Scott this year is that they didn't *just* emerge from bankruptcy! We now live in an age in which everybody is going around congratulating one another for emerging from bankruptcy. It's not enough to survive—then you need to invent. And Carson's invented a mouse, and a story, and the ornaments, and 18 kinds of merchandise and sweatshirts and everything else. Tootie Mouse & Friends. Is it the salvation of a department store to have what is not available anywhere else, that they designed themselves? Could this mouse be a Mickey? It had a *tremendous* salutary effect on everybody. The public was saying, "Give me that. What is that? I want that." The staff was proud. They raised $50,000 for a hospital, launched a whole new thing—does that look in any way like a store that's *just* made it through bankruptcy?

If you want blue skies, you need to *create* them. And you find this out by listening to your customers. You must ask your customers what's on their minds.

[LOUD GUNSHOT]

I'm going to share with you one minute from a focus group conducted by Tysons Corner mall, in which for the first hour and a half, customers sat around and said, "Well, we could use more stairs, we could use more shops." There was this kind of fake discussion. And just when the meeting was almost over, one customer raised her hand and said, "Could I just ask one question?" Here is the question a *customer* asked:

Q. "I know at one time, I think you know, when you put out your security brochures, has there been a problem with safety here? That's my concern. I think there was maybe an incident one time—did someone get raped or something?"

A. *"There was a rape last June."*

The rule has always been, ask your customers what they want and they will tell you. Do you know what Tysons Corner did? They immediately published a safety brochure, hired policemen and monitors, appropriated $180,000 a year to remove graffiti. Where does this money come from? The special events budget (sit on Santa's lap) has now been changed to the security budget. They are advising their customers of what's going on. They are dividing the facts from the myth. Nothing is as bad as what people imagine.

You need to inform your customers how safe they are. It is more important than 30% off and grunge and Santa and all the rest of it. Fear of violence will *kill* shopping unless we do something about it. There are no blue skies there, except that Tysons Corner took action!

How depressing is it? Here's a picture of an ant carrying the Empire State Building. That's the way I feel, talking to you about violence. But we mustn't allow ourselves to think that the problem is so huge that we can't do anything about it.

Fernando Mateo is one of 17 children running a carpet store in Manhattan who suddenly became the most famous person in America because instead of waiting for the police department and the government, he did gun-busting. People are trading in guns for carpets, football tickets, Bette Midler tickets, and running shoes. The story is that Fernando Mateo's SON, Fernando Jr., who's fourteen, said to his father, "Don't give me anything for Christmas, because I want you to spend that money collecting guns." Only a small, maverick retailer could do this...in the first three days they collected as many guns as the New York City Police Department has collected in 24 months.

I wondered if this affected his business. But while I was in the store talking to Fernando Mateo, I noticed this little kid running around, looking through carpet samples with his parents. And the parents said, "We're customers. We just bought a ten-room house, and we're shopping here because of what Fernando Mateo is doing."

Isn't that a funny way to advertise? But you see, advertising means you make a joyful noise, or maybe just a necessary noise. And the people come and buy your carpets.

[LOUD GUNSHOT]

The wife of the president of Paul Stuart menswear store founded the Friends of Island Academy, which goes down to the jail on Rikers Island—a place you never even want to see, which is JAMMED with thousands of teenagers—and it gives them sponsors and tries to place them and save them.

Well, Paul Stuart hired one of these guys, and I went to meet Marc Washington. One year ago, Marc Washington was on the streets selling drugs and going straight to hell by his own admission. He was put into jail, and now he is working at Paul Stuart.

I interviewed him, and I said, "What did you think about in jail?" He said, "I had eight months to do nothing but think and protect myself. I thought that I had two choices—I could become a better crook or I could become a better person.... I was turned down once before...." He and seven other kids had applied to a very famous, bankrupt department store (which starts with an "M," in New York) for jobs. And they handed in the applications that they had already filled out. The woman behind the window said, "You're not supposed to fill those out till you get here." And she tore them up and threw them in the wastebasket.

I said, "Marc, what did you feel like doing?" And he said, "I wanted to go down to the corner of 34th Street and Broadway and find an old lady and rob her." Now, his reaction wasn't right. The bankrupt department store's reaction wasn't right.

Paul Stuart is right.

Marc Washington is now writing poems. He never dreamed that he would get what he wanted. And do you know what he wanted? A job. He wanted to be a teenager, which he had never been. And he wanted to be in a fashion store like Paul Stuart.

So I said, "What would you say to the audience?" And he said, "Don't turn your back on me. Hire me."

It's a tremendous risk; there is no question about it. This, up till now, is a wonderfully loyal employee with a sense of value of his life that he would never have had without jail. Who knows what will happen? But Marc changed bullets into blue skies in his own life.

We know what customers want. We have the power to do it. We need to *create* blue skies, because there aren't any unless we make magic. You've got the power. You've got the job. Don't be depressed. *DO IT!* It's time to *act*. It's time to *create* blue skies and then we will have made our own blessed year!

INDEX